EAST AND WEST OF SUEZ

Nelson and his World
Chelsea Reach
Fighting General
Remember Nelson
The Young Nelson in the Americas
1945: The Dawn Came up Like Thunder

Travel
London Walks

EAST AND WEST OF SUEZ

The Retreat From Empire

Tom Pocock

THE BODLEY HEAD
LONDON

For Hugh and Mayda Pocock

British Library Cataloguing
in Publication Data
Pocock, Tom
East and West of Suez: the retreat from empire.
1. Commonwealth of Nations—History
I. Title
909'.0971241   DA18
ISBN 0-370-30615-5

© 1986 by Tom Pocock
Set by Eta Services (Typesetters) Ltd., Beccles, Suffolk
Printed and bound in Great Britain for
The Bodley Head
30 Bedford Square, London WC1B 3RP
by The Bath Press, Avon
First published in Great Britain 1986

CONTENTS

LIST OF ILLUSTRATIONS

Unless otherwise stated in the captions, photographs are by the author.

Introduction

The dozen or so British journalists who were regularly sent to report from the last outposts of the Empire during its final years often reflected the attitudes of their readers. We, too, had been brought up in the imperial ethos and, even if we affected to think of this as obsolete, it sometimes seemed to us strange that so many of those we had ruled with such benevolence should spurn the civilization we had imposed upon them in favour of what seemed likely to be chaos and corruption of their own making. Our bewilderment was compounded of surprise and a lack of understanding.

At the time it was, for me, a matter of waking early each morning in London to hear the BBC news and, in consequence, quite often starting to pack my bags. Within the hour, a telephone call from Fleet Street would tell me that my immediate presence was required at the seat of trouble. By mid-day I would be flying towards some far-flung outpost of empire—usually British, sometimes French—where decline was becoming a fall.

Then the preoccupation was with airline schedules, visas and permits, transport and, above all, communications with London. On arrival there would be briefings and interviews, assignations and expeditions that emerged as stories to be dictated over a tenuous telephone connection, typed on a cable form or punched on to a Telex tape. The pattern was much the same whether the scene was Malaya or Cyprus, Arabia, Borneo or Aden; it was different in Algeria and Indo-China but there we were guests at somebody else's debacle.

Only later did the two decades following the coronation of Queen Elizabeth II hang together as an historical sequence: the disintegration of the British Empire, and that of the French, which was prolonged at such cost in blood by their American successors. The long misery of Northern Ireland and the melodrama of the Falkland Islands were still to come but, by then, the British Empire we had known was gone. In its place was

I

something called the Commonwealth, an old comrades' association of the former rulers and the once ruled.

In recalling some of the events and the attitudes of that time, my memory has been supported by my notes and my reports published in *The Times*, the *Daily Express*, the *Sunday Dispatch*, the *Evening Standard* and various magazines.

Conversations with former colleagues and participants in what are now historical events have sharpened the focus and for these I am grateful to Mr Jasper Archer, Mr James Bishop, Lord Caradon, Lord Carrington, Mr Jack Cooper, Major-General Jack Dye, General Sir Charles Harington, Mr Denis Healey, Mr Louis Heren, Mr Owen Hickey, Mr John Lawrence, Vice-Admiral Sir Hector MacLean, Mr Iverach McDonald, Mr Stanley Meagher, Lieutenant-Colonel Colin Mitchell, Sir Philip Moore, Miss Jan Morris, Sir Edward Pickering, Mr Ian Samuel, Sir Robert Thompson, General Sir Walter Walker, Mr Michael Watkins and Mr Michael Weigall; and I am grateful to Mr Patrick Moore and Lord Wilson of Rievaulx for advising me on points of detail. My gratitude is due to Mr Charles Wintour, then editor of the *Evening Standard*, for putting many of these adventures in my way and for his understanding that prompted such sympathetic instructions to a returning war correspondent, somewhat frayed, that he now research and write a five-part series of articles about Hampstead. I am also grateful to Mr Louis Kirby, editor of the *London Standard*, for his encouragement; to Mr David Machin for his constructive advice; and to my wife Penny for compiling the index and, above all, for making life at home so much more enjoyable than ever it was in those exotic regions that we once regarded as British.

Tom Pocock,
Chelsea, 1986

Prologue

On the cloudy morning of 8 June 1946, exactly a year after the ending of the war in Europe, the victory parade marched through the streets of London. More than twenty thousand men of the armed forces of the British Empire, who had been assembled in a vast encampment under the trees of Hyde Park and Kensington Gardens, marched behind bands, or rode in tanks and the other fighting machines and transports of modern warfare. As usual, national and imperial opinion was distilled by *The Times* in a leading article, which declared that 'the procession epitomises the whole life of the British Commonwealth and Empire, because it was by the direction of their whole life to a common end that the war was won'.

I watched the procession from the top of the easterly of the three Decimus Burton arches at Hyde Park Corner, having the vantage-point to myself. The central arch was occupied by a newsreel camera and crew but I, wearing the war correspondent's uniform that was still necessary for travel in countries occupied by the victorious allies, followed them up their ladder and occupied a plinth to watch and to ruminate. For any young man of twenty, there would be mixed emotions that day for behind the enjoyment of pomp and spectacle were thoughts of friends and contemporaries who had not survived to enjoy this or any of the pleasures to come.

Such ghosts were swept along in the parade as familiar uniforms gave way to unfamiliar and the ruddy faces of the British infantry to the coloured skins of soldiers from the Empire. There were mixed feelings again as the Indian Army contingents swung past, behind the band of the Royal Garwhal Rifles, for India, 'The Jewel in the Imperial Crown' was, amazingly, to leave the Empire in little more than a year's time. But there were many who were not, one felt sure; many who remained grateful for British protection and guidance towards eventual self-government, perhaps some time in the next century. There would be the men of the

African regiments, the local defence volunteers from Cyprus, the Aden Protectorate Levies and the representatives of what were excitingly called Guerrilla Forces, from Malaya and Borneo.

Yet others *were* following India: Ceylon and Burma, we knew. Would Britannia watch, aghast and helpless, as her charges, barely in political adolescence, rejected her? Rather than face the humiliation of this, might it not be better to pre-empt the rejection, to have staged a farewell jamboree rather than a victory parade? Could not the British Empire end—if it had to end—with a fanfare and a flourish of mutual affection, rather than face slow erosion of loyalty and purpose?

While such treasonable thoughts passed through my mind, it began to rain. The pageant in the streets below had to march on but I scrambled down the ladder and sought shelter.

1

From Olympus

Across Queen Victoria Street from Printing House Square, the names of distant places were carved upon the façade of Blackfriars railway station: Paris and Berlin; Venice and Dresden; Genoa and St Petersburg. Boat-trains of the London, Chatham and Dover Railway had once served these, their passengers having sometimes crossed the road from their office to begin assignments as special correspondents of *The Times*. Another reminder of purpose was upon the pediment of Printing House Square itself: a great clock supported by sculptured scrolls bearing the name of the newspaper, the words 'Times Past' and 'Future'; above the latter, an ominous stone scythe.

The Victorians must have built the station here to serve what they regarded as a temple of civilization, and some of us still did. Certainly, at the beginning of 1953, it was at the heart of the British Empire, which was beginning to be known as the Commonwealth and Empire. To the west, the rulers and legislators of Whitehall, Westminster and St James's; to the east, the producers of wealth in the City and the greatest trading port in the world; here at Printing House Square was enshrined the ethos, if not the soul, of the Empire.

On this January morning, I crossed Queen Victoria Street to Printing House Square with awe and anticipation to join the staff of *The Times* and become known as Our Naval Correspondent. The newspaper might think of itself as the conscience of the nation, but the Royal Navy was its right arm and I was to represent each to the other. For a newspaper journalist in his twenties to be appointed to the staff of *The Times* at that time seemed akin to joining the peerage.

Printing House Square stood apart from Fleet Street in every sense. I had, of course, met *Times* journalists when a war correspondent in 1945 and, more recently, when reporting naval and military affairs for the

Daily Mail, but they had not seemed to be component parts of their newspaper as the rest of us were. This was partly because they wrote anonymously and, if reference to themselves was unavoidable, it was in the third person as 'your Correspondent'. It seemed as if they served, rather than contributed to, 'The Thunderer', as it had long been nick-named, which spoke from the depths of Printing House Square as from the grotto of an oracle.

What reverence that newspaper inspired! What other would disdain the flaunting of headlines and news on its front page and give that over to the personal announcements and advertisements of its readers? None other presented news with such clinical detachment, or its considered opinions in such sonorous leading articles. No other correspondence column commanded so close a scrutiny (whether for political denunciation, or news of the first cuckoo) and no arbiter of social precedence was as re-spected as its Court Page. Certainly no other newspaper would presume to print a limited daily edition on heavy paper destined for a readership implied by its title of Royal Edition. When *The Times* spoke, those who themselves commanded attention, listened.

Or so we thought. In retrospect, it is clear that the newspaper was now past its summit of power and glory, since its reputation still suffered from its policy of appeasing the dictators before the Second World War, dur-ing the editorship of Geoffrey Dawson. Yet, in manner and appearance, it seemed as august as ever; indeed, the regard—or, perhaps, self-regard— in which it was held could be seen as a reflection of the nation's self-esteem.

Within the doors of Printing House Square waited a porter, genial and ginger-haired, who might have been chosen for this post to reassure the timid visitor. Today I was not to see Sir William Haley, who had appointed me soon after he had taken up the editorship in October. This was something of a relief, since he was a daunting figure. Although aged only fifty-two, he had scaled Olympus, having been Director-General of the British Broadcasting Corporation during the wartime and post-war years, when it had been accorded the world-wide respect that the British felt was their due. Now he had ascended again: a lone figure, whose aura of self-confidence and commanding looks (wiry, grey hair and a gaze so implacable that legend had it that both eyes were glass) suggested that he would have been clad more appropriately in a toga than a subfusc suit.

My duties, as now explained, could hardly be so described because, it emerged, I was to write only when so inclined. I could comment upon news, when I felt that appropriate, and any contributions to the news pages would be gratefully received. From time to time, I might care to write a long 'turn-over' article for the leader page about maritime strategy, or allied topics, and perhaps initiate, or advise upon, leading articles on such subjects. In the latter activity, I might keep in touch with another newcomer, Robert Jessel, a brilliant young academic with a notable war record, who would be writing leaders on all aspects of defence, which had become a fruitful field for theory and speculation since the advent of nuclear weapons and the formation of multi-national military alliances. I might also keep in touch with Our Military Correspondent, Captain Cyril Falls, Chichele Professor of the History of War at Oxford University and Fellow of All Souls, with whom I would be sharing a room until his retirement at the end of the year.

This was on the second floor: a square, high-ceilinged room with two tall sash windows looking out upon Blackfriars and the river. When I arrived, an open fire was burning cheerfully in a wide Victorian grate, on one side of which stood a coal-scuttle; on the other, one of logs. Also to either side, was a large kneehole desk, one of which was to be mine. Later I was told that my predecessor, Rear-Admiral Henry Thursfield, had insisted on the precedence due to the Senior Service to occupy that nearest the window. But, since his recent retirement, Our Military Correspondent had presumably taken that position by *coup de main*, for he sat there now.

Captain Falls was at his desk, writing with a fountain pen. He was a trim, immaculately-tailored figure, his neat features decorated with a small, upturned moustache, like a porcelain hussar. As I entered, he peered over the gold rims of his half-moon spectacles, pen poised above page.

Having spent most of the past decade on the breezier side of Fleet Street, I was accustomed to the bluff approach and the early use of Christian names. Indeed, my second meeting with my editor on the *Daily Mail*, the tempestuous Frank Owen, had ended twelve hours later in a Mayfair night-club, from which he edited his newspaper via a white telephone amongst the bottles on the table, while despatch-riders brought page proofs from Fleet Street. So I introduced myself to Captain Falls with hearty fulsomeness. Having given my name and a sketch of my professional career, I remarked upon the honour of being appointed to *The Times* and felt that life here would be somewhat different from past experience. I would be grateful for his advice on all appropriate subjects and for his forbearance towards a newcomer; I was delighted to be sharing so spacious a room, which made such a nice change from the poky offices or open-plan editorial floors elsewhere; in any case, I had always wanted a room with a view of the river.

Captain Falls listened to this monologue in silence, pen still poised. When it ended, he inclined his head slightly and said, 'Falls'. Then he continued writing. I waited, standing before his desk, for him to say more, perhaps on concluding the sentence in his manuscript, but the scratching of his pen continued and his eyes remained upon the paper. So I crossed to my own corner to inspect my inheritance: the kneehole desk; another, smaller, desk upon which stood an antique typewriter (I was to learn that specialist correspondents were not expected to be able to type but summoned a girl from the typing pool when required); a glass-fronted bookcase and a large wall-map of the world suspended between mahogany rollers.

Realizing that my exchange with Captain Falls had come to an end, I sat down in my leather-covered swivel chair and stared at the map.

A fear of having to pontificate upon maritime strategy in the soaring columns of *The Times* was already upon me and, apprehensive of this and, even more, of a sudden question about naval policy from the silent Captain Falls, I decided to take this opportunity of considering global strategy and let my eye wander over the map upon which a third of the land area was coloured pink as dominions, colonies, dependencies and protectorates of the British Empire.

So much had changed eight years ago at the victorious conclusion of the Second World War. The United States and the Soviet Union were now the two giant nations—the latter an empire but not, like our own, divided by seas—while Britain recovered from the exhaustion of war. To most British minds, this loss of status applied to quantity rather than quality, to military and economic power rather than wisdom, experience and inventive genius. Harold Macmillan, the Tory politician, had started a vogue for talking of ourselves as Athenians; the Americans as Romans.

In 1945 the use of atomic bombs by the Americans had given the United States global dominance, but their monopoly of strategic power had ended four years later when Russia tested its own nuclear weapon; Britain had followed in 1952. Now a nuclear stalemate had been reached and, it seemed, another world war could break out by accident, or miscalculation. But a variety of conflicts, to which nuclear power was inappropriate, could break out and several already had.

Since the formation of the North Atlantic Treaty Organization, supported by American nuclear power, in 1949, war in Europe had become unlikely. Elsewhere, it was becoming clear, anything could happen: the unexpected was to be expected. To meet such contingencies around the world, the British felt themselves well prepared through their long preoccupation with what traditional strategists called Sea Power. This meant that the Royal Navy, and that remained second only in size to the United States Navy to which it felt superior in many aspects of technology and experience in everything from ship-handling to maritime strategy. In 1953, the Fleet—the capital letter was mandatory—seemed able to face any possible crisis since its heavy ships, in service or reserve, included sixteen aircraft carriers, five battleships and twenty-four cruisers. This was enough to fight another conventional global war.

Despite my own youth and only passing experience of war at sea, I felt well equipped to preach the doctrine of Sea Power, since I had learned it at my father's knee. He had been a schoolmaster at the Royal Naval College, Dartmouth, for many years and amongst the cadets to whom he had taught history were some of the present generation of admirals, including Lord Mountbatten. He had also recently written a series of newspaper articles about global strategy and these came to my mind now.

Apart from the ultimate duty of Sea Power to defend the United Kingdom against invasion, its principal task over the past two centuries had been the maintenance of what the Victorians and Edwardians had called 'The Lifeline of Empire'. This was the dotted line marking the sea route that linked most of the richest land areas painted pink on my wall-map. On leaving England, it passed briefly through the North Atlantic (now secure under the command of a British admiral, although subordinate to an American supreme commander) before turning sharply east through the Straits of Gibraltar.

That strange mountain, shaped like a crouching lion, often called 'The Rock', had long been a symbol of British maritime power as it held open the gates of the Mediterranean. Spain, preoccupied with its civil war for much of the 1930s, and a near-enemy throughout the Second World War, had only recently resumed its claim to The Rock, which the British had held since it had been ceded to them under the Treaty of Utrecht in 1713. General Franco, the sole surviving Fascist dictator in Europe, had finally ventured the suggestion that he would 'consider it a friendly act' for the British to return Gibraltar. He had, of course, been ignored.

Next, the Lifeline of Empire reached Malta after passing through the western basin of what we regarded as a British lake but allowed the French, who ruled both northern and southern shores, to think of as their ornamental pool, if they so wished. The Grand Harbour of Valetta was

9

still the base of the Mediterranean Fleet, now commanded by Lord Mountbatten—also, most gratifyingly, the NATO commander on the theatre—and young Prince Philip, the consort of the new Queen, who was to be crowned in the summer, had recently commanded one of the frigates. Malta seemed as secure as The Rock, but the Maltese Labour Party, which seemed to be gaining influence, had become tiresomely vociferous and surprisingly anti-British..

Eastward again lay another colonial island, Cyprus, which seemed as sleepy as its lemon groves. It had played little direct part in the Second World War, partly because it lacked a deep-water harbour, but there was now talk that one might be constructed so that the island could become a major British base covering the Levant. My father had written about Cyprus, describing the arrival there of a British parachute brigade as 'Richard Coeur de Lion's striking force all over again' in an historical allusion which reached farther back than usual. Since two-thirds of the Cypriots spoke Greek and boasted Greek ancestry there had, from time to time, been claims to the island from Athens but these were not taken seriously.

From here the Lifeline began to encounter difficulties. It had run through the Suez Canal since that had been completed in 1869 and Disraeli had acquired the majority shareholding. Since it could easily be blocked, it had to be defended by strong land forces and, until recently, these had been based on either shore: in Palestine and in Egypt, both having the use of major seaports: Haifa and Alexandria, respectively. But the British had left Palestine and were due to leave Egypt in three years' time.

Now Palestine was Israel, of course, and it was nearly five years since the British had thankfully abandoned their mandate, having had to fight Arab terrorists before the war and Jewish terrorists after it; these were now at each other's throats and Haifa was no longer a British naval base.

In Egypt, during the year just ended, the British garrison of 70,000 in the Canal Zone had, by its presence, provoked rising nationalism to violence: ferocious riots in Cairo had been quickly followed by the revolution, which brought down King Farouk and replaced him with a military government. The British had agreed to evacuate their troops by 1956 and the strategic base would then be split between Cyprus, Kenya and Aden.

So on through the Suez Canal into the Red Sea, memorable to the British for sweltering passages to India. To the west lay Africa, much of which belonged to the Empire: South Africa, Rhodesia, Uganda, Tanganyika, Somaliland and, across to the west, Nigeria, the Gold Coast and the rest. Colonial wars, great and small, had always troubled the Empire here and one had broken out a few months before in Kenya. The Kikuyu tribe had rebelled, incited by the Mau Mau secret society, which, with its obscene oath-taking ceremonies, might have been something from Rider Haggard, but for its scale: something like twelve thousand Africans were up in arms and outnumbering the British and African troops opposing them by nearly two to one. Like earlier colonial wars, this would doubtless be won when the troopships steamed out.

To the east lay nothing but the scorched mountains and deserts of Arabia, much of it unmapped—there was still the 'Empty Quarter' for intrepid British gentlemen-explorers to cross—its sparse and scattered population still living as in the Middle Ages. The whole southern shore of Arabia was coloured pink but valueless to the Empire, except for the port of Aden, which had been a coaling-station on the way to India and was now scheduled to become a major military and naval base, covering the Middle East, East Africa and the Indian Ocean. Its original purpose had, of course, ended when India had left the Empire but remained within the Commonwealth.

Burma, so valuable for its oil, teak and tea, had followed India into independence, and—as the British saw it—the wilderness, a year later. But, eastward, there was a new jewel in the Empire's crown set in tin and rubber: Malaya and the port and base of Singapore. There was trouble here that could be regarded as the last rumble of the Second World War. During the Japanese occupation the most effective resistance had been by the Chinese communist minority and they, like their fellows in Europe, were claiming the political fruits of victory. In 1948 subversion, sabotage, and then guerrilla attacks had led to the declaration of a State of Emergency. Now, five years later, a jungle war was still being fought between some five thousand Chinese—described as 'bandits' or 'freedom fighters', according to taste—and more than three hundred thousand soldiers, police and militia, of whom twenty-five thousand were regulars and conscripts of the British Army. Under the vigorous and imaginative direction of General Sir Gerald Templer, the British seemed to be winning, but it would still be a long war. Some years before, it had been a long haul on the North-West Frontier of India, so there was no undue dismay.

At Singapore, where the naval dockyard served the Far East Fleet, the Lifeline divided. It turned south-east to Australia and New Zealand, the Anglo-Saxon dominions, still much in the mind and care of the motherland, which they had so hurt, two years before, by signing a mutual defence treaty with the United States in tacit recognition of strategic realities; and north-east, past the jungles of Sarawak and North Borneo, towards Hong Kong, the busiest trading post of them all, and the myriad islands of the Pacific which still flew the Union Jack.

Dangers came not only from within, as in Kenya and Malaya, but from unexpected quarters. Until the summer of 1950 the mountainous peninsula of Korea had generally escaped British attention, but the American and Russian troops who had each occupied half of it since 1945 had left, and the communist North had invaded the capitalist South. In the fortuitous absence of the Soviet representative from the Security Council meeting in San Francisco, the United States had been able to declare a United Nations crusade against aggression and the Korean War had become international. The fortunes of war had been fickle to both sides but now the United Nations had restored the status quo at the cost of some thirty thousand American lives, and eight hundred British.

Here the Americans, and some of their allies, had faced the communists—albeit Koreans and Chinese rather than Russians—and held the line. Elsewhere in the East their allies in NATO, the European imperialists, were less successful. The Dutch had fought and lost a brief war to hold their Indonesian empire, which had declared its independence in 1949. The French were still fighting and losing theirs in Indochina.

Unlike Britain, the Netherlands and France had suffered under German occupation and their national pride was still sensitive. The British, however, could be smug in the assumption that, with the exception of two minor colonial wars, their own possessions were secure. The more advanced colonies would have to be led towards eventual self-government once their potential legislators and civil servants had been educated and instructed in democratic practice. But most—notably those in black Africa—would surely have to, and wish to, wait until the twenty-first century before having the apron strings untied. When this prospect had been questioned by Denis Healey, when secretary of the Labour Party's International Department, the Colonial Secretary, Arthur Creech-Jones, had told him, 'Kenya will not be independent in my lifetime, or in yours'.

It was not only that, by and large, the Empire was seen to be content. The British had the means and the will to rule. Indeed, the political scene in London was reassuring; it was almost as though the Labour victory of 1945 had been a dream, for Winston Churchill was again Prime Minister and Anthony Eden his Foreign Secretary. Other great names from the years of victory were back in the headlines: Field Marshal Earl Alexander of Tunis was Secretary of State for Defence; General 'Pug' Ismay, Secretary-General of NATO; Field Marshal Lord Montgomery as its Deputy

Supreme Commander in Europe; Field Marshal Lord Slim, the Governor General of Australia. The wide, confident grin of General Eisenhower was with us, too; recently back in Washington from Europe, where he had been Supreme Commander at Supreme Headquarters Allied Powers, Europe, instead of the former Supreme Headquarters Allied Expeditionary Force; he was now President of the United States. Finally, the seal was about to be set on British recovery from post-war exhaustion by the coronation of the young Queen Elizabeth II in June and, even among the cynical, there seemed to be the expectation of a new Elizabethan Age. All in all, there were grounds for confidence.

At this point, my reverie at Printing House Square was interrupted by the crunch of burned-through logs falling in the grate with a fountain of sparks. Later, I was to discover a bell beside my desk, with which to summon a minion to replenish them, but now this seemed an opportunity to strike up a conversation with Our Military Correspondent, who was still writing but not, I assumed, about the strategic problems of our own century.

'Excuse me,' I asked. 'Shall I throw another log on the fire?'

Captain Falls paused, then peered over his spectacles and replied. 'Pray do.'

Those were the last words I exchanged with Our Military Correspondent, for he retired soon afterwards, but I was not offended by his reserve, accepting it as an example of the manner to be expected. At Printing House Square it was not customary to converse with those to whom one had not been introduced, and if one did so, address by surname only was usual. Three years later there were still several of the twenty-odd who shared the second-floor corridor whose names I did not know and with whom I had not even exchanged nods.

Such behaviour was, by then, peculiar to a few surviving male institutions in England: the more distinguished London clubs and the common-rooms of the grander Oxford and Cambridge colleges, perhaps. Here it was appropriate as a sign of reverence to the newspaper we served but was sometimes regarded as arrogance. When I put this to the arts editor, John Lawrence, he replied, 'You must be arrogant if you are going to believe in your standards.' He was speaking with humour but there were other, familiar sayings in this vein like, 'It's not news until we have published it', 'It's not true unless you have read it in *The Times*', and the boast of the editor of *The Times Literary Supplement* that 'I've improved it — it's unreadable again'. But underlying the jest was belief.

The source of the last remark was Stanley Morison, in one of his several incarnations. His editorship of the *Literary Supplement* was brief and his occupation was usually given as that of typographer but, since he had designed the typeface of *The Times* before the war, one wondered what he did other than writing recondite monographs on subjects like *The Calligraphy of Ludovic degli Arrighi* and *The Alphabet of Damianus Moyllus*. He was sometimes known as 'The Sage', sometimes as 'The Conscience of *The Times*'; if any mortal spoke with the voice of The Thunderer, it was Haley, but Stanley Morison was the keeper of the sacred flame.

He was a spare, hunched man, looking older than his sixty-three years, always dressed in black, often with a black skullcap on his cropped white head. In youth, his views had been violently radical, by all accounts, but he had been received into the Roman Catholic Church and, whatever egalitarian attitudes he may once have adopted, he now enjoyed scholarly banter at the Garrick Club accompanied by champagne. Morison had been a friend and confidant of editors and proprietors and, to those below such rank, his opinions were holy writ.

So it was to Stanley Morison that one looked for a definition of the institution we served and his views were distilled in a testament written five years later, but which applied particularly to *The Times* as it was when Sir William Haley became editor:

> Obviously Great Britain cannot function without a strong, educated, efficient, informed governing class; *The Times* is the organ of that class. The due discussion of the country's affairs cannot be adequately conducted in Parliament alone so long as it is elected quinquennially and sits only for a few months in the year . . .
>
> The existence of a competent governing class is rightly said to be absolutely dependent upon *The Times* because no other newspaper attempts to rival it in self-respect, impartiality, independence, range of significant news, capacity to reason upon the matter printed . . . This was true a hundred years ago and it is true today.
>
> A country like Great Britain depends for its administrative efficiency upon its politically intelligent and professional men; these, in turn, depend upon *The Times* for the material upon which to reflect and, ultimately, act.

Such were the reasons for our supposed arrogance and such, too, were the reasons for the nation's confidence in its own present rôle and future destiny in ruling and guiding what was now a little less than a third of the world.

Yet while many of us believed implicitly in this creed, others did not and amongst them, it was later to emerge, was, amazingly, the man who seemed its personification, Sir William Haley himself. Soon after his appointment, he had summoned Morison, who was expecting to resume the relationship he had established with former editors, and told him that his views on typography, and nothing else, would always be welcome. Haley well knew Morison's beliefs and he did not share them; in his view, *The Times* should appeal to a much wider readership and become 'a balanced, interesting and entertaining paper for intelligent readers of all ages and classes'.

In trying to broaden the appeal of *The Times*, Haley had powerful friends and enemies. Amongst the former was Gavin Astor, the heir to Colonel John Julius Astor, the future Lord Astor of Hever, who had become proprietor thirty years before, following Lord Northcliffe's brief ownership. He not only supported Haley but wanted to diversify the family's and the newspaper's resources, even to the extent of investing in commercial television, which was then being planned. Amongst Haley's opponents — the believers in Stanley Morison's dogma — were, however, Colonel Astor himself and the manager of *The Times*, Francis Mathew. They understood the semi-mystical rôle of the newspaper and were not over-discontented that its circulation remained below a quarter of a million, or that its annual profit was not much more than £100,000.

This divergence was yet to be resolved. Certainly there was little evidence of change; the hierarchy still reflected the eccentricities of English social class. The Foreign and Imperial News Department was a cut above Home News; the former's correspondents were seen as gentlemen-journalists, living abroad at almost ambassadorial level and seldom, if ever, needing to be given instructions by the Foreign Editor; the latter's reporters were regarded as skilled and honest artisans. The Foreign Department's sub-editors were usually graduates of Oxford or Cambridge, whereas the Home Department's tended to be recruited from the better provincial newspapers, like the *Glasgow Herald*.

Indeed, the Foreign Department was something of a reflection of the Foreign Office itself. There was the same casual formality; the same air of knowing a great deal more than admitted. Even the reference library at Printing House Square was called the Intelligence Department.

Recruitment to the writing staff seemed haphazard. Stanley Morison had chosen the young editor of the *Cherwell* magazine at Oxford University as a likely lad and this he had proved to be since he was already half-way up Mount Everest, accompanying Colonel John Hunt's attempt on the summit. This was James Morris, a slight, wiry young man with lively, intelligent eyes and the air of nursing an amusing secret which he would share on better acquaintance. There was Peter Fleming, who arrived in well-cut tweeds, pipe clamped in square jaw, to sit at 'Colonel Fleming's table' in a lobby outside the Intelligence Department to write his gently witty 'fourth leaders'. He would then motor back to Oxfordshire in the old Rolls-Royce he had had converted into an estate car and which, he would say, had 'room for a stag in the back'.

There was one unexpected, but recognized, way to ascend the hierarchy and that was by becoming an acolyte at the shrine of The Thunderer in youth, or even childhood. Sir William Haley himself had once been a young telephonist at Printing House Square and two others, Louis Heren and Jack Cooper, both sons of senior printers, had started at even earlier ages as office boys. Heren was now Our Special Correspondent attending the war in Korea; Cooper, on the staff of the weekly edition of the paper. When the latter had returned from the war as a squadron leader in the Royal Air Force, it had been expected that he would resume his job of collecting and distributing cables from foreign correspondents and it was only with difficulty that he was accepted on the editorial staff. Now he felt something of a bond with the editor and, chancing to find himself alone with him in the ascending lift, ventured, 'Good morning, Sir William, you don't know who I am—'

'I know exactly who you are,' replied Haley, as the lift stopped and he opened the door and walked away. Ruefully, Cooper spoke of this encounter to Professor L. F. Rushbrook Williams, another Fellow of All Souls and the newspaper's authority on Indian affairs. Cooper should not worry about an apparent slight, urged Rushbrook Williams comfortingly, because he felt certain that Sir William had not intended such. Then he paused and his face clouded. 'On the other hand,' he continued, 'sometimes he calls *me* Rushbrook and sometimes he calls me Williams.'

Members of the editorial staff might never meet, and, since in the early days of Haley's editorship there were no editorial conferences, even the heads of departments rarely met to confer. When they did, it might be over a meal at the Private House, a Georgian house opening on to Printing House Square at the back of the office. Here they dined and drank, waited upon by uniformed staff and helping themselves to snuff from a porcelain snuff box decorated with a view of St Petersburg on the lid. While they were at table, the more bohemian members of the staff might be carousing a few yards away in a smelly little pub called the Lamb and

Lark, where the landlord would lock his door at closing time so that they could continue drinking his sharp beer, perhaps to the accompaniment of a guitar played by Geoffrey Green, Our Cricket Correspondent. Outside, at this hour, *The Times*'s trollop, a middle-aged painted lady, lay in wait beneath the gas-lamp in Printing House Square, hopeful of customers amongst the van drivers, her services available, it was said, for the price of a pint of bitter.

Journalists on *The Times* were poorly paid and the subject of money was regarded as slightly indecent. It had been assumed that the more senior would have some private money or, in the case of my predecessor, a rear-admiral's pension. 'You never talk about money,' John Lawrence had been told on joining the staff, and he soon found that, as he put it, '*The Times* gloried in poverty'. Sometimes newly-appointed specialists would seem surprised to hear that they were going to be paid at all; the honour was enough.

Some notable scholars worked for the newspaper. Our Museums Correspondent, Iolo Williams, a tall, donnish figure from the Athenaeum, was the leading connoisseur of his day in early English water-colours and also a botanist, ornithologist, poet and authority on the Welsh language. The senior leader-writer, Dermot Morrah, bristling with moustache, eyebrows and opinions, was yet another Fellow of All Souls and commanded an immense range of knowledge. This included heraldry, and he had recently been appointed Arundel Herald Extraordinary by the College of Arms along Queen Victoria Street; so, when *The Times* reported the Coronation in the coming June, one of its correspondents would be standing a few feet from the Queen, wearing a tabard.

At the opposite social extreme were the photographers, who were regarded as peasant craftsmen. While other Fleet Street photographers might be skilled at persuading young actresses to display more bosom or leg, *The Times* men specialized in views: lambs in springtime, daffodils in the churchyard, a headland presented to the National Trust, the last sunset of the Old Year. Such photographs of pretty, noble, often sentimental views would be printed large, often occupying almost half a page. The most discerning eye for such scenes was that of a tough old Cockney, who sometimes accompanied me to sea to take a photograph of the Home Fleet steaming in line ahead, a flapping white ensign in the foreground and seagulls overhead. He had an eye for other scenes, too. 'Seen the television?' he would ask with a leer, hauling from his pocket a key-ring from which dangled a tiny model of a television set made in coloured plastic. ''Ave a look in the screen,' he would command and, doing so, one would see through a lens a coloured photograph of a naked lady, who could be changed to another at the touch of a switch.

In all this Rowlandsonian gallery of savants and grotesques, the quintessence of all that was remarkable about specialist contributors to *The Times* was Our Astronomical Correspondent. Dr W. H. Steavenson, an old friend of my family, who knew him as 'Steave', was a bachelor in his sixtieth year but looking older, with his grizzled moustache and stiff, winged collar. One of his eyes was glass and the other bulged—perhaps, we thought, from gazing so long and hard through the telescope mounted in his little observatory which stood, like a miniature mosque, in a field outside Cambridge.

Steave had discovered a comet while a boy at Cheltenham College and it had been named after him. He had been President of the Royal Astronomical Society and was now Gresham Professor of Astronomy at London University. His presence at Printing House Square would first make itself known by a waft of evil-smelling fumes from the herbs he smoked in his pipe, which could also serve as a musical instrument; he could conjure squeaks from it and, due to the inexact fit of his false teeth, was able to whistle in parts.

But his visits were rare and usually to deliver his calculations for his regular contribution, 'The Stars of the Month'. Usually he was to be found at Cambridge, where he inhabited a small lean-to outhouse, which he had named Dustbin Lodge, in the yard of a lodging house near The Backs. The single room was furnished like a stage set with scenery for an eccentric professor's study, cluttered with telescopes and lenses, a tank of greenish water for aquatic plants and creatures, a brass microscope, desk, bed and stacks of books, astronomical charts, learned journals and his other favourite reading, the *Mickey Mouse Weekly*.

Dustbin Lodge was cold in winter. So, when seated at his desk by the window with its view of dustbins, he placed a lighted Bunsen burner, the flame shielded by a square of copper gauze on a little tripod, beneath his chair. At night he slept with his head beneath his pillow, a rubber tube running from his mouth to his feet beneath the bedclothes, for he had trained himself to inhale through his nostrils and breathe out through his mouth and the tube so that the exhaled air would warm his feet.

When astronomical reports reached *The Times* and his comment was sought, he refused to answer the telephone. Replying by letter to a written request, he would point out that he either knew about, or had forecast, the event and would have written about it himself had he considered it important; or, if he did not know about it, consultation by letter with other astronomers around the world would be necessary before he was able to express an opinion.

All recognized that 1953 was to be a significant year. The coronation of Queen Elizabeth II in the early summer was widely seen as a celebration of a British renaissance and there was little cynicism over this. But there were to be other, unexpected events which marked the year with historic importance. On 5 March Stalin, the communist emperor of Russia, died of a stroke at the age of seventy-three. Hope suddenly arose that the Soviet Union might at last reciprocate the goodwill that had been lavished upon it during the war and that the subject states of Eastern Europe might finally be able to choose their own forms of government.

Stalin's successor was to be Georgi Malenkov, a communist functionary unknown outside Russia, but who had a podgy face and a kiss-curl on his forehead, which seemed to hint that he might be less of a tyrant than his predecessor. Yet hopes were soon dashed. A week later, a Lincoln bomber of the RAF, on night exercises near the border of East Germany, was shot down by a Russian fighter and six of its crew killed. The fear of resumed intransigence was confirmed in June, when a rising in East Germany against communist domination was suppressed by Russian tanks.

Preparations for the coronation went ahead in a mood of ingenuous enthusiasm. But for the middle classes—particularly the executive class of the British Empire—life had not resumed its pre-war pattern. The impact of the Labour Government, which had been elected in 1945 and of the practical social reforms discussed so avidly during the war, had given the working class new confidence and the Labour politicians, despite the post-war economic handicaps and austerity, had acquitted themselves with credit. So the old ruling class was no longer omnipotent; young men could no longer aspire to the Indian Political Service, or the Indian Army, and the Sudan Political Service ('Blues ruling blacks', it was joked) was no longer recruiting. Even those joining the Colonial Civil Service did so with varying expectations, for a few of the more advanced territories might be granted independence before they came to the end of their careers.

Life in London was subdued but pleasant. Most staple foods were still rationed—although eggs and sugar returned to the free market during the year—but it was possible to eat well and cheaply in an increasing number of restaurants, some of them excitingly exotic to British taste. It was still a city primarily for Londoners, and visiting provincials, with a few foreign tourists. When, towards the end of May, foreigners began to arrive for the coronation celebrations, it again began to seem the capital of the Empire, as it would on such occasions; at other times coloured faces were rare. Now one was reminded of those patriotic tableaux in statuary, stained glass or coloured print that had glorified the imperial ethic: the monarch, graciously robed and crowned, receiving homage from assorted subjects with eyes gazing with devotion or downcast in humility. Now in place of the stock figures of that iconography—the submissive Indian princes, the noble sheikhs, the tamed savages, the bare-breasted Polynesian maids, the loyal rough-riders and the wise orientals— appeared a variety of multi-racial royalty and politicians, officials and officers, still representing more than a quarter of the world's population and owing allegiance to the nice, dutiful girl who was about to be crowned.

Flags flew, decorations swagged buildings and lamp posts and the city was invaded by the 30,000 soldiers, sailors and airmen who were to march in the procession from Buckingham Palace to and from Westminster Abbey or line the circuitous route. The most complete reportage of the event was, of course, to be by *The Times*, which had secured vantage points for thirty-three correspondents, ranging from Arundel Herald Extraordinary in the Abbey to the likes of myself along the processional way for 2 June. But it also offered its own tribute on a suitably grandiose scale and with impeccable timing. On 1 June a cable reached Printing House Square from James Morris, reporting that the summit of Everest had at last been reached, the two victorious climbers—neither of whom would claim to have been the first to scale the peak—being a New Zealander and a Nepalese Sherpa in reflection of the imperial polygenesis. Next morning the news was announced in headlines, bold as those announcing the coronation itself; one of them, 'The Crowning Glory'. As the *Annual Register* was to put it, 'If this was to be a new Elizabethan Age, its dawn was illuminated by a feat worthy of the boldest of Elizabethan adventurers.' At Printing House Square there was satisfaction but no surprise: everybody had expected Morris to carry out his assignment with appropriate competence and he had. Yet its leading editorial could only echo the surge of national sentiment, concluding its fanfare of prose to 'today's sublime ceremonial' and praise of the young Queen with the words, 'The splendid trophy brought to her from the summit of the world's highest peak is the earnest hope of a new heroic age.'

Along the processional way the waiting crowds were vast and did not thin when swept by chill, wind-blown showers. I was to report the scene in Regent Street and Piccadilly Circus and could watch it from a first-floor window above a shop in the former.

The spectacle was charged with emotion and, writing my report immediately afterwards, I could not resist a daring personal touch:

> Somebody began singing *Land of Hope and Glory* and another sang *Rule Britannia* and soon everybody seemed to be singing. The RAF men, lining the route, sang and the policemen sang and nobody seemed to mind the darkening rain clouds. People were smiling at each other and watchers on the rooftops waved to the crowds below and the crowds cheered back. Your Correspondent found himself possessed of an uncontrollable grin . . .
>
> Then, quite suddenly, the Queen was before us and cheering, like the thunder of surf, rolled along the processional way and burst into a great roar as her coach turned into view of the thousands massed in Piccadilly.

I wrote this at Printing House Square to which I had walked, shouldering my way through the happy crowds. Arundel Herald Extraordinary had arrived there before me by Underground train from Westminster and, through the open door of his room, I saw him seated at his typewriter dressed in the lace cravat, crimson tail-coat, white silk knee-breeches and stockings and buckled shoes that he had worn beneath his tabard in the abbey, a court sword at his side.

Later that day the Queen broadcast to the Empire, putting into words what the majority surely felt:

> The ceremonies you have seen today are ancient and some of their origins are veiled in the mists of the past, but their spirit and meaning shine through the ages, never, perhaps, more brightly than now . . . I have behind me not only the splendid traditions and annals of more than a thousand years, but the living strength and majesty of the Commonwealth and Empire, of societies old and new, of lands and races different in history and origins but all, by God's will, united in spirit and in aim.

When this was reported on the principal news page of next morning's *Times* it was accompanied by another report from one of her distant lands, Kenya, beneath the headline, 'Drive Against Mau Mau. 54 Killed in 24 Hours'. In the leader columns could be read an editorial echoing Rudyard Kipling's *Recessional*, which the newspaper had published after

the golden jubilee of Queen Victoria. 'The British people have had a
holiday from reality long enough,' it warned. 'The main reason why
Britain has not yet prospered sufficiently to lift herself above the safety
line is that the British people as a whole have not yet had the will to
prosper.'

Cassandra was not welcome at the feast, however, and the celebrations
were only just beginning. Foremost among them was to be the traditional
naval review at Spithead off Portsmouth, when, tricked out with fluttering bunting and burnished brass and to the sound of bugles and saluting
guns, the British displayed the realities of power. Two hundred warships
of the Royal Navy lay at anchor, including the beautiful battleship *Vanguard* and seven aircraft carriers, while three hundred naval aircraft
waited at airfields ashore to fly overhead as the royal yacht steamed
between the long lines of grey ships.

The review, which took place on 15 June, was a stately affair but lacked
the aura of omnipotence that the Royal Navy had formerly generated. All
eyes were drawn to a foreign cruiser, newer and bigger than any of our
own: the *Sverdlov*, said to mark the beginning of a vast naval construction
programme in Russia.

Passing down the lines in the sloop *Redpole*, which had been converted
into the Admiralty yacht, and watching the thousands of sailors, manning
the sides of the anchored ships, wave their caps to the ritual three cheers
as the royal yacht *Britannia* steamed ahead of us, I was unaware of any
lack of confidence amongst my fellow-passengers. These were the Board
of Admiralty and their guests, amongst them venerable admirals wearing
their old uniforms: gold-encrusted cap-peaks above sunken, or mottled,
cheeks, jackets sagging on their shrunken chests from the weight of their
medals.

If the Fleet assembled off the Hampshire coast appeared less almighty
than it once had, this could not be said of the old men aboard the Admiralty yacht, who had been smoked and weathered by the battle and the
breeze since childhood. There was Cunningham, who had watched his
fifteen-inch shells tear the Italian cruisers apart by the light of searchlight
and star-shell off Matapan; there was Fraser, who had watched the
Scharnhorst glow white-hot in the Arctic night; there was the most dashing destroyer man of them all, Vian, now also an admiral of the fleet,
whose air of disciplined ferocity had been slightly tempered by the pruning of the bristles that had sprouted from ears and nostrils.

In the British pantheon there were few more daunting gods than the
Sea Lords of the Board of Admiralty. On my appointment to *The Times*

several of them, together with some heads of departments, had gathered to meet me at the Admiralty, showing friendliness to me and deference to my title. But this was not always the case. The Royal Navy knew that it was the final arbiter of dispute; its weaponry, the decisive point of argument. This confidence was sometimes reflected in the manner of its senior officers, who considered their executive task superior to that of legislators, administrators, advisers, and chroniclers from Printing House Square. This I discovered on joining the flagship of the Home Fleet, the battleship *Vanguard*, which towered and gleamed in her pale grey paint like a tiered wedding cake, bound for exercises, which would take her to Gibraltar. The commander-in-chief was suited to his ship; Admiral Sir George Creasy was an old-fashioned naval officer of aristocratic style: white hair at fifty-eight, cold eye, hard mouth and aloof bearing. Yet, accustomed as I now was to a greeting on terms of equality, I was put out when not invited to meet the admiral until our last full day at sea.

The commander-in-chief sent word that perhaps the naval correspondent of *The Times* could report to his day-cabin at half past four in the afternoon; implying an invitation to tea, when I had expected a dinner party to be held, as was usual, in honour of my title. At the appointed time the flag lieutenant led me to the cabin door and asked me to wait a moment while he entered to announce my presence. For several minutes I waited; then the door opened and the admiral's steward emerged carrying a tray upon which stood silver teapot and jugs and a single, used, porcelain cup. The commander-in-chief had had tea! It was a stiff little interview—affronted pride on my side; condescension on his—about the general usefulness of naval exercises, unadorned by offers of tea, a drink or even a cigarette.

Sir George, who was later to accord me some wintry smiles, retired soon after, occasionally to be seen limping in the wake of the gun carriage bearing the coffin of another of his formidable breed, propping himself with an ivory-headed walking stick.

The *Vanguard* was also a show-piece, her fifteen-inch guns made during the First World War to fight another Jutland, and the new capital ship was the aircraft carrier. During the Second World War the Fleet Air Arm had been handicapped by the pre-eminence of gunnery officers who had regarded aircraft as useful in slowing the fleeing foe so that he could be destroyed by the terrible broadsides that were the British Empire's last word. But the Japanese and the Americans had proved otherwise and British naval aviation was now being accorded the resources it required to replace the obsolescent heavy guns.

Because of such shortcomings, the Board of Admiralty was demanding a yet more generous share of the defence budget for research and development, aircraft production and ship-building. This brought them into conflict with the Air Council which was bidding for a force of long-range jet-powered bombers to drop the atomic bombs which were now being delivered to the RAF. The air marshals were allowed their bombers, which were to be called the Valiant, the Victor and the Vulcan and, collectively, the V-bombers, but the admirals were disappointed. True, eight aircraft carriers were under construction but work was proceeding slowly on three cruisers, which had been laid down about ten years before, and the Admiralty maintained that at least seventeen were needed.

An even larger share of the defence budget had to be allocated to the bases around the world, each of which held a strategic theatre reserve and stocks of ammunition and supplies to fight a war for two months, by which time replenishments should have been shipped from the British Isles. In the Mediterranean this was shortly to move from the Suez Canal, when the Anglo-Egyptian agreement on its use ended in 1956, to the island of Cyprus, which was well placed to provide airfields. The Middle East, Arabia and East Africa were covered by the new base in Kenya and another in Aden. In the Far East were Singapore and Hong Kong. In 1954 and 1955 these British bases were to be welded into two new defensive alliances: first, the South-East Asia Collective Defence Treaty (SEATO) with Australia, France, New Zealand, Pakistan, the Philippines, Thailand and the United States; then the Baghdad Pact with Iraq and Pakistan. Both were linked with NATO in the west and with American alliances in the east.

These defences, designed to contain expansionist Russia and China, seemed formidable enough but already doubt was being cast upon their viability. In 1953 the Royal United Service Institution in Whitehall had published in its journal an essay by a Captain F. B. Ali of the Royal Pakistan Army which had aroused much comment. In this, the risk both to bases and to colonies producing such essentials as oil, rubber, manganese, wolfram, tin, mica, bauxite, cotton, hemp and jute from 'the rising tide of nationalism in the Middle East and Far East' was described.

Captain Ali wrote:

These countries will continue to strive for the attainment of complete independence. The Powers that retain positions of control, or even of influence, in these countries will continue to find themselves subjected to pressure tending to force them out. Should they seek to retain these positions, they will be faced with increasing hostility and opposition and, consequently, if they wish to utilize these positions strategically, they will have to resort to military occupation and the use of force. Short of this, the Powers that have been obtaining advantages out of these eastern countries will have to reconcile themselves to their cessation.

In another war, these bases will not be available or, even if some of them are retained till then, they will be of much reduced value as they are unlikely to be secure internally.

This view was regarded as alarmist or, perhaps, as an exaggeration, since there already were signs, here and there, of a rising tide. In addition to the troubles in Kenya and Malaya, Cyprus was beginning to grumble with the recurrence of the Greek-speaking majority's dream of union with Greece. The British garrison of the Suez Canal were still being harassed by occasional sniping, sabotage and pilfering by Egyptians but they were soon to leave. Elsewhere, other than Kenya and Malaya, insurrections were being mastered and the British territories along the Lifeline seemed in good order. Even the Korean war had petered out.

This was not so with our occasional friends and allies, the French, who were fighting a full-scale war against the Viet Minh communists to maintain their hold on Indo-China. This had begun when the British occupation troops, who had replaced the Japanese, left in 1946, and was now approaching a climax. At the end of 1953 General Navarre, the French commander, had established a strong force far in his enemy's rear—much as the British had in their campaigns against the Japanese in Burma—and garrisoned it with 16,000 men, who had to be supplied by air. The name of this fortress was Dien Bien Phu and it seemed impregnable until his opponent, General Giap, the Vietnamese commander, besieged and assaulted it with unexpected resolution and success.

By the spring of 1954 the French position—not only in Dien Bien Phu, but in all Indo-China—was desperate and they appealed to the Americans for direct military help, using air power and even atomic weapons. Churchill was aghast and begged President Truman to reject the request for a nuclear strike. But General Sir John Harding, the Chief of the Imperial General Staff, was sent to Washington to hear the French plead and to discuss with the Americans possible means of helping them. A conference was addressed by a French general. With impassioned oratory he told of the long and bloody struggle for the French inheritance in

South-East Asia, of the gallantry and the loss of life for the cause; it now was the moment for the United States and Great Britain to halt the catastrophe and come to the aid of the defenders of Dien Bien Phu: surely no nation of honour could refuse such a cry for help? He finished his oration, bowed to those assembled, walked stiffly to his chair, sat down, caught the eye of a British naval officer seated opposite—Rear-Admiral Hector Maclean, Director of Plans at the Admiralty—and he winked.

That instant symbolized, perhaps, the cracking of French resolution. They were not given Anglo-American aid and, on 7 May, Dien Bien Phu was finally stormed by the Viet Minh: the French had lost Indo-China. The British, facing no troubles that required the presence of their warships, felt free to turn briefly to that ceremonial they enjoyed so much and, a week later, sent the Home Fleet to welcome the Queen from a six months' voyage round the world to receive the homage of the Commonwealth and Empire. I was again on board the *Vanguard* (a jollier Commander-in-Chief, Admiral Sir Michael Denny, having succeeded Creasy) and watched from the bridge as the *Britannia* materialized through the heat-haze and saluting-guns threw out their plumes of smoke. Admiral Denny had prepared a dignified signal of welcome and this was now flashed in morse code to the royal yacht. After a short while, the signal lamp on *Britannia*'s bridge flickered Her Majesty's reply: 'Are Lingfield races running today?'

The commander-in-chief was pleased with the ships' evolutions and the smart bearing and brisk cheering of the sailors manning their sides. He was in an expansive mood, ready to share his views on world affairs, and did so in the vast day-cabin, cluttered with dozens of dolls dressed in the national costume of the countries he had visited, which he had requested as mementos from his hosts instead of the customary signed photograph. I was particularly anxious to hear about the Russians, because the First Lord of the Admiralty, J. P. L. Thomas, had recently announced that their naval tonnage exceeded our own and was second only to the Americans'. But Admiral Denny was dismissive: 'Remember Tsushima,' he said, recalling their obliterating defeat by the Japanese fifty years before. 'The Russians aren't seamen—they'll never be able to compete.'

As it happened we would both be able to put his view to a test in the coming autumn, when the British and Russian navies were to exchange visits and I was to accompany Denny and a squadron from the Home Fleet to Leningrad. It was to be the Royal Navy's first call at a Russian port since the war and curiosity was unbounded. The admiral was taking the minelayer *Apollo*, two destroyers and the aircraft carrier *Triumph*, and the latter would probably be the largest ship to make her way so far up the river Neva.

The visit took place in October as the sun had begun to set early over the Baltic. In view of this the navigating officers of the squadron were anxious to make good time on passage up the Gulf of Kronstadt so as to steam up the narrow, winding channel of the river to Leningrad in daylight. Yet the Russian pilot, who boarded the *Triumph* at the naval base at Kronstadt, began insisting on reductions in speed to delay our progress. So it was not until dusk that Captain Varyl Begg was able to take his big ship into the Neva and we could see the reason for the delays: on either bank spread vast naval dockyards and building slipways, just visible in the gloom. The Russians had not wanted us to pass these in daylight when photography would have been possible.

Our arrival in Leningrad on 12 October 1955 was strangely moving, however much it may have been contrived. In the lamplight, along the embankments, vast crowds watched silently, sometimes chanting, in English, 'Long live Queen Elizabeth!' The exchange of visits began immediately. The more senior officers and the correspondents were taken on tours of the Hermitage galleries and restored Tsarist palaces; the sailors, warned by their officers to be on their guard against over-indulgence in vodka, were offered none but shown a film about industrial production and monuments to Soviet heroes in the Park of Rest and Culture.

A frequent visitor to the ships was a renegade Englishman, Ralph Parker, who had been Moscow correspondent of *The Times* during the war and had become so uncritical of Soviet propaganda that he was eventually dismissed. This was not such a shock as might be supposed: other *Times* men had travelled this road; Claud Cockburn in the same direction; Stanley Morison in the other; Kim Philby was also to go all the way to Moscow. Parker was a pathetic figure, to be seen pacing the Neva embankment between two Russian escorts, deep in conference, before coming aboard to ask questions about the intelligence officers in the *Triumph*, notably one who wore a heavy beard and was thought to be of Russian origin.

The visit ended with a banquet in the city, after which the guests had difficulty in returning to their ships, for a gale had started to blow and the Neva was threatening to flood its banks. The high-sided *Triumph* dragged her moorings and her stern was blown ashore, while the river rose eight feet and burst over the embankment, flooding streets. So, while moving his ship back to new moorings, Captain Begg was amazed to be told by the Russians that he would not be able to sail, as planned, in the afternoon, while it was still light, but in the dark at two o'clock in the morning of the following day. He protested, at first in vain, that it would be dangerous to attempt the passage down-river at night-time, particularly since the first few miles would have to be covered stern first, and that the gale would almost certainly blow the ship ashore. Indeed, he refused to sail that night; wisely so, for the ship again dragged her moorings in the storm.

Realizing that the British would only sail in daylight, the Russians were forced to relent, finally agreeing that the ship could leave at two o'clock the following afternoon. The rest of the squadron sailed without trouble, then the great bulk of the carrier began to move. We already knew that she was the biggest ship to lie off Leningrad but she was also the highest and our hosts had realized that the upperworks above her bridge would command a clear view of their naval dockyards, including whatever was normally hidden from ordinary passing ships behind dockside warehouses. This had been understood by the Naval Intelligence Department before we had sailed from England and that part of the ship, out of bounds to all but the intelligence team, was said to be packed with cameras and electronic devices.

Captain Begg performed a remarkable feat of seamanship in extracting the 14,000 tons of his ship from the Neva. The gale would catch her and swing the 700 feet of her hull across the river, once to within touching distance of a moored merchant ship.

We passed the naval dockyards in daylight and were amazed by what we could see. There lay four cruisers like the *Sverdlov*, which had been at Spithead, and other big ships building; there were ships armed with rocket-launchers (something far into the future for British warships), and destroyers and submarines. In a desperate attempt at some concealment, the conning-towers of submarines were draped with tarpaulins but, otherwise, all was plain to see and, presumably, photograph. Then, as we watched, smoke began to spurt from the docksides and billow into a smokescreen. The smoke cannisters must have been damped by rain and were slow to ignite and, when they did, the wind whirled the smoke away. It was not until the ship had passed the dockyards that the smokescreen took effect and, as the *Triumph* headed for the open Gulf of Kronstadt, the greatest naval base in all Russia was enveloped in smoke.

Since the defeat of Germany and Japan it had seemed that the task of the Royal Navy might now be limited to an occasional small-scale war, erupting unexpectedly, like that in Korea. But now, as we had seen in the dockyards of Leningrad, a new challenge was being prepared. The realization that a potential enemy was, for the first time, taking to the high seas on a scale to match our own tradition, was thrown into relief by the decision of the British Government that had marked the climax of Sir Winston Churchill's premiership. At the beginning of March he had led the debate in the House of Commons on the proposal to produce the hydrogen bomb. The Labour Party, which had in 1945 ordered the production of the British atomic bomb, was alarmed and cautious, but the House had supported the Government. Sir Winston had spoken with sombre optimism of the policy of deterrence when 'safety would be the sturdy child of terror and survival the twin brother of annihilation'. *The Times* had thundered in support, 'The policy of deterrence . . . is the only way through uncharted perils.'

It seemed probable that the nuclear stalemate would prevent major aggression by the Soviet Union against countries covered by the NATO guarantee although the Russians, having lagged behind the Americans in the development of nuclear weaponry, had tested their own hydrogen bomb in 1953. But the scale of the naval construction at Leningrad demonstrated that this did not mean that the Russians would be content to remain within their own, and their empire's boundaries.

The future seemed uncertain in other ways. Back in Printing House Square there was a restlessness. Partly it was that Haley's appointments and editorial changes were not enough to match the aspirations of the younger journalists, including those, like myself, he had recruited. It was not only that we were poorly paid, but that we were pinioned: we were not permitted to write under our own names elsewhere; broadcasting, television appearances and the writing of books were forbidden to members of the staff.

There was a wider restlessness in London. The rising generation— those who had grown up over the past decade and so missed the disciplines of the war years—were beginning to assert themselves. There were stirrings in popular taste and entertainment: commercial television had started and was already challenging the canons of the BBC; the English Stage Company had been founded to produce radical plays; rock and roll music had been heard for the first time, causing frenzy amongst the audiences watching a film called *Rock Around the Clock*; amongst the new books, Graham Greene's *The Quiet American* pointed to the assumption of British imperialism by the United States, and Vladimir Nabokov's *Lolita* stretched the bounds of sexual propriety; the young were forming their own society, independent of their seniors, gathering in a new sort of establishment that catered for them: coffee bars. No longer was I so awe-struck by my own employment. Now, at the end of 1955, it was time to move on.

A farewell dinner party was given for me at Rule's restaurant where we were joined at table by a solitary diner, Graham Greene, who had been an Imperial and Foreign sub-editor on *The Times* before becoming a novel-ist. I had never met him before but neither I, nor those of my older com-panions who remembered him, felt in awe of the famous writer; he and we were equally in the shadow of what was now for him and me 'Times Past', as on the stone scroll on the pediment of Printing House Square. For all his charm, Graham Greene had about him the air of doubt and questioning that showed in his novels, so that we seemed to share a feeling that the future would probably be difficult; possibly dangerous; certainly different.

2

State of Emergency

By one o'clock each weekday El Vino's bar in Fleet Street would be crowded with journalists and lawyers but a stretch of the bar-counter near the door would be left free for a party that always arrived at a quarter past. Then in would burst half a dozen or more men, laughing loudly, to take this place, order double measures of spirits and briefly glance, grinning, around the room before resuming their boisterous banter.

Their leader was a stocky, middle-aged man with black, crinkled hair and a wide, thin-lipped smile on his pink face, wearing a belted camel-hair coat. This was Arthur Christiansen, editor of the *Daily Express*; his companions his assistant editors, political correspondent, gossip columnist and any other senior journalists who might have joined the group as they left the editorial conference. They excited envy and admiration amongst other journalists, just as those on *The Times* had inspired reverence.

These were the men who produced the most virile newspaper in Fleet Street. The circulation of the *Daily Express* exceeded four million and it prided itself on the full, if idiosyncratic, coverage of world news, reported by twenty staff correspondents stationed abroad supported by some three hundred part-time correspondents, or 'stringers', and a phalanx of special correspondents, as *The Times* could have called them, here known as 'firemen', to make lightning dashes to the scene of sensational news.

This was presented in a dramatic display of bold, black headlines, blown-up photographs, cheeky gossip and old-fashioned political opinions; the *Daily Express* wrote of the Empire as if it were still in its prime. These, of course, were the opinions of Lord Beaverbrook, its proprietor. It was he who gave the *Daily Express* the vulgar verve that made it the antithesis of *The Times*. When I was invited to join the staff as a fireman, the temptation was irresistible.

So early in 1956 I returned to Fleet Street itself and entered the black glass palace of Beaverbrook Newspapers, through an entrance hall resembling both an Art Deco night-club and Cleopatra's tomb as imagined by Hollywood. On a marble plinth in this bizarre antechamber stood a small bronze head, its eyes coldly appraising those approaching. This was Beaverbrook himself and was the nearest he now came to entering the offices of his newspapers. He controlled them from a variety of lairs: from a flat in St James's, overlooking Green Park, or Cherkley Court, his country house near Leatherhead; otherwise he might be found on Cap d'Ail in the South of France, in Jamaica, or the Bahamas, or in the Canadian province of New Brunswick from whence he had sprung.

As with Haley, there was something of the Roman in Beaverbrook, but of a very different type. Here was a clever, spoiled emperor, omnipotent, capricious; kind or cruel, as the mood took him. I had heard about him from a Canadian friend, Jack Golding, who had worked as his personal assistant after the war and had delighted in his tales of life at court and the jesters and sages, rogues and vagabonds, and the fascinating women assembled there. A memorable story had been about Beaverbrook's sudden arrival at Cherkley, striking fear and arousing excitement around him, and ordering his butler to check on the stock of rationed food in the larder. When the butler reported that there was less cheese in hand than there should be, his master—in the manner of Captain Bligh—accused him of stealing it. When this was denied, Beaverbrook asked who else had the key to the larder and was told: the chef. So, while the butler waited, Beaverbrook summoned the chef and said, 'The butler tells me that you have been stealing my cheese. Do not do so again.' And with that, he sent both men back to the servants' hall.

His politics, too, were not so eccentric as they often appeared, but Victorian, for he still treasured the ideal of the British Empire. Indeed, his view of the Empire—as expressed in the leading articles of his newspapers—was far more reverent than it can have been at Printing House Square since the turn of the century.

Soon after my arrival at the *Express* I was summoned by Beaverbrook to his flat in St James's, where he stood, as was customary on such occasions, at a lectern by the window. On this were spread the morning's newspapers and, beside them, the microphone of his recording machine into which he dictated comments and memoranda, which were transcribed and sent to those concerned on strips of flimsy paper, which could stop the guilty heart as they were taken from their envelope. As with royalty, one did not initiate conversation with Lord Beaverbrook and there was no small talk. On this occasion I was given an assignment which was to be a first lesson in the perils of reporting for the *Daily Express*. For no longer would a visit to a foreign capital begin, as a matter of course, with a private briefing from the British ambassador; now it was more likely to be the tradesman's entrance, and an aptitude for cat burglary might be an advantage.

On Sunday 12 February 1956 there had been a demonstration by students in Madrid against the rule of General Franco; it had led to violence, shots had been fired by the police and one student had been killed. The *Express* carried only a brief news-agency report but Beaverbrook had sent Christiansen one of his strips of paper asking what steps he had taken to report the trouble in Spain. He had taken none, so I was summoned on the following Wednesday and ordered to Madrid. Fog had closed the airports and, after vainly waiting for it to lift, I had made the journey by rail, arriving on the Saturday morning. Since there was no *Daily Express* on Sunday, my first report could not appear until Monday, more than a week after the event that had taken me there.

But perhaps there would be another riot this weekend? Was Madrid, as the *Express* would put it, a seething cauldron? It was not. I walked around the streets where the riot had taken place; they were almost deserted but for an occasional pair of policemen; I interviewed some diplomats. Whatever the discontents in Spain, it was highly unlikely that I would find anything exciting to report this week or next.

Had I been writing for *The Times* there would have been no report to send but, perhaps, a few days to spend preparing a 'turn-over' about the state of unrest in Spanish universities. But popular newspapers demand that correspondents report from the first day of an assignment and they become adept at giving a sense of importance and immediacy to informed speculation. So, with the use of such words as 'suspected', 'potentially' and 'could', I dictated to London a report on the apparent split in the Falange Party between the dedicated fascists and those supporting Franco's hopes of restoring the monarchy.

Next day, the London newspapers were expected to arrive at the Madrid news-stands in the afternoon and all but the *Daily Express* did so. That it had been banned became apparent when I telephoned to say that there was nothing more to report and ask how the first despatch had been presented. It had led the main foreign news page, they said, beneath photographs of Spanish tanks (taken at some military parade), of General Franco and of myself. The headline had been 'FRANCO FACES CRISIS PLOT' with the byline, 'Expressman Tom Pocock flies into Spain for this report on a flare-up in Madrid that now threatens the biggest explosion since the civil war.'

Happily the foreign editor added that I could now leave for Gibraltar. Happily, too, a sleeping berth was available on the night train but it was on arrival at the station that it became apparent that I was not alone. A small, lean man with broad shoulders, dressed in a tight-waisted coat and wearing black gloves, was speaking to the guard with sidelong glances in my direction. When I emerged from my compartment as the train pulled out of Madrid, he was standing at the far end of the corridor, watching me; next morning he was still there, perched uncomfortably on the conductor's tip-up seat; he did not leave me until I boarded the ferry at Algeciras.

The Rock was as reassuring as ever. The gleaming brass on the belts of the British sentries; the policemen dressed like London bobbies; the red pillar-boxes; the grocers' window-displays of Twining's tea; the distant bugle calls and the Union Jack fluttering against a blue sky; all this announced that this was the first great stepping-stone along the Lifeline of Empire.

For three years General Franco had been renewing his claim to the sovereignty of Gibraltar, and the recent trouble in Madrid suggested that this would be increased to divert public attention. My task was to report on the attitudes of the Gibraltarians which, the British Government always declared, would dictate the future of the colony, but which were not taken seriously, the British attitude being that they were lucky to live under the benevolence of the British Empire. There was a proprietorial instinct within the individual British. The source of this was apparent in various testaments of faith as vividly as the duty of *The Times* was seen by Stanley Morison. In a recent book, *The British Colonial Empire*, W. E. Simmett had written,

> The ultimate responsibility for the government of the Colonial Empire rests with the Colonial Office in London, which is thus an *imperium in imperio*. The political head of the Colonial Office is the Secretary of State for the Colonies, who is a Cabinet Minister. The Cabinet is responsible to Parliament, and Parliament to the electorate. That is to say, since this is a democratic country, the men and women voters of Great Britain are, in the last analysis, responsible for the Colonial Empire.

Gibraltar was the first and most dramatic of the three sentinels guarding the seaway that bound the Empire together as it passed through the Mediterranean, where it was vulnerable to attack by envious European rivals; the other two being Malta and Cyprus. There had never been any question of their devotion to the Crown; this was taken for granted in London, and with satisfaction, so long as the Gibraltarians, Maltese and Cypriots remembered their place. Indeed, there was hilarity in Whitehall when my interview with Mr Joshua Hassan, the leading politician among the 18,000 Gibraltarians, who was later to become Chief Minister and a knight, was published. 'We are as British as the Cornish, or the Welsh!' he declared. But who, in 1956, could imagine anybody with a name like Hassan being British?

As with Gibraltar, so with Malta. So gratifying was the loyalty of the Maltese that their Prime Minister, Dom Mintoff, the leader of the Labour Party, had been in London to urge that the island be fully integrated with the United Kingdom, sending its own Members of Parliament to Westminster. When lobbying in Fleet Street he had been accorded an enthusiastic welcome by the deputy editor of the *Evening Standard*, John Junor, who had seen his proposal as an echo not only of the apparently successful granting of full citizenship of France to all peoples of the French Empire, but of the similar policy in the Roman Empire. But his leading article welcoming the idea brought a swift rebuke from Lord Beaverbrook. To Junor's surprise, and enlightenment, his proprietor was not such an all-embracing paternalist as he seemed. Such a plan would never do, said Lord Beaverbrook, because the Maltese would have to be given all the benefits of the British welfare state, including those of the National Health Service. If the Maltese received such bounty so would all the other citizens of the Colonial Empire. To Beaverbrook, Junor realized, the British Empire meant Canada, Australia and New Zealand, the dominions of Anglo-Saxon stock; all else was peripheral.

Early in 1956 the Maltese voted in a referendum in favour of such integration but, as Beaverbrook had foreseen, negotiations with the British Government foundered on the issue of financial support for the island. At this, Mintoff announced that he would instead lead 'the fight for independence' and, resigning the premiership, launched the Maltese Liberation Movement to sever all ties with Britain.

The desire of Cyprus for integration came as even more of a surprise to most of the British, who were forced to recognize that, in this case, the motherland was not Britain but Greece. For the island, together with its history, had largely escaped popular attention, particularly since, although surrounded by battles during the Second World War, it had never itself been directly involved.

In the Colonial Office this hankering after an idealized ancestry had long been recognized; indeed, it had sometimes been encouraged as a healthy trend, for most senior civil servants had been educated in the Classics and regarded Athens as the fountainhead of western civilization. Most of the men of the British ruling class had been taught to read, write and speak Classical Greek and their organ, *The Times*, kept the typeface in its composing room, mostly for use in the correspondence columns, where Classical allusions and tags were printed without translation. My father had been so deeply imbued with love and respect for ancient Greece that he counted his first sight of the Parthenon as one of the greatest moments of his life and, when I was born, tried to persuade my mother to engage a Greek nanny so that I would take more naturally to the language.

Although compulsory Latin and Greek had now faded from most school curricula, the more senior administrators, army officers and traders who lived and worked on the frontiers of the Empire had all been subjected to a smattering of the Classics in their youth. This survived as hackneyed and half-understood phrases like 'The Greek Ideal' and 'The Glory that was Greece', dimly remembered as having had something to do with the origins of democracy, an austere purity in architecture and the stiff upper lip displayed by Socrates when drinking hemlock.

So to encourage the Greek ideal amongst islanders they considered to be Greek-speaking Levantines the Colonial Office was happy to recruit teachers from Greece to staff Cypriot schools and to allow the preaching of the doctrine of union with Greece—known as *enosis*—from the pulpits of the Orthodox Church of Cyprus as a robust aspiration which, so long as it remained no more than that, could seem akin to that of the Boy Scout movement.

Cyprus had been remarkably easy to govern since Britain had taken over its administration, but not, at first, the sovereignty, of the Turkish island as part of defensive measures against Russia in 1878. Then when Turkey took the German side on the outbreak of war in 1914, Britain formally annexed the island and it became a colony. The Greek-Cypriot hope for eventual union with Greece soon became apparent; more so when Greek refugees from Turkish persecution fled to the island in such numbers that, before the outbreak of war in 1939, four-fifths of the half-million Cypriots regarded themselves as Greek, most of the remainder being Turkish and seeing the island as a geographical appendage of Anatolia.

When the idea of *enosis* again excited the Greek-Cypriots after the Second World War, the British saw it as an understandable response to the shifting of power in the Levant—the departure of the French from Syria and Lebanon, the British from Palestine and the transfer of the Dodecanese islands from Italian to Greek rule—and to the belief that the new Labour administation in London was sympathetic towards self-determination for colonies. Even though the Greek Government supported this aspiration, the Colonial Office was not unduly alarmed. In 1954, Henry Hopkinson, Minister of State at the Colonial Office, told the House of Commons in words that few British noticed but which echoed through the churches and schools of Cyprus that 'nothing less than continued sovereignty over the island could enable the United Kingdom to carry out its strategic obligations in Europe, the Mediterranean and the Middle East'. That, so far as Her Majesty's Government was concerned, was that.

Yet plans for a Greek-Cypriot rebellion were already advanced and, in 1951, its joint leaders had begun to plot. They were an oddly-contrasting pair: Archbishop Makarios III—the son of a Greek-Cypriot shepherd, but now Ethnarch of Cyprus; still in his thirties but a daunting figure in black robes and black beard, his hooded eyes, watchful and intelligent; the other, Colonel Grivas, late of the Greek Army but passed over for promotion, perhaps because of atrocities committed by his men during the recent civil war. The official British description of him—eventually circulated with a price of £10,000 on his head—ran: '*George Theodorus Grivas. Age about 58, height 5 feet, 6½ inches; medium to broad build, strong broad face, small Hitler-style moustache, chestnut hair, bald on top (hair greying above ears and on temples), chestnut eyes, dark and bushy eyebrows. Ears are large and set low on head; wide, shut mouth with firm jaw.*' In the coming struggle for *enosis*, Grivas would be the mailed fist, Makarios the velvet glove.

While the archbishop stirred Greek-Cypriot emotions, pleaded and threatened, as need arose, with London and Athens and caught the attention of the United Nations, the colonel recruited and trained guerrillas and terrorists for his *Ethniki Organosis Kuprion Agoniston*—the National Organization of Cypriot Fighters—that became known by its initials, EOKA. Arms were smuggled into the island from Greece and the uprising planned for 1955, to coincide with the transfer by the British of their General Headquarters, Middle East, from the Suez Canal Zone in Egypt to Cyprus. This move was made on 1 December 1954, when the headquarters moved into barracks outside Nicosia until the building of permanent quarters at Episkopi was completed. Exactly four months later, in the early hours of 1 April, EOKA bombs exploded in many parts of Cyprus—all aimed at military or strategic targets—and the rebellion had begun.

Later Makarios was to claim that he had hoped to limit military action to sabotage and to avoid loss of life, whereas Grivas always planned for both. Whether this was so, or not, the violence mounted, assassinations began and, in October, the first British soldier was killed. The British reaction was surprise followed by indignation and the Foreign Secretary, Harold Macmillan, sought to buy time by proposing that the British, Greek and Turkish governments should discuss possible ways towards partial self-government for the island, although sovereignty would remain with Britain 'for the foreseeable future'. But, since the Turks would not countenance *enosis* and the Greek-Cypriots would accept nothing less, the wrangling would clearly be prolonged. Meanwhile the unexpected problem of internal security had to be tackled and, to organize this, Field Marshal Sir John Harding, the recent Chief of the Imperial General Staff, was recalled from retirement and appointed Governor.

Increasingly it had been possible to imagine the British Empire as a reflection of its educational system: the dominions as universities; the more advanced colonies as public or grammar schools; the more backward as state secondary, or elementary, schools; the mandates as, perhaps, subsidized schools for which other worthy bodies were primarily responsible. Like many schools some colonies went through their 'difficult' periods when a new headmaster with a strong personality and firm ideas on discipline might have to be appointed. One such was Sir John Harding: immediately likeable, clearly fair-minded and approachable; a tiny, bright-eyed man but a disciplinarian ready to inflict corporal punishment when necessary. The application of school metaphors to Cyprus was particularly appropriate not only because of associations with the Greek ideal, but because the unrest had begun in the schools and the first television broadcasts of the troubles that reached Britain were of rioting schoolchildren.

The pace of events quickened. Harding now had some 12,000 soldiers at his disposal in the island and many of them were used to sweep through the Troodos mountains in an operation code-named *Foxhunter* in an attempt to capture Grivas. It almost succeeded, for the quarry was seen and fired upon; he escaped but, amongst his belongings lost in flight and found by the British were his diaries, which implicated many with EOKA, amongst them Makarios. More British soldiers were sent to

Cyprus, bringing the total to 17,000, and Harding chose this moment, at the beginning of 1956, to talk peace with the Archbishop in the hope that the show of strength, combined with sensible man-to-man talk, would lead to a compromise between Greek-Cypriot aspirations and British strategic needs. This failed, whereupon, in March, Makarios was deported to the Seychelles in the Indian Ocean.

I now found myself on the edge of these events when, on my return from Gibraltar, I was appointed Middle East correspondent of the *Daily Express*, based on Cairo but to relieve the busy reporter in Nicosia for a fortnight every six weeks. Events dictated otherwise for, a few days after my arrival in Egypt, General Glubb Pasha, the commander of the Arab Legion in Jordan – the most effective indigenous army in the Middle East — was dismissed by King Hussein at the prompting of his Arab neighbours. The sequence of action and reaction that was to make 1956 so memorable a year in the Middle East had begun and, as other *Express* correspondents arrived, I spent the spring moving between the eastern capitals: Cairo, Baghdad, Damascus and Beirut.

James Morris, now covering the Middle East for *The Times*, was sometimes a companion on these journeys. In Cairo he and his beautiful wife Elizabeth and their babies lived on the Nile in a Victorian paddle steamer, which had carried Kitchener towards Khartoum, and were waited upon by a magnificent Sudanese servant. The Morris family had made themselves at home with the nonchalance the educated British had often shown in exotic places yet the charming, clever and amusing James, whose idyllic domesticity I, a bachelor, envied so much, still seemed to be nursing some curious little secret. I speculated but soon gave up trying to guess what it could be.

On 13 June the rearguard of British troops left the Canal Zone, leaving vast stockpiles of arms and ammunition, to which they would have right of immediate access in an emergency as agreed under the Anglo-Egyptian Agreement of 1954. On 19 July the British and United States governments announced that they would not, after all, finance the building of the great dam at Aswan, which was to store and regulate the flow of the Nile's water to increase immeasurably Egyptian agricultural production. Six days later Nasser announced that he had nationalized the Suez Canal, taken over its control and assets and that its revenue would be used to finance the building of the dam. The Egyptians had already announced that this would be done in twelve years' time when the existing agreement, under which the Suez Canal was operated, expired.

The response was outrage. Sir Anthony Eden, supported by Hugh

Gaitskell, Leader of the Opposition, expressed indignation, the latter, mindful of the Labour Party's own nationalization of essential industries, adding that it must be seen in the light of President Nasser's boasts of creating an Arab empire from the Atlantic to the Persian Gulf. The Admiralty and War Office found themselves short of contingency plans, so quickly had the *coup* followed the withdrawal of British forces.

It was not only outraged pride that inflamed the British and the French, their partners in the construction and operation of the canal. More than half the British imports of oil were shipped through the Suez Canal, and reserve stocks in the United Kingdom would last only six weeks. As my father had put it in a newspaper article just before the crisis (and had drummed into the naval cadets at Dartmouth, who were now captains and admirals, wondering what to do next), 'We have got to hold the canal—the very life-line; the jugular between East and West.' It was not only being asked whether the Egyptians might close the canal at whim, but whether they were capable of keeping it open. Would they be able to keep it dredged, let alone regulate the flow of traffic and pilot the ships, without European help?

The energy generated by this apprehension was channelled into diplomacy at the United Nations, the American proposing, as a compromise, a Canal Users' Association to take control of the waterway; this to be denounced by Egypt and the Soviet Union on the same day in September. Indeed, Russian involvement was becoming a new and dangerous aspect of the crisis; increase in trading leading to enormous purchases of Soviet bloc armaments and, finally, the financing of the Aswan dam by Russia. So, while the Foreign Office tried to find a legitimate excuse for British forces to re-occupy the Suez Canal Zone under the 1954 agreement, the Ministry of Defence and the Admiralty, War Office and Air Ministry began planning to re-occupy it by force.

As the drift of the crisis set strongly towards some form of armed intervention, I was back in London reporting news of reservists being recalled and warships ordered to the Mediterranean. Expecting to return to the Middle East—Cairo and Nicosia were the vantage-points for journalists— I was not surprised when, after a mid-day editorial conference in September, the editor, Arthur Christiansen, asked Donald Edgar, who had, until recently, been the 'William Hickey' diarist, and myself, to remain behind. He told us that there might be military operations in the Middle East and, if so, the *Daily Express* would send two war correspondents and he had chosen us.

While the British Government was referring the crisis to the Security

Cyprus, 1958. The Greek-Cypriot men of Paralimni, a village near Famagusta,
are herded into a barbed-wire compound by the Royal Ulster Rifles to be scrutinized
and some to be interrogated. EOKA suspects sit beneath the eucalyptus trees in
the background; the principal quarry, their leader Grivas, was absent.

The arms of the law: the brave but vulnerable British police in Cyprus. Sergeant Nicholas Joice (left) introduces his successor, Sergeant John Griffiths, to the village of Ayios Amvrosios from which he will attempt to keep order in three villages and 85 square miles of hillsides. Their pistols are tucked away under their bush-jackets.

When the British soldier has embarked in the landing-craft lying off the Cypriot port of Kyrenia, one of the few reminders of the British presence will be the red pillar-box on the water-front, of a pattern familiar throughout the British Empire.

Malaya, 1960. The war against the Chinese communist guerillas is almost won
and supply-drops are amongst the few operations still in progress.
Supply-packs to be parachuted from a Valetta of the Royal Air Force
stand ready at the aircraft's door.

Supplying Fort Chabai, a Valetta dives over the jungle outpost to parachute its
load. Low-level flying among the steep hills had become routine for aircrews and
the young soldiers who manhandle the supply-packs.

Council of the United Nations, where any Anglo-French proposal would be, and was, vetoed by the Soviet Union, secretly the two governments were plotting with Israel to concoct a *casus belli*. This was to be the Israeli action against Arab guerrillas on their border with Egypt, which led to the Anglo-French ultimatum to both Israel and Egypt, then intervention in the guise of peacemakers. At the end of October Donald Edgar was suddenly flown to Cyprus; the RAF began bombing military targets on the night of the 31st, as a result of which Nasser blocked the Suez Canal by scuttling forty-seven old ships filled with concrete. At dawn on 5 November British and French parachute troops were dropped around Port Said and, next day, landings were made from the sea.

The collapse of the expedition to Egypt, once Sir Anthony Eden had surrendered to American financial pressure and ordered a halt and cease-fire at midnight on the day of the landing. It came when forward British troops were only twenty-five miles from Suez at the far end of the canal. The United Nations announced that the British must withdraw and be replaced by their own 'emergency force', which would be assembled immediately at Naples, which was where I, too, had to go.

Weird was the scene that greeted passengers on the British European Airways flight on landing at Capodichino airport. A military tattoo appeared to be in progress against a background of Vesuvius and the Bay of Naples. Little parties of polyglot soldiers were marching, running about or throwing themselves on their faces as they practised platoon attacks; on closer inspection these proved to be Danes, Colombians, Canadians, and Norwegians whiling away the time while waiting to fly to Egypt in Swiss aircraft. They did not finally leave until the early hours of 15 November—giving the waiting journalists time for sight-seeing in Pompeii and a visit to Capri—and their arrival at the former RAF airfield in the Canal Zone added a final touch of irony.

The humiliation of the British and French withdrawal and the accusations of duplicity, inefficiency and stupidity that at once began to be directed at both governments was often to be seen as an historical watershed. The fiasco had been brought about by Sir Anthony Eden's insistence on behaving as if he were a British prime minister at the flood of imperial power.

In *pizzicato* accompaniment to these events, the murderous news continued to arrive from Cyprus to focus British attention on the tumult of the region. Shock was heightened by contrast, for the killings were often performed before scenery that had seemed beautiful, reassuring or domestic. The British deaths hurt most, of course: the boy on his way to

the bathing beach; the middle-aged man watering his roses; the foot-
ballers blasted by a bomb; the couple shot on a picnic; the RAF man,
turning to fetch a mug of water for the Greek-Cypriot, who then shot
him dead; unarmed Servicemen shot while shopping, notably in Ledra
Street, which the headline-writers called 'Murder Mile'. Harding himself
was lucky to escape being blown to pieces by a bomb his Greek-Cypriot
manservant had hidden beneath the mattress on his bed.

Hitherto there had been no understanding of Greek-Cypriot aspirations, now there was no sympathy.

As the white ensign of the Royal Navy disappeared over the horizon
from Port Said, westward-bound, another lull, heavy with the certainty
of future trouble, descended over the Middle East. Even Cyprus calmed,
for the year began with the publication of a plan for the island's future
proposed by Lord Radcliffe's committee in London. This suggested a
far greater degree of self-government than hitherto but left defence,
external affairs and internal security in the hands of the British and self-
determination remained a distant possibility. Because of this, the Greek
Government and EOKA rejected it at once, but the Turks responded
more favourably as, when the plan was debated in the House of Commons, the Colonial Secretary had mentioned the partition of the island,
which was the Turkish aim, as being 'among the eventual options'. While
this further divided Cypriots of Greek, or Turkish, descent, another
sedative was administered with the release of Archbishop Makarios from
detention in the Seychelles and his arrival in Athens, for he was still
barred from Cyprus. Grivas had promised to suspend terrorism in this
event, and the island began to enjoy a peaceful summer. Trouble began
again in October with more murders, riots and strikes and, the following
month, Sir John Harding handed over the governorship to Sir Hugh
Foot, the former Governor of Jamaica and a member of the celebrated
radical family.

Foot could be seen as a different sort of headmaster from Harding:
friendly, easy-going and expecting the best motives and actions from
everybody. Beneath this relaxed appearance he was a man of uncom-
promising honour who felt the Empire had brought guilt upon itself by
evacuating Palestine in 1947, leaving Jew and Arab to fight it out, as
others felt the ruling princes of India had been betrayed by the British
withdrawal. On arrival in Nicosia Sir Hugh visited hostile areas infor-
mally, sometimes riding with a small retinue of civilian horsemen, or
taking his family into the country for picnics. On one of these the Foots
were sharply reminded of realities, when their children, led by their little

son Paul, raced ahead to lay, and spring, an ambush on their parents. With Sir Hugh was walking his armed aide-de-camp, and Paul leaping out of the bushes, found himself looking down the barrel of the officer's pistol.

Shortly after Foot's arrival in Cyprus, and three years after the terrorism had begun, I made my first visit to the island, but not for the *Daily Express*. Life with the *Express* had been as exciting as expected but shadowed by demands to write in support of the real, or supposed, obsessions of Lord Beaverbrook, which had become enshrined as house dogma. Only the editor, Christiansen and, when he suffered a heart attack, his successor Edward Pickering, and a few favourites, could discuss and, perhaps, argue an issue with him; otherwise, it was often the assumption amongst others that what Beaverbrook had remarked some years previously must be developed into *Express* policy; as often, the word did come from on high, on those flimsy slips of paper bearing typed orders dictated by Lord Beaverbrook. So it was that I found myself interviewing Lord Templewood—the former Sir Samuel Hoare, Foreign Secretary in the 1930s—in defence of the Duke of Windsor, or General Lord Ismay, attacking Field Marshal Lord Alanbrooke and Sir Arthur Bryant for daring to criticize Churchill. I was becoming a Beaverbrook mouthpiece and it was time to move on. So, with some regret I resigned to spend two years dipping into more varied aspects of journalism. This included writing for the *Sunday Dispatch*, which tried to be a successfully sensational, yet not too vulgar, newspaper but had only been able to survive by running, as a serial, a flashy historical novel called *Forever Amber*, which had become a minor sensation of that prim period.

The third anniversary of the EOKA rising, 1 April 1958, was the occasion for a general strike in Cyprus, riots, bombings and murder. Foot had sought a secret meeting with Grivas, who initially showed his interest by declaring a brief cease-fire, but then, suspecting a trap, remained in hiding and ordered the killing to continue. News from the island was again in demand and in May I began the first of four spells there.

Flying across the Mediterranean towards the darkening eastern sky for an introductory encounter with terrorism, so familiar at second hand, produced a *frisson* of apprehensive anticipation. The stars were glimmering when, below, the first faint lights seemed to reflect them and the pitch of the engines changed as the descent into Nicosia began. It was then that I saw the flame. From that height it was impossible to judge its size, but it was a fierce tongue, flickering bright. Probably it was a bonfire of old olive trees but, to me, it could only be a burning police station. Then began the fearing of the worst.

43

So, down on the runway, the taxi-ing towards bright lights that floodlit barbed wire and silhouetted figures with guns and out into the dragon's breath of a hot Nicosia night. Police in starched khaki and dark blue peaked caps: a few pink-faced British, the rest sallow and black-haired, either Turkish and presumably trustworthy, or Greek and presumably not. Past the barriers and barbed wire and out into the forecourt, scented with pine, wild herbs and motor exhaust. There, in the glare of headlights, the British awaited the new arrivals; the men in open-necked shirts with pistols stuffed into their belts or trouser pockets; the women in sleeveless summer dresses.

I hailed a taxi. Was the driver Greek, or Turk? Either way, I scrambled into the front seat beside him on the assumption that, with a British target so close, he would take the safest route; if he were Greek, the lurking assassins would not shoot at me for fear of hitting him. We swept off towards Nicosia, the headlights showing only empty streets of villages and suburbs since, as I had heard at the airport, a curfew was in force. Sometimes the headlights would gleam in the eyes of a cat and, occasionally, a British soldier, holding a gun with both hands, would step back into the shadows. Nicosia was deserted, too, with light glinting behind closed shutters and a roadblock to halt us for a soldier to see the driver's curfew-pass and tell me to apply for one next day. Skirting the circle of Venetian fortifications that enclose the old city we turned into the drive of a large hotel, ablaze with lights, the Ledra Palace.

This was where the correspondents stayed and where those who wished to meet them had to come; it was also where EOKA had thrown a bomb at the Caledonian Club Ball. It was a theatrical setting, whether for tragedy or farce, with several scenes between which the performance moved. First was the front hall with its dark and silky receptionists and Savvas, ever-smiling with a flash of gold. He was the night porter and a Shakespearean chorus to whatever history, tragedy or comedy, was being enacted. Savvas was always the first with news of a murder, a demonstration, an arrest; Savvas always knew where most people, other than Grivas, could be found and perhaps he knew that, too; Savvas would hire you a car, send messages and, on at least one occasion, wrote and dictated a news story to London for a journalist prevented from doing so by intoxication.

The bar was the forum of intercourse: the passing of news, debate, laughter, gossip and convivial drinking. It was a large room, opening on to the garden and tennis court, heavily panelled and furnished in wood that gave it a faintly Austrian air. Behind the bar stood smiling Greek-

Cypriots in white jackets, who were assumed to be agents of EOKA; at the end by the windows sat another, an elderly building contractor with a grey moustache who, since he would sit drinking and exchanging occasional banter with the British, was assumed to be Anglophile. Standing, or perched on stools along the bar, were the journalists: mostly men aged between thirty and fifty; they appeared quite tough and capable; a few running to seed and mottled by alcohol; all genial.

There were, of course, other centres of activity in Cyprus—the governor's study, Grivas's lair, the general's operations room—but all the news that left the island passed through the bar of the Ledra Palace. The news during May and June was again swinging to the winds of politics. In London, Harold Macmillan had succeeded Eden as Prime Minister in April and made new proposals that the Greek and Turkish governments be associated with the British in governing the island with separate assemblies for the Greek and Turkish communities for an interim period of seven years. Both sides rejected this plan, rumours of a Turkish invasion brought out the mobs and communal rioting started.

News of trouble on the border of the Greek and Turkish quarters of the old city was brought into the bar by Celia Henderson, a girl who worked for the official radio station—so hated by the Greeks—who bravely lived alone off Ledra Street. It was just some Turkish boys getting overexcited and throwing rocks and setting light to things, she said airily. Anyway, she had been met only with chivalry and a young Turk with a brick in each hand had come up to her, told her that she should not be out in the streets at such a time and insisted on escorting her through the tear gas and flying stones to her front door. Celia had seen another Englishwoman among the crowd in Ataturk Square: a middle-aged woman in a pink cardigan, with a small dog on a lead; she had waited while the dog sniffed a lamp post and lifted its leg, before walking on through the mob as if it were a shopping crowd. Celia had no idea who she was; one of the middle-class pensioners who had settled in Cyprus before 1955, having found it such a sunny, quiet spot, she assumed; probably a regular customer at the teashop, the Mad Hatter, still kept open by an English couple in Kyrenia.

But the mood could change quickly in the bar, as when a Greek-Cypriot press photographer, whose comments on the news of the day were valued since it was assumed that he was involved with EOKA, came to deliver a message. Reports in some British newspapers that Greeks were attacking Turks in Cyprus were resented in certain quarters, he said quietly, and, as the customary noise of talk and laughter died away, continued that, unless the reporting of such lies was stopped, those thought to be responsible would, certain persons had told him, be shot.

All the British in Cyprus felt vulnerable, for EOKA assassins sometimes mistook identities, or were just looking for a soft target, and newcomers felt most vulnerable of all. From my bedroom window I looked over flowering shrubs and palm trees, behind which lurked, I felt sure, gunmen; the moment I left the hotel, my shoulder blades drew together at the expectation of a bullet in the back. Soon I learned the precautionary habits that were to become automatic from Donald Wise, who had lived and worked under terrorism longer than any of us. Watch out for young men wearing raincoats—particularly unbuttoned raincoats—on a dry day: there might be a gun underneath; be ready to jump if a young man puts a hand inside the breast of his jacket. Watch shop windows for the reflection of somebody approaching from behind. Before shopping, make up your mind exactly what you want before entering the shop, stay inside as briefly as possible and stand facing the door: a gunman appearing from the street may hesitate to shoot if you are looking at him because, if you survive his attack, you could recognize him. Sit with your back to a wall in a restaurant, facing the entrance and with another door, or window, nearby as an emergency exit. When walking beside a road, walk on the side nearest to the approaching traffic so as to lessen the risk of an assassin's car approaching from behind. Always watch your back.

Such behaviour became habit, the eye and ear attuned to danger, muscles ready for a leap to shelter. Other senses might provide warnings, too. Sitting outside a café in the sun and drinking a bottle of beer (back to wall; close to door; eyes on passers-by) the crowds in Metaxas Square are busy and preoccupied when an electric shock seems to run through them: nothing to see or hear but a *frisson* that sets people running and empties the streets. Soon police cars race by; then soldiers, running. Somebody has been shot dead in the markets, out of sight and earshot, but we knew.

Riots would begin with crowds of men milling and shouting slogans. These I soon recognized as Greek or Turk; but on a first encounter, I had replied, 'No, thank you' to a man I thought had asked, 'Taxi?' He had, in fact, shouted, '*Taksim!*' the Turkish word for partition, which was painted on the walls of their quarters just as 'EOKA' was daubed by the Greeks, who also painted out all English words on signs, or shopfronts, to substitute Greek script. The riot, once started, was almost preferable to walking alone, since only sticks and stones were involved, and there were doorways, or a line of British soldiers, for shelter.

It was impossible to know whether the day would be one for riots, shootings, bombings, or arson, or any combination of these. In April it had been bombing—with seventy-five explosions to twenty-six murders, or attempted murders. In May it had been the shooting of Greek communists opposed to EOKA, with twenty-seven murders, or attempted murders, to fifteen bombs. Now, in June, it was fighting between Greeks and Turks. The bloodiest encounter took place on 12 June in the fields around the Turkish village of Gunyeli on the road between Nicosia and Kyrenia, known, appropriately, as 'the village of the butchers' because of the local industry.

It had all been an appalling mistake. Some fifty Greeks had gone to the village of Skyloura where, they had heard, there had been fighting with Turks. They had been misinformed but, on arrival, were arrested by the British for unlawful assembly and taken to Nicosia. As it seemed to their captors that, on reflection, there was no viable charge to bring against them, they were given the usual 'cooling-off treatment' of being driven into the countryside and told to walk home. On this occasion the British set them down on the far side of Gunyeli. The Greeks set off into the fields to skirt the butchers' village; while the Turks imagined that an EOKA war-party was deploying to attack, armed themselves—mostly with butchers' cleavers—and set out to meet them. Nine Greeks were killed—one decapitated, another hacked to pieces—and others wounded; naturally EOKA claimed that the British had deliberately deposited the unarmed Greeks outside Gunyeli for them to be slaughtered by the Turks.

This was, of course, major news, but two days earlier there had been a curious incident. A second lieutenant of the Royal Horse Guards, on duty in some dusty village, where Greek might fight Turk, had happened to be standing in front of his armoured car when its machine gun fired without its trigger being touched, activated, perhaps, by the extreme heat. The young officer had been badly hit, and was now in hospital, where he was not expected to live. His name was Auberon Waugh, son of Evelyn Waugh, and it was said that his father might fly to Cyprus; in the event, his mother came out and stayed with the Foots, and the young man survived. But the possible arrival of Evelyn Waugh at the Ledra Palace delighted those who had read *Scoop* and alarmed those who had heard that his combative friend Randolph Churchill, son of Sir Winston, was also due to arrive as a roving correspondent for the London *Evening Standard*. As one remarked, on hearing of Churchill's arrival, '*This* is all we need.'

Randolph Churchill arrived, two days after the Gunyeli massacre, from Ankara, where he had been interviewing the Turkish Foreign Minister, Zorlu, and was at once invited to dinner with the Foots at Government House. Next day was to be busy, because the Mayor of Nicosia, Dr Themistocles Dervis, who had once declared, 'We are all EOKA now!', was to hold a press conference at the Ledra Palace to speak about the massacre; however, as public assemblies had been banned, the police might regard this as illegal.

Next morning the sun rose early, glaring hot, and I dressed quickly to get down to the dining-room to hear the overnight news, read the English-language newspapers, look at the correspondents' notice-board and see whether the survivors of Gunyeli (unshaven young Greeks with black armbands over their white shirt-sleeves) would again have been sent by EOKA to eat toast and marmalade amongst the journalists. As I locked my door the neighbouring one opened and there stood, in pyjamas, a strange figure with the head of a ravaged sphinx, purple pouches beneath the eyes.

'Good morning, I do not think we have met,' it said, in a husky, cultured voice. 'My name is Churchill.'

I introduced myself.

'But, of course. I know your work well and admire it greatly. Are you about to breakfast? Might I persuade you to breakfast with me? I would so much like to talk with you.'

Flattered, I agreed and was beckoned into his room, expecting to wait until Randolph Churchill dressed. Instead, he asked, 'Coffee? Orange juice, eggs and bacon, toast and marmalade?' and, when I nodded, picked up the telephone and ordered a single breakfast from room service.

'Forgive me,' he said to me, 'if I breakfast on something else.' And he disappeared into the bathroom, returning with a tumbler half full of whisky.

'I was dining at Government House last night,' he continued, as if by way of explanation, then, 'Do you get about the island much? I know the people at Government House and they tell me everything. Perhaps we could work together?'

It was the custom, when two correspondents who did not directly compete with each other—like those of a London evening and national Sunday newspaper—might help one another, each covering an aspect of the day's events, then meeting to share their information. To give the *Evening Standard* first-hand reports of happenings around the island, in return for political forecasts, would be ideal. But before I could agree he went on, 'Pocock, may I ask your help? You know, it may seem extraordinary, but I cannot compose my article and type it at the same time. I have to cable my account of seeing Zorlu and Hugh Foot this morning. Might I ask you if you would, most kindly, type it for me?'

I could hardly refuse, so balanced his portable typewriter on one twin bed, sat on the other, tore a Cable and Wireless form from a pad and typed, 'press urgent collect evestandard london churchill nicosia monday begins . . .' Churchill paced to and fro in his slippers, tumbler in hand, and began to dictate, 'An almost unnatural calm enfolds this beautiful island. Often in life, when one fears the worst, things go much better than expected. So it may be tomorrow, when the Governor, Sir Hugh Foot, makes his long-awaited statement as to Britain's new policy.'

As he paced, he would stop talking, then stop walking, to consider his next sentence, while I sat waiting, beginning to realize that I could be sitting here for some time. Then, as Churchill came to the Turkish rejection of the British plan and his own visit to Ankara, he asked himself, 'Shall I be naughty? Yes, I will.' He continued dictating, 'When Mr Zorlu, the Turkish Foreign Minister, told me this on Friday in Ankara, I could not refrain from saying to him, "Your Excellency, with great respect, permit me to say that I was brought up to believe that the Turks were adult-minded, but it seems to me that you are now behaving politically like a bunch of Greek children . . ."'

At this point my breakfast arrived, but Churchill, in full spate, motioned the waiter to set it on a table, and carried on, 'He smiled a smile of superior incredulity . . .' The report was now one of a conversation, in which Churchill quoted himself more than the Foreign Minister: 'I argued with him for nearly an hour . . .; "Fun is fun", I said. "But you go too far, Your Excellency." I regret to say that I then went so far as to accuse Mr Zorlu of humbug; Mr Zorlu, who is a very grown-up person, naturally didn't like this but took it in very good part'.

I had now been sitting, typing for about an hour and had given up all thought of breakfast, but, despite my annoyance and frustration, felt bound to carry out my agreement to type his report. At last he finished, asked if he could read it through, then, as if suddenly realizing that my breakfast had arrived, apologized profusely for keeping me from it. Mustering a smile, I said that I was no longer hungry, that I had work to do and Dr Dervis's press conference to attend. As I backed towards the door, Churchill added, 'My dear fellow, you wouldn't be passing the cable office, would you? If you are, you wouldn't be so kind as to drop this in?' And he handed me the pages I had just typed.

All thoughts of working in partnership with him had been replaced by the urge to escape and, taking the typescript, I ran down the stairs. Having sent his cable, I returned to the Ledra Palace, where the press conference was making news before it had begun. The British chief constable had arrived, cap on head, cane under arm, to declare it an illegal assembly. Dr Dervis angrily protested, more than thirty journalists waited and finally the chief constable changed his mind and allowed the meeting to begin, whereupon Dr Dervis ordered his town clerk to read out a long statement, blaming the British for the Gunyeli massacre.

At this point Randolph Churchill appeared in the doorway, looking bemused, as if he had been seeking the bar and lost his way. Then, seeing me, he pushed through the crowd and asked, in a hoarse whisper, what on earth was going on. I began to explain, but, before I had finished, he was on his feet, booming, 'Your Worship! Do you make the suggestion that the British procured the death of these people?' Startled, the Mayor of Nicosia replied that he did not know, that he was just giving the facts and the journalists could draw their own conclusions. At this, Churchill declared, 'In that case, Your Worship, you and I cannot remain in the same room', and he strode out, making for the bar, followed by some of the journalists, who thought the son of Sir Winston Churchill more interesting than the Mayor of Nicosia, while Dr Dervis began shouting that he did not care whose son his interrupter was, even if he was the son of Stalin, because he was only interested in telling the truth about the British imperialists.

Randolph Churchill, finding the bar congenial, spent much of the day there and, although trying to keep out of his way, I felt a hand on my arm and heard him ask, 'My dear fellow, I so enjoyed our talk this morning. Perhaps you could breakfast with me tomorrow?' Mumbling excuses about an early start for distant troubles, I declined. This was true, for life at the Ledra Palace, with much talk but little involvement with the events we were reporting, was beginning to pall. Seeking the quickest way to plunge into realities, I had accepted an invitation to spend a day at an isolated police station in a hostile country district.

In the hotel bar we had often heard echoes of what sounded like the Wild West that came to our notice as reports of shootings and ambushes in villages and on country roads, and continued, whatever was taking place in Metaxas Square, Ataturk Square and Government House. Once I had heard a police inspector say to an army officer—both sunburned and dusty from such regions—over pints of beer, 'I'd like you and your boys to come into town with me tonight. I'm expecting a little gunplay.'

If I was looking for such dramatics, it was suggested, I should call on one of the 200 British policemen who had volunteered to spend two years in Cyprus with the rank of sergeant and were mostly alone and in charge of remote districts. A group of three villages in the north-east of the island was recommended as being particularly hostile.

The road to Ayios Amvrosios, Kharcha and Kalogrea ran across the baking plain to the dragon-back ridge of the Kyrenia range, across it and eastward along its northern slopes which ran down to the dark sea, beyond which stood the mountains of Turkey. It should have been charming country, bright with oleander, hibiscus and jacaranda and other points of colour, the blue and white, or red and white of Greek or Turkish flags, which proclaimed the allegiance of each village. In either case, these were dull and dusty, the only activity being at the coffee house, where old men with sweeping white moustaches—the Turks in their black, baggy trousers—sat in the sun and watched the passing car without expression. I was reminded of a British officer's belief that he could identify an EOKA man by looking into the eyes of every young Greek-Cypriot male he passed: 'If they look away they are probably only collaborators. If they meet my stare boldly, they are EOKA.'

The three villages proved much like the others and with no doubt as to their loyalties, for a Greek flag flew from the church in Ayios Amvrosios and its walls were daubed with fresh EOKA slogans in blue paint: another fifty had appeared the previous night, I was told. Near the old police station was a new, concrete one, half-built and half-demolished because, while the builders worked by day, EOKA came by night and had, so far, undone their labour with ten bombs. Two rooms had been completed and here lived Sergeant Nicholas Joice, a strapping man of thirty, who was about to hand over his command to Sergeant John Griffiths, a twenty-six-year-old from Cardiff, before returning to his wife and children in County Durham. Both were tall and strong, wore military moustaches and, at first, made light of their task with dismissive humour.

But their life here was dangerous and uncomfortable as no amount of flippancy could disguise and both were soon describing it with detachment. Except when handing over to a successor, the sergeant lived here alone; his Greek-Cypriot sergeant and three constables remaining at the old police station until the new one was complete. Since the Greeks were either in league with EOKA, or brave men risking their lives to collaborate with the British, he had to do the more risky work himself.

51

Sergeant Joice would tour his territory of the three villages and eighty-five square miles of hillside in a Land-Rover, noting likely ambush sites along the road, tracing hidden paths into the villages, searching caves and setting up his own checkpoints by parking across the road and standing beside it with his Stirling sub-machine-gun. All this he did alone, but the true test of nerve was in the villages. These were dominated by loyalty to, or fear of, EOKA. A few days earlier, gunmen had walked into a coffee shop and seized an elderly man and a youth, accusing them of helping the police. They had been taken into the street, where the villagers were assembled, ordered to spit in their faces and then to beat them. The old man died and none of the villagers would dare to dig his grave, or even carry his coffin. Joice shook his head sadly, as he told the story, and added that neither had helped the police but perhaps it had been, as it was quite often, the settlement of some private vendetta.

It was in the main streets of the villages, where such things happened, that the British sergeant's nerve was under particular stress. He had to dominate the village, or try to do so, and he could only do this by showing himself to be unafraid. He would therefore have to walk alone each evening, down the main street of each village, slowly and calmly, knowing that he was probably being watched by armed men who wanted to kill him. 'Some nights are worse than others,' he said. 'Sometimes you can feel the eyes watching you from the darkness.'

Like a sheriff in the Wild West, he relied both on his own bearing and on his skill with a pistol. There were snap-shooting contests for policemen at Kyrenia, where he had learned to put six bullets into three oil drums in six seconds. In his room at the police station he would clear space amongst the camp-beds, refrigerator, cooker, chairs, wardrobe with its rack of clean, pressed khaki uniforms, Stirling gun and riot gun for firing tear-gas grenades, and the table with its stack of paperbacks and framed photographs of his family, to stand at a distance from a long, upright looking-glass. There he would practise drawing his pistol, faster and faster. 'Don't look at the gun—keep your eye on the target,' he explained.

Before Nicholas Joice began his walk, he would decide whether to carry his pistol beneath his khaki bush-jacket, leaving the bottom button undone so that the black butt stood clear; or to buckle the belt and holster over it for a quick, unimpeded draw. If the walk seemed likely to be peaceful, he would leave it underneath; only if trouble seemed probable would he walk with gun displayed. Sometimes trouble had been all too obvious; as when a shouting crowd had stoned the police station and

Joice had buckled his pistol over his jacket and gone out with the Stirling in one hand and the riot gun in the other. But just as challenging had been the quiet evenings when he had to take his long, slow walk down the village street, enter the crowded coffee house to arrest a man, and walk him back to the police station. In a few days' time, he would be back in County Durham, perhaps as a village policeman with his bicycle propped against the fence of his cottage, and all this would seem as unreal as it did to his neighbours.

It was easy to write about Sergeant Joice and, as heroes are popular with Sunday newspaper readers, his story appeared in the *Sunday Dispatch* under the enormous black letters of the headline 'GUN LAW', for Wild West movies were popular with the readers, too. But heroes must be matched with villains and, for the British, the blackest of these was their opponents' hero, Grivas.

By now he had become one of the great patriotic outlaws of history and fiction. Despite the continuous efforts of thirty to forty thousand troops and police, much of the Turkish community and the Secret Intelligence Service, he remained at large in an island half the size of Wales. Rumours would run through Nicosia that he had been seen disguised as a priest riding through Kyrenia on a donkey; in Larnaca, walking with a limp; or had actually preached a sermon in a Nicosia church. All that the British knew for certain was that he had been seen, but such was the size of the island and the scale of the search, he must have only just succeeded in escaping many times since then.

The scale of his terrorism had fluctuated according to the military success and political initiative of the British. By the beginning of 1957 Harding had inflicted a serious defeat on EOKA, almost wiping out its mountain gangs. While the numbers of guerrillas and assassins was always small—not much more than a thousand men under arms, with a core of about three hundred effective, well-organized fighters armed with modern weapons—these had the support of a high proportion of the Greek-Cypriot population.

The early autumn of 1958 brought a veering of the political wind. The Turkish Government decided to support the latest British plan and Macmillan decided to implement it, despite Greek opposition. Makarios, fearful of being presented with a *fait accompli*, immediately changed tack and, with the support of the Greek Government and to the surprise of all, renounced *enosis* as his principal aim and declared that he would accept independence for Cyprus instead. Grivas was outraged and responded in his own way: not only were as many British as possible to be killed, but this would now include women. On the morning of Friday 3 October the wives of two British sergeants, Mrs Cutliffe and Mrs Robinson, out shopping in Famagusta, were shot in the back; Mrs Cutliffe died.

The news shocked and appalled the British. Complaints from the Greek-Cypriots that soldiers had at once sought revenge, pouring into Famagusta to attack any young Greek males they could find with their fists, were brushed aside: the British had used their fists, not guns, as other vengeful armies would have done. When the first agency reports reached Fleet Street, I was there and was summoned by the editor of the *Sunday Dispatch* who, as expected, said that he wanted me to return to Cyprus immediately, but added, to my amazement, 'I want you to find and interview Grivas.'

'Right,' I agreed, and departed. In retrospect, my instant acceptance of so absurd an assignment sprang from two instinctive reactions. One was that, particularly in times of stress, the Englishman brought up to believe himself heir to the Empire tended to obey orders instinctively; the other was that, still thinking of myself as a *Times* man, I regarded sensational journalism as unworthy and, ashamed of myself for practising it, disdainfully avoided discussing such a stunt.

When I thought about the assignment I reassured myself that I might arrive at the very moment when Grivas decided that he wanted to broadcast his views in an interview. Supported by such optimism, I returned to the Ledra Palace. But how to make contact with EOKA and present my request for this interview? The only answer was that which had solved so many little problems before: ask Savvas.

Behind his desk in the lobby the smiling porter flashed a gold tooth in welcome and, when I whispered that I wanted to speak to him privately, beckoned me into a little cloakroom and cocked an attentive ear. 'I want to interview Grivas,' I said. Savvas did not flicker an eyelash, but nodded and said, 'I see what I can do.' There being nothing more that I could say, or do, I returned to the bar and awaited developments.

The next morning the telephone rang in my room and a man with a Greek accent said, 'This is what you will have to do. You will walk out of the front door of your hotel and you will take the taxi that you will find waiting there. You will be driven to a bar in the old city. There a man is waiting for you.' And he rang off. This was the real thing; the fantasies in the newspaper office coming true; with a tightening of the throat and stomach muscles, I did as I was bidden. Savvas did not look up as I passed his desk; a taxi was there and the driver was expecting me; we drove around the Venetian walls, then turned through the Paphos Gate into the old city. Two bombs had exploded in Nicosia that morning, the city was tense; in empty streets soldiers stood in doorways, fingering their guns. In a narrow and deserted street, the taxi stopped outside Charlie's Bar, well known for its lavish *mezedes* dishes in quieter times, but now deserted; except for a dark young man in a white shirt who sat alone at the far end of the bar, sipping coffee. He looked up as I approached and spoke my name. Then he whispered, 'I am taking you to meet the brother of the man you wish to see.'

We hurried through the streets littered with EOKA leaflets, along Ledra Street, and then into a quiet street beyond and stopped at a tall house with double doors decorated with iron grilles, 57 Alexandra Road. A nameplate announced in Greek script that this was the home and consulting room of Dr Michel Grivas; so there was nothing secretive here. A servant girl peered through the bars and opened the door, and as she led us across the cool, dim hall and up a creaking wooden staircase, my companion whispered that of course Dr Grivas spoke English but wished to speak Greek; he himself would translate. There must be no political questions.

Dr Grivas rose to meet us; a broad-built man with a strong, sad face and thick, grey hair; intelligent, friendly eyes peered through heavy, horn-rimmed spectacles. 'You wish to ask about my brother?' he asked. Then, with only occasional prompting from me, he talked of their childhood as sons of an Anglophile grocer at Trikomo below the Kyrenia range and how George had been a stubborn, aggressive little boy, always the leader of a gang and playing soldiers, although an Englishman had taught him to play cricket. He had excelled as an athlete (particularly at sprinting) but his favourite subject was the heroic mythology of Greece, including that of the War of Independence. At nineteen he had declared his intention of joining the Greek army and, when his father threatened to disinherit him if he did, worked as a labourer, saved his wages to pay his passage to Athens, and ran away. Eventually he wrote to say that he had won a scholarship to a Greek military academy, adding, 'Do not forget that Cyprus is under slavery and I do not exclude the possibility that one day I may be useful.'

'I last saw my brother in 1952,' said Dr Grivas, 'when he was in Cyprus for six months.' I had known that he had been in the island the year before and was thought to have made a later visit before his final return for the EOKA campaign, but this seemed a promising line of inquiry. 'My brother came for a medical examination at the hospital,' volunteered the doctor. 'He had a bad heart and was ordered to give up smoking. He also had trouble with his stomach and had an X-ray examination here.' Perhaps Dr Grivas's own interest in medicine had prompted this disclosure but, whatever his motive, this suggested a clue to follow.

If that had been his state of health six years ago, Grivas was likely to be in need of medical attention now. If this was so, then the most likely source would be the general hospital in Nicosia, which treated sick and wounded EOKA men as it would any other patient, Greek or Turk. I met Greek-Cypriot doctors and one who remembered Grivas's visit in 1952. From him more evidence emerged: Grivas had suffered from a duodenal ulcer and a form of diabetes: the former must surely have worsened under the stress of his subsequent activities; the latter might now demand a regular supply of insulin. Here, surely, was a warm trail?

The degree of stress he must have undergone became apparent when I talked with soldiers who had taken part in the manhunt across the Troodos mountains which had almost trapped him four years before. It was then that the trail had petered out; since then there had been no first-hand reports of Grivas, even from EOKA prisoners; no hand-written orders or despatches had been captured; nor had there been fresh photographs of him in Greek newspapers.

Now a new rumour was heard in the Ledra Palace: that Grivas was in hiding somewhere near Famagusta. Perhaps it might be more than a rumour for, one evening, several of us were called out of the bar by an Army public relations major who, after swearing us to secrecy, told us to be dressed and ready to leave the hotel at four o'clock next morning but on no account to ask the hotel staff for an early call. So, in the half-lit lobby a dozen of us assembled (others, whose loyalties, or views, were thought suspect, had not been invited) until the headlights of Land-Rovers lit the drive, we climbed aboard and were driven away. As the sky lightened, our conducting officer told us that we were bound for a big village called Paralimni, near Famagusta, where two battalions of the Parachute Regiment and another of the Royal Ulster Rifles, supported by armoured cars of the Royal Horse Guards, were about to conduct a major cordon and search operation. Important EOKA men were thought to be in Paralimni. They might include Grivas.

While we had been waiting in the lobby of the Ledra Palace, the troops had surrounded the village and six buglers of the Royal Ulster Rifles, wearing plimsolls, had tiptoed into the market place by the church. There, in the stillness before cock-crow, they had come to attention, raised the bugles to their lips with a flourish and sounded reveille. Immediately police cars drove through the streets, loudspeakers booming orders for all the men of the village to report at once to the schoolhouse. Lights came on and doors opened, Irish pipers began to play a quick-march and, as the men of the village, dazed from sleep, emerged, hustled them into large barbed-wire compounds erected on the school playing-field.

The sun was up and the eucalyptus trees casting long shadows as we swung off the Famagusta road on to the dusty track that led to Paralimni. All eyes were on the road surface for it was loose and suitable for mine-laying. This had been the latest EOKA campaign and we were all familiar with the crumpled Army trucks with blood-stained cabs that had been the result.

A few miles on, reassuring signs of the British Army appeared: sand-coloured armoured cars of 'The Blues' and the distant red and green specks of the berets of the infantry as they moved in and out of the houses they were searching. On the outskirts of Paralimni, rolls of barbed wire had been spun out to form a large, rectangular compound. Here the men of the village sat, cross-legged in rows, to be summoned, one by one, for questioning by Special Branch officers who sat at a table beneath a clump of eucalyptus trees. After their interrogation they joined another group, similarly seated but with their backs to the others; or, if wanted for further questioning, were ordered to lie on their backs in the sun.

We were greeted by the Ulsters' colonel, a trim, black-moustached figure, electric with confident energy. He explained the progress of the search and added, 'As you can see, we are not being brutal, but we are not using kid-glove methods, either.' We could see what he meant: the rows of Cypriots sitting in the sun were being kept in place by a corporal swinging a riot-baton and ready to use it; as each man was called for interrogation he ran between coils of barbed wire, speeded by a cut from a knotted leather thong, swung with zeal by a soldier waiting for that purpose.

Four arrests were made at Paralimni but there was no sign of Grivas. Back in Nicosia I realized that, even if he was receiving medical attention, I had not, as yet, found a trail to follow. It was then that a new idea occurred. Walking down Ledra Street and watching the reflections in shop windows, my eye was caught by a cardboard cut-out advertisement in a shoe shop's window display. It was the figure of a sprightly, striding man in bowler hat, black coat, striped trousers, swinging an umbrella and wearing a black moustache that momentarily reminded me of Grivas. Beside him was the slogan, 'Walk the Barratt Way!' This was familiar since it was the climax to the successful strip-cartoon advertising campaign—

57

almost as well known as that suggesting that 'night starvation' could be avoided by drinking Horlicks at bedtime— showing a sufferer from uncomfortable shoes meeting the bowler-hatted Northamptonshire shoe manufacturer, Mr Barratt, who advises him to try his own product and 'walk the Barratt way', which he does with success and mutual congratulations. There was, however, a sad piquancy about the lithe figure of Mr Barratt, who seemed to grow younger each year, because in fact the real shoe manufacturer of that name, of whom this was a flattering portrait, had been dead for some time.

Staring into that shop window I forgot, for a moment, to watch the reflection of the street behind me. There it was, the solution to the mystery. Like Mr Barratt, Colonel Grivas was dead! Suddenly, all the pieces of evidence fell into place: that he had been a sick man six years ago and had not been seen for two years; that no direct clues to his presence in the island had been found since that time; that he had avoided detection by tens of thousands of soldiers, police, intelligence agents and informers. Grivas was dead but, like Mr Barratt, his soul went marching on, leading the Greek-Cypriots towards *enosis*. Somebody else, using his name, was commanding EOKA, confident that the leader his enemies sought could never be found.

Charged with excitement, I collected a few more relevant scraps of evidence and flew back to London. There I visited a doctor, a friend now a specialist at the National Heart Hospital, and showed him one of the most recent, but least familiar, photographs of Grivas. He did not recognize him, so I presented my medical evidence: the man was now aged sixty; six years ago he was suffering from heart trouble, a form of diabetes and an ulcer and I repeated details of the symptoms I had been given. Assuming this to be so, what might his health be like now? He thought for a while, then replied, 'From the symptoms described he is suffering from ischaemic heart disease—the narrowing and hardening of the arteries—which is often linked with the form of diabetes he is reported to have had. Pain, such as he experienced, is often caused by this condition.

'At any time since 1952 he might have died from coronary thrombosis. Physical exertion—such as running, or climbing—could cause great pain. Nervous stress and excitement could also bring on heart attacks. The chances that his health could have survived six years of very active life are remote, but he could have survived if able to lead a quiet, gentle life free from stress.'

That decided it. I put my theory to the editor of the *Sunday Dispatch*, who listened with mounting interest. This was a major story, he announced, which I would write to spread across two pages on two consecutive Sundays. This I did: telling the story of my search in the first article and presenting my theory in the second. Aware that, contrary to the evidence, I might be wrong, I announced the death of Grivas as only a possibility, ending the second article with a question mark.

The first article was published on 19 October, beneath the bold announcement 'Another Great Scoop . . . In Search of the Most Wanted Man on Earth. I keep an astonishing rendezvous . . .' The pages were illustrated by a small photograph of Grivas and a large, full-length figure of myself, striding as purposefully as Mr Barratt. Slightly ashamed by this, but excited at what seemed a journalistic triumph, I left for Paris on another assignment. The following Sunday, returning to Heathrow and riding into London on the airport bus, my eye was caught by enormous posters: a grim face of Grivas and, in huge black lettering the words: 'GRIVAS: THE WHOLE FANTASTIC TRUTH'. At a news-stand I tore open the *Sunday Dispatch* to see the bold, barefaced headline, 'I SAY GRIVAS IS DEAD'. The question-mark at the end of the article had disappeared.

The hot wave of shame and its undertow of guilt broke, then settled into a calm that reflected a radiance of congratulations. How amazing that nobody had tumbled to the truth before, when now it seemed so obvious! How clever of me, and how brave! Even in Fleet Street there was that grudging praise for somebody else's scoop. Even James Morris, home from the Middle East and resigned from *The Times*, thought the theory plausible, at least.

Nemesis was four months away. A run of success for the British Army in Cyprus was matched by political progress. In December the foreign ministers of Britain, Greece and Turkey met in Paris at the invitation of NATO, which had its own strategic reasons for wanting a settlement between its three member states. Here Selwyn Lloyd agreed to the island's independence on condition that Britain could maintain two sovereign base areas at Episkopi and Dhekelia in the south and south-east of the island. Greece and Turkey agreed and, without the support of Athens, the ideal of *enosis* withered, leaving Makarios no choice but acceptance. In February 1959 formal agreement was reached.

But EOKA and its leader, whoever he might be, were anguished with frustration. Outnumbered by about thirty to one, his guerrillas and assassins had not been defeated and, despite recent reverses, could have continued the campaign and, indeed, wanted to. Compared with conventional war, losses had been small: more than five hundred killed, about a third of them British. In the British Isles the agony of Cyprus had been reported in greater detail than any previous colonial conflict so that its fear and pain seemed part of the domestic scene.

Watching developments from London my own interest became intense as, at the end of February, Makarios prepared to return to Cyprus from Athens and the EOKA leadership to emerge from hiding. On 1 March the Ethnarch flew back to Nicosia to a frenzy of welcome, a slim, sinister figure, pale of face and robed, veiled, hatted and bearded a dead black. His first gesture must, all agreed, be to meet and hail Grivas and the British braced themselves for the demon king to spring upon the stage. But he did not. A day passed, then two and three and, whatever they were wondering in Cyprus, I began to nurse a bud of hope that I really had been right after all; when a week passed without sight or sign of him, it began to flower. On the 9th a leaflet appeared, apparently from Grivas, ordering EOKA to lay down their arms. But a fortnight went by and he had still not materialized. Then, on the 17th, Colonel Grivas, haggard as befitted an elderly man with his medical record but looking exactly as long imagined, made his appearance, gave a press conference and flew to Athens.

'How clever those Greeks are,' said a kind friend, 'to have kept his double up their sleeve for this moment.' But there, all too alive, was Grivas, soon to talk of his exploits, his escapes and hiding-places, one of which had been in the house of the building contractor who had sat drinking with us for so many hours at the end of the Ledra Palace bar.

In my embarrassment, I did not draw any parallel between my own ridiculous blunder and the mistakes at an infinitely higher level which had led to the Cyprus tragedy. All were guilty of a blindness to the aspirations and abilities of those who did not think as we did; particularly of those to whom the Greek Ideal meant more than it did to us and for whom the call of the motherland was as strong as the bonds we believed bound us to the Empire.

So the British departed; at least from Government House. Just before he boarded the destroyer off Famagusta, Sir Hugh Foot, the benevolent headmaster, broadcast some final man-to-man advice: 'There are a few who say that the island will go down in a sea of blood and hate—but I don't believe it. People who have been to the brink of hell don't want to go over the edge.' At first it looked as if he might be right. Certainly Archbishop Makarios, who was to be the first President of the Republic of Cyprus, was picking up the right mannerisms. As the Foots were preparing to leave, the Archbishop called at Government House, inspected a guard of honour mounted outside by the Black Watch, and later sent a message to the guard commander: 'His Beatitude's compliments. An excellent turn-out.'

Cyprus would be an independent republic within the Commonwealth—whatever that might mean—but, at the time, it seemed that the loss of the island to the Empire was a British defeat. Later reflection showed that this was not so: the Greek-Cypriots had failed to attain *enosis* and the British had kept their military bases, which had been all we had really wanted to keep.

3

Dust of Empire

Plumes of dust rose above the palms as the column started to move, obscuring the mauve silhouette of the distant mountains. The afternoon sun had raised the temperature to 120 degrees Fahrenheit and the metal of the trucks and armoured cars was too hot to touch. But it was the dust they would raise—fine as flour, gritty as iron filings—that would be the worse discomfort and the three of us in the open Land-Rover tied scarves over mouths and nostrils and pulled goggles down over eyes. The colonel, sitting next to the driver, turned to me, perched among the kitbags, bedrolls and jerricans of petrol and water at the back and said, 'What bliss to do this with lancers and pack-mules!' He was a sophisticated fellow with a romantic feel for the ways of the old Empire.

Once a fortnight the column left Aden with supplies for Dhala, beyond the mountains, eighty-three miles to the north and five thousand feet above sea level. This summer day in 1959 the thirty three-ton trucks would, as usual, cross the desert of Lahej, then spend the night at the fortified camp of Nobat Dhakim before taking the dangerous course through the mountain passes next day that would involve infantry, armour, artillery and air cover. Now the whole column was on the move, all but the leading armoured car plunged into choking dust that obliterated all but the back of the vehicle in front, scrubby trees at the roadside and, occasionally, a lurching camel train.

Once this route was said to have been known as the Incense Road, because of the loads of spices carried by the caravans through the passes on their way across Arabia to the Mediterranean and Europe. It had always been dangerous for travellers, particularly through the mountains between Aden and Dhala, where the hill tribes had long levied tolls on the passing trade and tried to kill those who would not pay. For most of the time since the British had annexed Aden in 1839 this irritant had been ignored because the Lifeline of Empire crossed the sea and ships stopping to refuel at Aden could carry whatever cargoes were necessary.

Just occasionally, when the tribesmen ventured too far from their mountains, or killed a European, a small punitive expedition had been necessary. For the past thirty years these had been rare because the imposition of such minimal discipline on the tribal territories had been the duty of the Royal Air Force. Here, as on the North-West Frontier of India, British rule was enforced, literally, from on high. Aircraft showered leaflets demanding the payment of fines, or the surrender of hostages, and, if there were no response, inflicted punishment: sometimes the shooting of cattle, camels and goats from the air, or the bombing of an emir's house, but always after a warning by leaflet of the wrath to come.

Until 1955 this had seemed enough. But then the message of the impending British departure from Egypt had reached Arabia, the tribes had become more self-confident and, in one of several raids and ambushes, two RAF officers were killed, when out of their element on the ground. Then began a series of punitive expeditions mounted from Aden, involving not only the locally-raised Aden Protectorate Levies but British troops, including regiments with a sonorous roll of battle honours from the farthest frontiers of Empire: the Seaforth Highlanders, the King's Own Yorkshire Light Infantry, the Gloucestershire Regiment, the Queen's Own Cameron Highlanders, the Durham Light Infantry, the King's Shropshire Light Infantry, the York and Lancaster Regiment, the Royal Lincolnshire Regiment, the Prince of Wales's Own Regiment of Yorkshire and the quaintly-named Queen's Own Buffs, who owed their name to the colour of their uniform in the seventeenth century. There were several set-piece battles with British soldiers storming the rocky heights of a *jebel* with the bayonet, losing a few men and winning a few medals. Nobody seemed to express any surprise that British boys not yet twenty and only a few months away from life on a Lincolnshire farm, or down a Durham mine, should find themselves fighting wild mountainmen in country as remote and savage as any that faced their predecessors when they were pushing outward the bounds of the British Empire.

The trouble was not only caused by the unruly subjects of the emirates and sheikhdoms but by the fierce neighbour whose frontier ran to within fifty miles of Aden, the Yemen. The four million Yemenis, once freed from Turkish rule by the British in 1919, had begun to assert themselves, claiming sovereignty over both Aden and its hinterland, which they called South Yemen. No amount of aerial disciplining by the RAF could keep the Yemenis out of the British protectorate and their expulsion became one of the duties of those old and illustrious regiments of infantry. Only two battalions were available for internal security in Aden, 'peace-keeping' up-country and keeping an eye on the four battalions of Levies, who were regarded as unstable and once had 500 men posted as deserters. Yet the British infantry—supported by the resident cavalry regiment's armoured cars, known as 'The Metal Box Company'—joined the Levies in providing three garrisons in the protectorate. These, code-named 'cricket pitches', were at Beihan, Mukeiras and Dhala, the only one of the three that could be supplied overland. It was near these, particularly the latter, that most of the fierce little actions were fought. The last of the battles had been necessary to raise the siege of Dhala, the capital of the emirate through which ran the Incense Road, when in the spring of 1958 the Buffs and the Levies had carried the commanding heights of the Jebel Jihafi. A year later, as another Dhala convoy set out, the state of war had relaxed marginally into one of ferment.

Long experience had given the British expertise in fighting and winning such colonial skirmishes, but now there was a far more worrying possibility: a threat to Aden itself. Since the withdrawal from Egypt in 1956, Headquarters, Middle East Command, had been moved first to Cyprus then, on independence, to Aden, where it covered a vast area including the Red Sea, Arabia, the Pesian Gulf, the Indian Ocean and all the African territories including Kenya and Rhodesia. The port, visited by some 5,000 ships each year, remained an important bunkering station for the Navy and, nearby at Little Aden, a new oil refinery capable of handling five million tons of crude oil a year had been built to replace the vulnerable refinery at Abadan in Iran. The airfield at Khormaksar had been enlarged for use by long-range troop-carrying aircraft and strategic bombers. Aden State was regarded as another Gibraltar and its population of 250,000 as even more docile than the Cypriots had been thought to be. But 80,000 of these were migrant workers from the Yemen and 95,000 were Arabs and so subject to the summoning up of nationalism and Islamic fervour broadcast by Cairo Radio. Moreover, this cause had taken hold of the trade union movement which, encouraged by the British as part of the progression towards increased self-government, now controlled 22,000 workers.

As Britain had lost the goodwill of Arabs through supporting Israel, and by the Suez war, so the political restlessness in Aden grew, resulting in strikes and rioting. In an attempt to harness these energies, the British pressed forward with plans for the building of a viable nation out of Aden and its hinterland, which would remain loyal and so eventually qualify for a higher degree of independence within the Commonwealth.

So it was that, at the beginning of 1959, the six wild little states of the

Western Aden Protectorate were joined together in what was called the Federation of Arab Emirates of the South, which was to have its own capital and legislature at Al Ittihad, just outside Aden. Eventually this would become the capital of the new nation, including the three sultanates of the Eastern Aden Protectorate and Aden State itself. The Yemenis objected, realizing that the success of the federal plan would end their hopes of annexing South Yemen, and accused the British of breaking a standing agreement between them of maintaining the *status quo*. In a sense they were right, for they had taken the treaty to refer to the *status quo* within the frontiers of the protectorate and of their own country, while the British assumed that it referred to that on the frontier itself. The Yemenis were therefore increasing their border raids and arming the tribesmen, concentrating on those inhabiting the roadless, and mostly unmapped, mountain regions to either side of the Dhala road, which were known collectively as the Radfan.

So, just before sunset on this June evening, as the Dhala convoy, powdered with dust from the desert, reached its staging point at Nobat Dhakim there was a faint feel of danger in the air. The camp was built on a bluff above a dry riverbed and, beyond its barbed-wire perimeter, the ground fell away in steep slopes of grey shale on three sides. Within, drab-green tents sheltered behind breastwork sangars of rock and sandbag so that only the pointed roofs protruded; my own had been slashed open by a sniper's bullet so that I could lie on the camp-bed and see the stars.

Next morning the column climbed the gentle gradient of a road running up a wide valley bordered by bare hills that led to the fort of Thumier, where the warlike operations would begin. The fort itself, whitewashed and reminiscent of Beau Geste, was used as a residence by the British political agent covering the Radfan and as a command post during the passage of convoys. Here waited more armoured cars of the Life Guards that would increase our escort to twelve, together with a company of British and Arab infantry; somewhere along the fifty miles of road between Thumier and Dhala would be two field-guns covering the heights above a pass vulnerable to ambush and, down on the airfield at Khormaksar, Venom jet fighters were ready to fly in our support; so, if necessary, were the big, four-engined Shackletons, maritime reconnaissance aircraft which could be used as bombers.

Here the convoy took up battle formation and all weapons were loaded. The colonel in my Land-Rover took a sniper's rifle with a telescopic sight from its canvas case and laid it across his knees and, since the rules of the

Geneva Convention forbidding the carrying of arms by war correspondents could hardly apply here, I loaded my own Beretta pistol and tucked
it into the pocket of my bush jacket. 'Oh, to be doing this with Gatling
guns,' sighed the colonel, 'so that I could order, "Mr Smith, be so good
as to rake the crest with your piece."'

The road to Dhala now ran along riverbeds half-choked with boulders,
beneath the sheer flanks of jagged ridges, and finally reached the bottom
of the fearsome Khoreibah Pass, which reminded old soldiers of the
Khyber. Here the column halted for the infantry to dismount, the Arabs
scampering up the mountainsides while the British hitched the webbing
straps of their equipment on to their bare, brown shoulders and plodded
in file along the verges of the narrow road. This was where ambush could
be expected and binoculars swept the heights, then focused on tiny
figures on the skyline high above. The officer in the wireless truck called
to the air support, 'Gloworm calling Venoms ... Gloworm calling
Venoms!' Then somebody interrupted, 'It's friendly troops—the high
pickets from Dhala.' But a moment later a pair of Venoms came whipping
over the camel thorn, opened their throttles to rocket up and out of the
valley and circle in high, wide arcs, wings flashing as they caught the sun.

The column climbed the pass in the traditional way: high pickets
manned the commanding heights ahead and, when the convoy had
passed, scrambled down the mountainside to be collected by trucks at the
rear. At the head of the pass stood the twenty-five-pounder guns, ele-
vated to bombard; but on this occasion they were not needed, nor did the
Venoms have to fire their 'sparklers', the special mixture of ammunition
loaded into their cannon for these purposes. In late afternoon the column
rolled on to a high, green plateau below the bulk of Jebel Jihafi, which the
Buffs had stormed a year before. In a shallow green bowl beneath surrounding hills lay Dhala; above it on a shelf of land stood the fortified
camp of a battalion of the Levies; and above that again, and commanding
it with mortars as a precaution, the smaller camp of a company from the
Royal Warwickshire Regiment.

Here, too, the camps were surrounded by barbed wire and sandbagged
weapon pits, the tents sunk within sangars. Even so, they were regularly
attacked: two men had been killed in their tent by a mortar bomb a few
days earlier and sniping was so commonplace that new arrivals had to be
warned not to shine a torch when making nocturnal visits to the latrines.
But on this calm evening all was still and silent but for the distant barking
of a dog. How pleasant were the simple comforts of the camp: washing
away the dust and annointing the head with oil from a barber's shop in St

James's; cleaning the boots with saddle soap and the pistol with its neat little brush; putting on clean clothes not impregnated with sand. Then a stroll through the camp for drinks with the non-commissioned officers before dining with the British colonel commanding the Levies.

In the Life Guards' lines, two corporals of horse were in a reflective mood. One of them, who had commanded the armoured cars that had travelled with us from Aden, was a big, muscular man in early middle age, nut-brown from standing in his gun turret stripped to the waist. The Dhala convoy was, he said, almost as enjoyable as the Lord Mayor's Show, with which he had ridden through the streets of London, but could not match his first experience of public duties more than twenty years ago. That had been riding in the mounted escort at the wedding of the Duke of Kent and Princess Marina of Greece. It was not so much the wedding procession itself that he liked to recall but, after dark that night, escorting the couple to the railway station and a waiting train. The young trooper in cuirass and helmet, sword drawn, had ridden his charger through the crowded streets and never forgot what it was like. 'All those faces looking up at you in the lamplight,' he mused. 'I felt the world belonged to me.'

In a sense, of course, it had, for every young Briton had felt a proprietorial familiarity with much of the world that was the Empire, if only through an uncle who had soldiered in India, or from the broadcasts on Christmas Day by the King's subjects in distant places. His friend was less romantic but equally rooted in his country's past. 'Just give me beer from the barrel and Fulham and I'm happy,' he said. 'Good old Fulham.'

The colonel was waiting for me with canvas chairs set outside his tent and whisky and soda ready. He too was in a reflective mood as the sun went down, throwing the ridge of mountains beyond Dhala into sharp purple silhouette against a red and yellow sky. 'Don't worry about any sound effects at night,' he said. 'There's usually some shooting but not necessarily at us. They might be having another go at the Emir's palace; or at each other, for that matter. You must remember that the only territory we can claim to control all the time is behind our own wire.' He gestured towards a valley, now only visible as the shading of purple mountain into black, and added, 'If I wanted to go up there, for example, I would have to take a brigade group with air support.'

It was then that he told me the strange story of The White Women of Radfan, that was halfway between news and legend and recalled those myths of the Empire's frontiers that I had occasionally heard from old men, long retired from those regions. Not so long ago, it seemed, several

67

of the more adventurous tribesmen of the Radfan had made their way to Aden, found work and eventually been taken aboard a passing ship in some menial capacity as what were known to the British as lascars. They had learned a little English and, when their ship had eventually docked at Cardiff, they had been able to engage Welsh girls in some conversation. One, at least, had apparently been able to give the impression that, despite appearances, they were men of consequence; if not Arab princes, then, perhaps, the sons of sheikhs. The impressionable girls having memories of Hollywood actors in the well-laundered robes of the desert Arab, eventually agreed to accompany them to what they may have imagined to be their silken tents, but whether as wives or concubines was not known.

They had passed through Aden and had been seen boarding one of the rickety buses which occasionally rattled up the road to Dhala. As they had not been sighted here it was assumed that they had alighted somewhere in the Radfan and made the rest of the way to their husbands' villages on foot, doubtless, said the colonel, getting accustomed to carrying the luggage for their masters. Wherever they had gone, a shock had awaited them, for the mountain villages were without sanitation or medicines, or, indeed, any of what the girls would have considered the essentials of life. They had not been seen since.

From time to time, continued the colonel, a signal arrived from Aden asking the political agent at Thumier, or himself, or their predecessors, to make an effort to find them. But short of sending an expeditionary force, there was nothing they could do beyond hoping that reports would filter out of the mountains and be heard by an Arab intelligence agent. All that had been heard were occasional reports of fair-haired babies in one of the most inaccessible hill villages. There had been a time when this case might have provided a convenient excuse to impose British administration upon the region, but now that would bring us into further confrontation with the Yemenis, and the rest of the Arabs, and that was to be avoided. The girls would have to live with their mistake, if they were still alive.

Why they might not be alive, the colonel went on, I might be interested to see for myself. Next morning he had arranged for me to visit a couple of frontier forts, where there had been trouble over the past few days. Somewhere up there I was likely to meet a young Army doctor who, as well as attending to gunshot wounds and a variety of septic cuts and sores amongst the soldiers, had his private patients in the mountains. He, and he alone, was able to penetrate the Radfan and visit the villages, where he attended to the sick and so had won the trust and, apparently, the friendship of the people. It might be possible for me to go with him.

Next morning a patrol of the Warwicks was to 'show the flag' along a stretch of the Yemeni frontier, calling at the fort at Sanah that stood just across the border from the garrison town of Qataba, which had been the source of much trouble. A few months ago a British fighter, flying on the Protectorate side of the frontier, had been hit by anti-aircraft fire from there; in revenge, Venoms had attacked the barracks at Qataba and, thereafter, their squadron's standing orders had included a new section under the heading 'Tit for Tat'. That had stopped the anti-aircraft fire but not the sniping and, only a few days before, an Arab officer of the Levies had been shot through the head while standing on the ramparts of the fort.

The patrol travelled in Land-Rovers through the camel-thorn of the sandy, rocky plain, surrounded by mountains, on which both Sanah and Qataba stood. The fort would have been familiar to soldiers of the Middle Ages and, indeed, of the Ancient World: a square, stone tower with two floors for living space and stores and a tent on the flat roof, from which flew the new flag of the Federation. From the battlements where the officer had died we gazed upon the plain to the white walls and flat roofs of Qataba, quaking in the hot air; such must have been a soldier's view of a hostile city throughout the centuries.

Two young British officers were living at the fort and they invited me to lunch in their mess. This was a stone-walled room with two unglazed windows opening towards Qataba, and they said that, at night, when the hurricane lamps were lit, the shutters had to be closed as a precaution against sniping. On the walls hung the portrait of the Queen, familiar from the messes and offices of the servants of the Empire across the world, and a battered bugle. This, it was explained, was a Yemeni bugle, captured in action and now sounded on guest nights when the appropriate toasts had been drunk and the glasses refilled.

Also at the fort was the doctor, a good-looking young man, unmilitary in white shirt, shorts and suede desert boots. He was going into the hills that afternoon and, although he looked askance at the military cut of my khaki bush-jacket and slacks, agreed that I could accompany him. We were to travel by Land-Rover but the Arab driver from the Levies wore the turban and striped *lunghi* waist-cloth of the hillman. Thus we set off, trailing the dust-plume that would announce us to watchers in the mountains ahead.

Like their equivalents in Europe, the villages stood on their hilltops, their stone walls and towers suggesting a scorched and arid Tuscany. No walls surrounded the villages but only slits of alleys led between the tall houses and the windows were high and tiny; unglazed, of course, but surrounded by a rim of a whitewash that apparently discouraged flies. It was at the foot of a dusty path leading to one of these that we stopped and, as we did so, three men with rifles walked towards us from the village. They were thin and sinewy; bright, dark eyes glinted above aquiline noses. Each man wore a brightly coloured turban, *lunghi* and jacket, across which were slung bandoliers of rifle ammunition and a belt from which dangled a curved dagger.

The doctor greeted them in Arabic and our driver announced us and introduced me at length. The tribesmen listened impassively, then beckoned us to follow them up the path to the village. As we walked, carrying ammunition boxes filled with medicines and medical paraphernalia, the doctor said to me, 'This is quite a privilege. The Army would have to fight their way in here. They have gradually come to accept me as they have seen that I really can help them sometimes. But if they thought we were spies, or that we were armed, our lives would not be worth a fig.' It was then that I remembered the pistol, thrust into my trouser pocket, but concealed by the skirt of my bush-jacket. There was no disposing of it now and, rather than upset arrangements at this stage, I determined that it should remain hidden until we were safely back in the Land-Rover.

The village street was some ten feet wide, stony, rutted, and littered with garbage, including the freshly-severed feet of slaughtered goats. Following our escort, we ducked through low doorways into the dark and stinking interiors where, as the eyes became accustomed to the gloom, women and children could be seen. 'They have every imaginable disease and then a few more,' said the doctor as he squatted to examine a baby. The sores and rashes, the swollen stomachs and diseased eyes, the emaciated and distorted limbs confirmed his pessimism as he worked quietly for an hour and more; feeling joints, listening with his stethoscope, injecting with his hypodermic syringe, rubbing with ointment and dispensing medicines while his driver interpreted his instructions.

Expectation of life hereabouts was not more than forty years at best, but this, he felt, was a beginning. The last child he tended, he had first seen a week before, being carried out of the village for burial; now there was a chance that it might survive. There was gratitude in the fierce faces of the armed men who stood in a ring around us and, when the last child had been handed back to its mother, their leader motioned us to follow him and led us farther up the steep and filthy street to the biggest house, which belonged to the headman. In a small room we were received by him and, still surrounded by his fighting-men, invited to sit on mats spread over the stone floor for coffee to be poured by a slave from a large brass pot. As I lowered myself to sit cross-legged there was a clatter as my pistol fell from my pocket; at once I sat on it, remembering the doctor's warning and hoping that, in the dim, crowded room nobody had noticed. Thus perched in discomfort I smiled, sipped coffee and bowed to our host while trying to edge the pistol back into the pocket when eyes were upon the headman, the doctor or his interpreter. I was successful and we were able to make our farewells and, escorted by the riflemen, walk down to the waiting Land-Rover and depart in a cloud of dust. As we jolted over the desert, the doctor spoke of his self-imposed task. 'Whenever I treat an Arab child,' he said, 'I hope that it will live to grow up and say that it remembers the British because they came with pills that healed it, as well as with the guns over at the camp.'

An echo of the doctor's sentiments came next day when I was received by the Emir of Dhala in the stone house that passed as his palace. He was not an impressive man; small, thin, without the proud presence expected of an emir, but with restless, expressive eyes. Conscious that he was being interviewed for a newspaper that would be read in Whitehall, he declared, 'The British send us soldiers and for this we are grateful. But we need more than this. We need medical supplies and now we need food for there has been little rain and the harvest is very bad. The British give much money to other nations in the Middle East, so why will they not give more to us, who are their friends?'

There was a chance that Whitehall might cock a sympathetic ear, for there was a need to demonstrate that the new Federation was more than the buffer state between Aden and the Yemen that it clearly was, and some civil aid was likely to come their way. But the British would have difficulty in ensuring that the money was used for its intended purpose, so aid might have to be in kind and that would mean supervision and supervision would mean even more of a military presence to protect the supervisors. How far could these people be dragged out of the Middle Ages?

Now, perhaps, the lone political officers in the federation would be joined by civil aid administrators and medical missions, who would try to persuade the tribes to grow more wheat instead of the stupefying drug *qat* and to try remedies other than branding for treatment of the sick. But before this came about the Emir of Dhala and the five other rulers would each choose six representatives for the world of secretariats, negotiations and press conferences down at Al Ittihad.

Down in Aden—a twenty-minute flight in a light aircraft—the Radfan still seemed infinitely remote, providing good training for the soldiers; somewhere any young officer would give his eyes to serve. There was satisfaction in the little shows of sabre-rattling that had been staged in support of the Federation. 'I have given up prophesying but I will state a fact,' a senior British official told me in his air-conditioned office. 'It may not be saying much, but the British position in the Middle East is now stronger than it has been for ten years. We have achieved this by showing our friends—and our enemies—that we are at last ready to back our words with deeds. We are going in for a little *realpolitik*. We let it be known that so long as we need oil from the Persian Gulf, and so long as there is a danger of war with Russia, we will remain in Aden.'

As the Statement on Defence in the 1957 Estimates' white paper had put it, 'Apart from its own importance, the Middle East guards the right flank of NATO and is the gateway to the African continent. In the Arabian peninsula, Britain must at all times be ready to defend Aden Colony and Protectorates and the territories of the Persian Gulf for whose defence she is responsible. For this task, land, air and sea forces have to be maintained there and in East Africa.' Those in Kenya had been transferred to Aden, which had become the keystone of the central arch of a defensive arcade stretching from the British Isles to Australia and Hong Kong. Moreover, now that trooping was by air, Khormaksar had become an essential link in the chain of fuelling stops on the route to the Far East, the transports also landing at Tobruk, in Libya, to the west and to the east on the new airfield at Gan, a scrap of coral in one of the atolls making up the Maldive Islands in the Indian Ocean, south of Ceylon. Those two were little more than fuel-points but Aden was a main base, where troops could be staged and aircraft repaired.

Certainly, despite recent unrest, Aden appeared reassuringly stable. At night—all night when a passenger liner lay in the harbour—the lights of the duty-free shops, selling cameras and electronic gadgets around the curve of The Crescent, glared. British families could spend all day at their beach clubs, feeding on mixed grills and chips. In the expatriates' club the revolving fans ruffled the flimsy paper of the airmail edition of *The Times* and members would occasionally rise from the creaking wickerwork armchairs to peer at shipping at anchor through the brass telescope that stood on a tripod in the window. From my balcony at the Crescent Hotel I looked across the flat roofs to the ugly outline of Mount

The Royal Warwicks at Sanah in the Radfan, 1959. An Arab officer has been killed on the ramparts of the fort by a sniper and a show of force, which can be seen from the Yemeni garrison town of Qataba, is in progress.

The Dhala Column halts at Fort Thumier. The 30 three-ton trucks have been escorted by armoured cars of the Life Guards on the 83-mile journey from Aden, lasting two days. Here the last, most dangerous stage of the journey begins.

Through the Radfan. In a haze of dust, the column passes hill-villages which are still trying to levy tolls on passing caravans and, in doing so, have found themselves in confrontation with the laws of the British Empire.

The kindly face of the old Empire. In a remote village among the mountains of
the Radfan, the young Army doctor is an honoured guest, although the Army itself
would have to fight its way here. He treats sick children, carrying his medicines
packed in an ammunition-box.

The war correspondent. No battlefield was complete at this time without the presence of Clare Hollingworth of *The Guardian*. Here she looks out over the Radfan during the 1964 campaign, before accompanying the vanguard of the Royal Anglian Regiment.

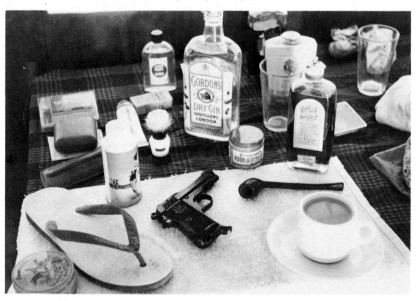

Still-life at the Dhala camp. The author's equipment includes foot ointment, sun-burn oil, powder, saddle-soap, disinfectant, aspirin and sunglasses. The pistol is a Beretta.

Shamsan, the extinct volcano that dominates Aden, rising into the strong blue sky from the haze of the maximum humidity possible. 'Should terrorism ever start here,' I thought, 'it will become a very unpleasant place indeed.'

For me it was a return to London in a Comet jet transport of the RAF, the route skirting the border of Egypt to an outcrop of rock in the Sahara, known as 'Nasser's Corner', then flying up the western side of the Libyan border to refuel at Tobruk, a journey of about four thousand, five hundred miles.

The stability of the strategic air route that ran through Aden had come to seem as important as the sea route always had. This was now the long reach and calming hand of the British that could be laid swiftly and firmly anywhere in the region known as 'East of Suez'. There, as anywhere still coloured imperial pink on maps of the world, the correspondent of Beaverbrook Newspapers was conscious of being under the unblinking eye of its principal shareholder. Lord Beaverbrook's interference with the *Evening Standard*, which I had now joined, was less than with the *Daily Express*, partly because of its tradition of partial independence and partly because it had a strong editor in Charles Wintour. But the little typed slips of dictated instructions and comment arrived from time to time and there were occasional summonses into his presence.

Dinner with Lord Beaverbrook could not have been in more marked contrast to dining with Colonel Astor (the future Lord Astor) at Carlton House Terrace, when courtliness prevailed and the only tension or embarrassment for his guests was in conversing amongst themselves when the old gentleman dozed in his chair after dinner. The host at Cherkley Court thrived on tension and embarrassment.

One such occasion at this time began with a telegram sent to me at eleven o'clock on Saturday morning that read, 'LORD BEAVERBROOK INVITES YOU TO DINE WITH HIM AT CHERKLEY AT EIGHT OCLOCK TONIGHT'. I was staying at my cottage on the Norfolk coast that weekend and the invitation did not reach me until I returned from sailing in late afternoon. It was impossible for me to reach London, change into my dinner jacket and reach Cherkley, near Leatherhead, by eight so I telephoned Lord Beaverbrook's butler with my apology and explanation. This I repeated on the following Monday to his personal assistant, who replied that Lord Beaverbrook understood the circumstances and, in any case, liked his staff to get away to the country at weekends; he hoped that I would be able to dine with him on another occasion. At this I said that should there be any possibility of another

invitation for the following weekend I would be glad to know as soon as
possible as I had guests coming to stay in Norfolk and would have to can-
cel these arrangements.

Next Friday, as I was about to leave for the country, the telephone
rang and I was told that Lord Beaverbrook invited me to dine with him at
Cherkley the following evening at eight. I therefore travelled to Norfolk,
welcomed my guests and left them on Saturday afternoon to obey the
summons. This was only the beginning of the lesson I was to be taught.

Cherkley Court, embowered in wooded hills, was a sombre house, furnished in the manner of an old-fashioned gentlemen's club. Lord Beaverbrook greeted me with grave courtesy and introduced me to his other
guests. Lady Dunn was a former *Daily Express* secretary who had taken
the fancy of his friend, the Canadian millionaire Sir James Dunn; now a
lean, aquiline widow of aristocratic bearing and richer, it was said, than
Beaverbrook himself, she was a frequent guest; they were to marry two
years later. An elderly American couple, Malcolm Muir, an editor and
columnist of the magazine *Newsweek*, and his wife had just arrived from
New York. Finally, Anne Sharpley, a brilliant reporter for the *Evening
Standard*, dazzlingly handsome and able to enchant Lord Beaverbrook
without a suggestion of coquetry, made up the party.

A reminder that small-talk was not in order for staff journalists came
early when I stopped myself remarking on the delightful view of the garden by noticing that it was dominated by a cross and remembering that
this marked the grave of the first Lady Beaverbrook. I had, in fact, taken
the precaution to assemble several weighty topics of conversation, most
of them with direct bearing upon the standing and responsibilities of
Great Britain at the beginning of the 1960s. When the moment came, it
was for the weightiest of these that I would reach.

Roast beef was being served and as the gravy was about to be offered to
Mrs Muir she turned suddenly, knocking the silver tray and sauce-boat
to the white carpet where the gravy spread, dark and greasy. As staff bus-
tled about with buckets of hot water, Lord Beaverbrook assured her that
it was of no consequence and the flustered Mrs Muir engaged me in small-
talk. She always loved England, she said, because of the wonderful way
we spoke English which was so different from anything they heard back
home. On the contrary, I replied gallantly, the most beautiful English
was often spoken by educated voices in New England, where phrases had
survived intact since the eighteenth century.

At this Lord Beaverbrook snapped from the head of the table, 'What's
that young man saying?'

'Why, Mr Pocock has just said that we Americans speak more gracious English than you do right here in England,' she chirped.

'Explain yourself,' Lord Beaverbrook ordered me.

I repeated what I had said to Mrs Muir but that was not enough.

'Let us have an example of what you mean,' he demanded.

At this my mind went blank and, groping in a void of memory, not one word, let alone expression, that would illustrate my point could be found. Lamely I said that I would compose a speech in eighteenth-century English for delivery next time we met.

'In future,' declared the rasping Canadian voice, 'support your case with evidence.' And he changed the subject.

Very well, you old bastard, I thought, if you want heavyweight conversation, you can have it and I reached for the weightiest topic of them all. There was no hurry, I could await a suitable moment. When it came I asked loudly, 'I wonder what each of you would consider the most dangerous threat facing the British Empire and the Western world today?' I looked boldly at each in turn and continued, 'I must add that— surprisingly, perhaps—it is not Soviet Russia or international communism. What then?'

There followed a stunned silence; gratifying at first but then prolonged to the point of embarrassment. 'Very well then, I will tell you,' I went on. 'In the view of some privy to the highest level of intelligence sources, it is something to which few can have given even a moment's thought. It is the possibility of an eventual economic and then political union between Japan, Indonesia and China. The industrial might of Japan exploiting the natural resources of Indonesia to meet the immense demands of the Chinese masses. Such a union would be more powerful than any other in the East or West and its effect upon the future of mankind would be incalculable.' And I stared across at Lord Beaverbrook with a light of challenge and triumph in my eye.

The silence continued. Clearly, all were lost for words. Now I must follow with penetrating questions. Just then Beaverbrook turned to Malcolm Muir and said, 'Why don't you come visit me at Cap d'Ail.'

That, however, was the end of the lesson I was to be taught. Later that evening, when the first edition of next day's *Sunday Express* arrived, Lord Beaverbrook talked with easy familiarity about politics but it was the politics and politicians of the past; not once did he refer to the problem that now beset the Empire he had loved, or even the news reaching London from 'East of Suez', where I was about to return.

This news was often from Malaya where, as elsewhere, the troubles

had been called 'The Emergency' and were seen as a direct legacy of the
Second World War, after which different political factions in countries
that had been occupied by the enemy fought each other for predomi-
nance, as in Greece. In Malaya the communists among the Chinese
settlers had offered the most effective resistance to Japanese occupation
and this had been recognized when their leader, Chin Peng, had marched
through London in the Victory Parade wearing the ribbon of the Order
of the British Empire. Their insurrection against the colonial government
had started in 1948 when the British had announced limited independence for the country in a Federation of Malaya made up of the Malay
states ruled by their traditional hierarchies, which would offer little, if
any, political expression to the Chinese, let alone the communists.

Chin Peng found response among the Chinese minority, about four-
tenths of a population of five million, which now feared that it would be
even more firmly dominated by the Malay majority than hitherto. They
formed a terrorist and guerrilla army—known as the Malayan Races'
Liberation Army; its supporting network, the Min Yuen—armed largely
with British weapons parachuted into Malaya for use against the Japanese five years before —launched their first offensive in June 1948. British
officials, planters and policemen were murdered; Chinese and Malay
workers in the rubber plantations were forced to stop work and the trees
were slashed; attacks on plantation and tin-mine offices and police
stations were followed by ambushing of road traffic and sabotage of
railways. The British response was hindered by the violent deaths of two
High Commissioners—Sir Edward Gent in a mid-air collision over
London as he was arriving for consultation; Sir Henry Gurney, his successor, in a terrorist ambush in Malaya—and only took effect under the
leadership of two remarkable soldiers, Lieutenant-General Sir Harold
Briggs and General Sir Gerald Templer. The former drew up the basic
defensive plan of concentrating the Chinese villagers, living on the edge
of the jungle, into defended settlements, so cutting off the guerrillas'
supplies of food; the latter intensified this and led the counter-offensive,
which was combined with a civil aid programme to win the 'hearts and
minds' of the population and the promise of early self-government for
Malaya.

Although the Chinese communists never mustered more than 6,000
guerrillas and terrorists, far more than the usual ten-to-one ratio in
manpower was needed to defeat them. When Templer had brought in
reinforcements from Australia, New Zealand, East Africa and Fiji as well
as from Britain, and, of course, Gurkhas from Nepal, the strength of the

security forces including police and local defence volunteers exceeded a quarter of a million. Of this total about 45,000 were soldiers, more than half of them from the British Isles. This huge effort, conducted with subtlety, had effect; in 1952, for example, nearly a thousand communist terrorists (called CTs by the military) were killed. By 1955 the back of the insurrection had been broken and elections held in that year put the Malay leader, Tunku Abdul Rahman, and his party, recently expanded to include Chinese and Indians, in a position to offer Malaya strong self-rule after independence, which was achieved in 1957.

In 1960 victory was almost complete but at a high cost. Although, over the past twelve years, nearly 10,000 insurgents had been killed (some 7,000 of these deaths being confirmed), more than 500 soldiers, 1,400 police and 2,500 civilians had also lost their lives and the cost to the economy had proved almost crippling. But now only a few hundred guerrillas were still active in the jungle; about a hundred of these were still in Malaya, the rest operating from the comparative safety of Thailand. There had been no terrorist attacks reported since half a dozen throats had been cut six months ago.

The first stage of the counter-offensive—the resettlement of rural Chinese in new, corralled villages—had been primarily a matter of organization; the second stage had been the attacks on the enemy in the vastness of the jungle. This had demanded soldiering of the highest order from the young soldiers of the British Army, two-thirds of them conscripts; youths of eighteen and nineteen, fresh from barracks in the British Isles and sent to fight in the jungle, after only six weeks' training and acclimatization. The most effective soldiers were the Gurkhas, of whom some 12,000 of the 15,000 inherited by the British from the Indian Army were on active service in Malaya throughout the campaign.

Before each British battalion arrived an advance party of officers and non-commissioned officers was sent on a month's course at the Jungle Warfare Training School in Johore, largely staffed by Gurkhas. There they were taught how to move silently through the undergrowth and how to make bivouacs of branches; how to lay an ambush and how to avoid one; the dangers of booby-traps, such as the tendril of undergrowth that, when pushed aside, would detonate a hidden grenade; which berries and fungi were nutritious and which poisonous; how to remove leeches, swollen with blood, with a lighted cigarette. They would spend days and nights in the jungle to be taught to think and behave with the wariness and cunning of a hunting, or hunted, animal.

Most took to this daunting environment with fortitude, good humour and even skill. By this time it was not so much fear of the enemy but of the jungle itself that had to be faced. One young second lieutenant of the Queen's Own Royal West Kents, who had been through the Jungle Warfare School and been trained further by an experienced battalion of the Scots Guards, confessed that he could never feel at ease in the jungle. 'It's the perpetual gloom and the smell of corruption that is so awful,' he said. 'Everything stinks of rotting vegetation. You are always wet through; it rains like hot pennies six times a day and the leaves never stop dripping. In dense secondary jungle it is good going to cover a hundred yards in an hour and you cannot see the enemy an arm's length away. But most terrifying of all is at night, when you are one of a patrol's four sentries. It is the blackest darkness and you can make no noise and certainly not communicate with your neighbours, twenty-five yards away. There is an intense loneliness. What I loathe most, and have never got used to, is living like an animal; wet, filthy and hungry. But an even worse fear is that I might let my men down; that keeps me going.'

It was not England that this young man dreamed about, but a pair of dry socks. Nor did he feel any particular animosity towards his enemy; indeed, he had never seen his enemy; or, if he had, it had only been once. Many times he had lain in ambush, watchful and sodden under the leaves—sometimes for days and nights on end—but no strangers had ever walked into his gun-sights. Then, one day, they did; a group of people who should not have been there. To him they looked like a village family, young women amongst them; certainly they did not seem to be carrying weapons. Perhaps they were carrying concealed explosives, or were members of the Min Yuen carrying food to CTs in the jungle? In any case, his orders were to open fire. 'I didn't give the order to fire,' he told me. 'I let them walk past and I never reported what I had seen.'

There were others who did not feel as he did. In jungle camps he had met thin, sinewy, cunning-eyed young men with skins sallow from living in the twilight of the jungle. These belonged to the Special Air Service, a wartime regiment, specializing in surveillance and sabotage behind enemy lines, which had been re-formed for The Emergency. 'There was an animal-like light in their eyes,' the second lieutenant recalled. 'They would go into the jungle for, perhaps, three months and come out yellow-skinned, haggard and covered with ulcers but very proud of themselves. They could not wait to get back into the jungle because they had learned to live and think like beasts of prey and they loved it. They were men apart.'

Others for whom the jungle held few terrors were the Gurkhas, the best soldiers of the old Indian Army, who now fought under contract, for the War Office, rather than for the King-Emperor.

By the spring of 1960 there were few warlike operations for the visiting journalists to watch. Here, as in South Arabia, they had now been reduced to the level of those necessary to maintain the frontiers and out-posts of a far-flung empire and so, for the second time within a few weeks, I found myself taking part in the routine relief of one such out-post; indeed, the dropping of supplies to remote jungle garrisons by the Royal Air Force was the only military diversion on offer.

Flying began early, before the sun burned away the morning mist and sucked the still clouds that spread in calm layers across the sky into the towers of cumulus and the thunderheads of afternoon. Two Valetta transports—stubby, twin-engined aircraft, the military version of the Viking airliner, which had been developed from the wartime Wellington bomber—stood on the bright green grass of Kuala Lumpur airfield, loaded with helicopter fuel and rations for Fort Chabai, one of ten such jungle outposts that could only be reached by air. The flight began plea-santly over sharp peaks thrusting through the virgin jungle above the sil-ver gleam of rivers; a battlefield recently won from the enemy in one of the 'rolling offensives' that had finally driven them from the forests and the rubber plantations and tin mines that made Malaya so important.

The pilot chain-smoked (against regulations), occasionally removing the cigarette from his lips to speak to me, or to somebody on the ground through his microphone. He had the manner and grimy looks of a mecha-nic and enjoyed his work, being without ambition to do more than fly. 'I like doing this,' he remarked. 'This is Old Time flying; flying by the seat of the pants. You will see what I mean.' Back in the cargo-space five young soldiers in black overalls and green canvas jungle boots laced up their calves—a forced landing could mean days, or weeks, of walking through the forests—fastened 'monkey-chains' round their waists in case they fell out of the aircraft when despatching their loads. They were some of the last conscripts (National Service was to end that year) and when they found themselves in the Royal Army Service Corps they little imagined how they would be spending their mornings. But they had become accustomed to the routine and sat staring out of the open door at the woolly, green surface of the tree-tops below, or at a comic, extracted from the hip pocket, folded into a wad of sweat-soaked paper.

The pilot pointed ahead to the other aircraft, which was banking, and then below to a cluster of buildings in a clearing, shaved of jungle, beside a river. That was Fort Chabai and he passed me his pilot's notes to read:

Approaches in either direction are obstructed by high ground but the saddle to the east clearer of trees ... A steep hill to the north runs alongside the airstrip and the dropping-zone is normally situated between the strip and this hill. Approach to the starboard side of this hill until well past the Fort on downwind leg heading west. Start turning port when almost adjacent to goal-post trees on top of ridge. Descend sharply as ridge is passed, turning on to the dropping-zone heading when Fort buildings rapidly come into view ...

We were diving towards the summits of ridges standing in parallel rows and, on one, the 'goal-post' trees stood: a gap where trees had been felled on the crest of a high knife-blade of rock. 'If we tuck a wing in there, we'll come out over the DZ,' said the pilot. He turned the aircraft on its side and sliced downward towards the ridge until the wing-tip flicked between the trees. Behind us the despatchers had manhandled towards the open door the first of seven loads to be parachuted, and awaited signal by light and bell. I heard the orders on my headset: 'Turning in ... Red light on ... Stand by the bells ... Three bells! Now!' Three rings and a voice shouted 'Pack away!' Below, Fort Chabai flashed past and we were flying down a deep, narrow valley, seeing nothing through the side windows but leaves, almost touching the wing-tips. The pilot hauled on the control column, bringing the nose up and a wing down so that we climbed, banked and finally soared clear of the hills, sweeping over them in a wide arc to begin the second of seven runs to parachute our loads.

It was as exhilarating as flying in a fighter. But, at the back, the despatchers had settled down on the floor, backs against the side, reading their comics, picking their noses, or just staring vacantly through the square of the open door at the tropical jungle, the needle-pointed peaks and the gleaming towers of white cumulus building above them in the heat of the mounting sun. Those boys, none yet nineteen, looked out at that panorama, which I found so awe-inspiring, romantic and grand, as if it were the view from a bus taking them through the council estate to the youth club. For a little while they had joined the other inhabitants of the jungle, the *ulu*, both indigenous and temporary—the aborigines and the CTs—and gave it a semblance of familiarity by giving the particular map references within it, where they happened to be, jocular call-signs for their radio messages: Easter Bunny, Gyppo Queen, Desperate Dan and Home James.

Perhaps they had been bred to expect such sights—or their parents or grandparents had—and had passed on the folk memory. Illustrations in *Brave Deeds that Won the Empire*, *The Wonder Book of Soldiers* and fly-spotted prints seen in junk shops had prepared the generations for this. The Empire, which, over the centuries, had given many tens of thousands of the British experience of its infinite variety—hardship and sensuality, beauty and horror; extremes of climate; scenery that could hardly be imagined—was now, in its final years, presenting a concentration of this to their final successors, as scenes from the life of a drowning man are said to flash before his dying eyes. Plucked from the cosy certainties of home, sent East of Suez along the Lifeline of Empire, these boys were being given an opportunity to understand the scale of their ancestors' achievements while it was still possible to see.

As in South Arabia, young soldiers in Malaya were taken to the limits of physical experience. Here it was the jungle: the dim, damp colonnades of the primary jungle, where tree-trunks soared to one or two hundred feet before spreading into the green canopy that filtered the light; the dense, continuous thickets of the secondary jungle that had grown, when the original timber had been felled, to become what adventure stories described as impenetrable. This was where, for a dozen years, British soldiers had fought and, finally won. As an army briefing officer at Kuala Lumpur had put it to me, pointing to an area of a map that was occupied by the East Anglian Regiment: 'If you walked down a jungle trail just there this morning, the chances arc that you would be shot to tatters by a teenager from Swaffham.'

The hard-earned self-satisfaction apparent in Malaya was not, however, reflected in Singapore, where the headquarters of the Far East Command and the main naval and air bases were established. While Malaya was now a self-governing federation within the Commonwealth, the island of Singapore remained a Crown Colony, ruled by able, sympathetic British administrators, who could still impress the indigenous politicians by taking them to sea for a day to watch an aircraft-carrier fly its squadrons. But it was a depressing place; haunted by the ghosts of 1942, having changed little in eighteen years. The once-white villas of the colonial officials and expatriate merchants were now stained green by the tropical damp and the city seemed as scrofulous as its masters had been after their long captivity.

Everywhere, there were reminders of that horror: the great, grey Cathay Building, which had been a keystone of the British presence, standing like a cenotaph above the low, tiled rooftops; Raffles Hotel as elegant as formerly but without self-confidence; the whitewashed monuments to those who had done their best—like the Argyll and Sutherland Highlanders, who had been the only British troops to learn jungle fighting before 1942—but a best that was not enough.

There was hostility in the air. Walking in the lamp light through the hot, humid night air of the streets, Chinese youths would stop chattering as I passed and stare without curiosity. There was no fear, as there had been in Nicosia; simply recognition of dislike and disdain. The British had been defeated by Asians but they had returned; it was time for them to go; their time was past. This feeling was articulated, if only indirectly, when I lunched with a Eurasian doctor, who was also a successful novelist and one of the most influential women in the Far East. Han Suyin's name had not been mentioned at Printing House Square in my time there but some knew of her because of her love affair with Our Far East Correspondent, Ian Morrison. When he had been killed while reporting the Korean war she had written a novel about him, *A Many Splendoured Thing*, which had become a best-seller and made into a film, with Morrison's name changed to 'Mark Elliott'. She had married a British police officer—an authority on Chinese criminal secret societies—but most of her friends were Asians of influence: Pandit Nehru; Chou En-Lai, Prime Minister of China; the kings of Cambodia and Nepal. Her subsequent novels reflected a rejection of the final traces of the Empire; one, *And the Rain my Drink*, was set in the Malaya of The Emergency and its principal character was a CT.

Han Suyin was an attractive woman with a beautiful face, owing more to the Chinese than to the Dutch half of her parentage, and fine legs. Her conversation was as lively, intelligent and sophisticated as one would expect but there was an underlying hostility in her as in the streets of Singapore. She remarked that the British in the East were 'fading away gracefully'; so what did the Asians feel about them now? 'They hardly notice them.' But had she any feelings about the Empire and its achievements? 'Like Mont Blanc—a little white at the top and a mass of brown, black and yellow beneath.' She admitted that she was lonely in Singapore and that life in London and New York, among her literary peers, would be more exciting but, she added fiercely, 'As an Asian, I want to live in Asia.' Some had said that she was a communist; others that she was simply anti-colonialist; was either true? Certainly the latter, perhaps the first, but all she would say was, 'I have my views.',

Later, I wondered whether she would have regarded that decent young subaltern of the West Kents with disdain, seeing his humanity as a sign of irresolution in contrast to the ruthless dedication of her CT. If so, this attitude would have been both widely shared and new, for the British Empire, in which I had been bred, inspired awe, anger, pride and even fear but not disdain. This dismissal of its achievements could be seen to have its roots here in Singapore, germinating at the great surrender to the Japanese and, equally, in the loss of the Indian Empire and the Indian Army, which, with the Navy, had been the foundation of British power East of Suez.

No longer had the likes of Han Suyin even a grudging admiration for the British imperialists and this void could be sensed in what had once been called the Mother Country a decade after the coronation of Queen Elizabeth. For those seeking signs and omens of decline, they abounded. For some it was to be the irrelevance of Great Britain in the confrontation of the Soviet Union by the United States in the crisis of 1962 over the Russian missiles in Cuba that seemed to bring the Third World War into the realm of probability rather than possibility. For others it was to be the rebuff of the British attempt to join the European Common Market by President de Gaulle in the following year, even as we planned to abandon our robust old currency in favour of Continental decimalization. And the end of a reassuring Anglo-American relationship came with the assassination of President Kennedy and the resignation of his friend (and, some said, mentor) Harold Macmillan, who together had personified the new optimism and the old urbanity. Now there was no more talk of Athenians and Romans.

4

Aux Barricades!

Red roses on the wallpaper, a brass bedstead and a view from the window across the rooftops of Paris. The prospect of a few weeks at this hotel, lunchtime drinks at the Crillon bar, and an expense account to spend, was as exciting that evening as it had been in the morning when Charles Wintour, the editor of the *Evening Standard*, had asked me to take over from Sam White, who was to visit Algiers. Piquancy was added to the assignment because on several occasions since I had joined the staff of the London evening newspaper three years earlier I had been sent to Paris to help our correspondent. My task had been to report *manifestations* on the streets: riots, plastic bomb campaigns and, in 1961, the expected airborne invasion by the rebellious generals in Algeria. Sam seemed to lead *la vie Parisienne* of one's dreams and was envied for his richly varied social life and the just acclaim accorded to his weekly column which was sometimes dictated from the white telephone on the bar at the Crillon.

So there was unworthy satisfaction in the thought that I would now be in that position, while Sam took to some far more dangerous streets. Correspondents who had been to Algeria had returned with shaking hands; one friend had suffered a nervous breakdown on his return, haunted by visions of a lynch mob, convinced that he was its quarry, and finally committed suicide on Hampstead Heath. By all accounts Algeria was worse than we could imagine; in comparison, the killing in Cyprus would seem like Agatha Christie murders.

British interest in news from Algeria was, of course, partly morbid curiosity and the pleasure of watching an old rival in difficulties. But in the new strategic context Algeria was important to Britain, and the rest of NATO, too. The convoy battles of the Second World War had enforced a new awareness of the Mediterranean shores and that those to north and south of the western basin were French, even if the insistence that Algeria was an integral part of metropolitan France did seem far-fetched.

So the nationalist rebellion—and fears of communist involvement—

84

threatened an ally: a vast country of mountain and desert, farmland and, as was being discovered, rich deposits of oil and natural gas; some fourteen million people, of whom one and a quarter million were European settlers; sea and air bases with a hitherto secure industrial base. It had begun at the end of 1954 with a few ill-coordinated acts of terrorism, much like those that began in Cyprus six months later, by the 800 Algerians who had formed the *Front de Libération Nationale*—the FLN—who it seemed could easily be rounded up, or contained, by the French Army, which had returned, defeated and restive, from Indo-China a year before.

But atrocities against the European settlers, involving disgusting mutilations, so enraged the avenging soldiers that the scale of massacre by automatic weapons matched quantity of deaths to the quality of cruelty by the other side. The fighting was mostly confined to the remote mountainous eastern regions for two years, then spread to the capital city of Algiers. There the French matched cruelty with cruelty when the parachute division, commanded by General Jacques Massu, was ordered to defeat the urban terrorists. This, as always, depended upon intelligence and that, in this case, upon information extracted by torture. General Massu's electrodes and paratroopers won the battle for Algiers and, in the countryside (the *bled*) the French seemed to be winning. But the settlers—the *pieds noirs*, so nicknamed because of their sun-burned feet (or perhaps because of the black boots worn by the conquering French soldiers 130 years before)—fearing a compromise settlement with the FLN, launched their crusade for *Algérie Française* with the support of the army. This had led to near revolution in both Algeria and France and the overthrow of the Fourth Republic. General de Gaulle again became President of France in 1958, having been heard to cry, '*Vive l'Algérie Française!*' and so leading the *pieds noirs* and the soldiers to believe that he shared their hope.

As it was realized that de Gaulle planned to negotiate with the Algerian nationalists the *pieds noirs* rebelled against him too. In 1960 they seized the centre of Algiers after a massacre of French *gendarmes* and, the following year, threatened to seize Paris by *coup de main* after mutinous troops had been flown to the capital's airports. When they failed even to attempt the latter, they formed their own terrorist *Organisation de l'Armée Secrète* to throw Algeria, and any plans for a negotiated settlement, into such confusion that de Gaulle would be forced to impose French military rule. This, they believed, would mean the final defeat of the FLN, and the establishment of strong, permanent French rule and in the spring of 1961, the OAS—under the command of the renegade

General Raoul Salan—began their campaign of murder, sabotage and intimidation both in Algeria and in France itself.

Within a year killings in Algeria by the OAS mounted to a total of 533 in one month—while the FLN, knowing that it was winning, was limiting itself to selective assassinations and the occasional target of opportunity. Amongst British foreign correspondents there was a saying that a crisis could be regarded as critical when an *Evening Standard* correspondent arrived. So, on Sunday 11 February 1962, Sam White was ordered to Algiers and myself to Paris.

From my room at the cosy old hotel near the Madeleine I telephoned Sam to wish him luck and a safe return, although not too soon. He gruffly thanked me, suggested I come over for a drink and added, 'There has been a change of plan. I have decided that the main story is here in Paris. *You* are going to Algiers.' That evening I walked to Sam's flat on the Left Bank with a sense of queasy excitement and of doom. Crossing the Tuileries gardens I looked up the Champs Elysées, already a river of the red and white lights of advancing and retreating traffic, to see the sky turning blood red as the sun set behind the Arc de Triomphe.

Sam White appeared as indestructible as ever and as I now wished I was. Since I had known him as an energetic Australian war reporter in 1945 he had matured into a shrewd foreign correspondent of the breed now almost extinct, his Russian-Jewish childhood and his Australian youth combining to give him a detached and mordant point of view. The looks and build of a boxer and his cosmopolitan air made him attractive to women. Indeed, he was an heroic, mythological figure even to us. This was only marginally due to his fostering of his own legend for he liked to profess that he had forgotten the family name which his parents had anglicized when they fled from Russia during the Revolution, although he would occasionally admit that he could remember the fear of the last of the Russian pogroms. He had been in Paris since 1947 and an important ingredient of the legend was that he could speak little French and that Lord Beaverbrook, on hearing this, had exclaimed, 'At last we have a correspondent in Paris who will not be fooled by the French!'

At fifty he was still a glamorous figure. Ronald Payne, a *Daily Telegraph* correspondent in Paris, could recall his first sight of Sam a dozen years earlier: 'At one very smart party, he made his entrance after midnight with a dazzlingly elegant woman on his arm. He wore a dinner jacket and she a long black dress—figures straight out of Scott Fitzgerald. *That*, I remember thinking, is the sort of journalist I want to become.' His reputation as a lady-killer was envied but exaggerated.

Once on a visit to London he had been seen to leave a party late with the most attractive woman in the room. But next day she complained that they had taken a taxi, Sam telling the driver to drop him off at his hotel on the way to her address. As he clambered out he turned, clapped a hand on her silken knee and growled, 'Thanks, old boy.'

So it was amongst a gathering of his admirers and fellow-journalists that I found myself next day at noon in the Crillon bar, while awaiting my Algerian visa, and again in the evening as another OAS *plastiquage* rattled the windows and Sam explained his own admiration for the ruthless statesmanship of President de Gaulle.

The pleasures of Paris, which had so recently seemed at my command, were next morning relegated to the toy cupboard by a brief ceremony at Orly airport when passengers for Algiers were led to cubicles and searched before boarding the Caravelle. Now the adrenalin began to pulse and apprehension was replaced by anticipation. Yet this was not to be immediately fulfilled, for Algiers was a city of teasing cruelty and today it only hinted at what was to come. On the taxi ride from Maison Blanche airport, I sat beside the driver, half expecting, as in Nicosia, the windscreen to be shattered by bullets. But the streets were deserted; the shops shuttered; the cafés closed; no buses ran; the pavements were deserted; the OAS had imposed a general strike for the day.

Algiers was bigger, grander and cleaner than expected. From my parents, who had spent their honeymoon there, I gathered it to be picturesque in the Moorish taste, with a slightly louche Mediterranean charm. But the French heart of the city was tough and smart: gleaming white cliffs of stucco-fronted apartment blocks, swagged with plasterwork, encrusted with cupids and caryatids, built for a provincial *haute bourgeoisie* in Parisian style with balconies for the hot weather. Here were brash brasseries, vulgar department stores, chic boutiques and little bars with their names written in blue neon light. Here were pillared palaces for officialdom approached by avenues of palms and squares where the grass was green and mown and the flowering shrubs glossy. To the north, the primary blue of the sea; to the south, white houses climbing the hills; westward, the Casbah and the FLN.

Along the road we passed patrols in battle order and, in the city, parked half-tracks mounting heavy machine-guns. The French deployed a variety of soldiers and police in Algeria. Conscripts from line regiments in khaki denims and field equipment; paratroopers in lizard-green leotards; but the Foreign Legion's white *képis* were at the moment being kept out of Algiers. In the city were Zouaves, the European-colonial troops (flame-red forage caps) and the smart, fresh-faced young men of the *Compagnies Républicaines de Sécurité* (dark blue battledress and forage caps), the older heavyweights of the *Garde Mobile* (First World War crested helmets), or the Algiers *flics*, much like those in France but swarthier. They were tense with watchfulness, like the British in Cyprus, their eyes restless, both hands on their guns.

'A neat little war with a good hotel' was what foreign correspondents—myself included—liked to report. The Algerian war was far from neat but the Hotel Aletti was all we could ask. A white concrete block in the centre of the city, equidistant from both the *Gouvernement Générale* building and the Casbah, it was an Art Deco citadel of slightly decadent comfort. The bar where the journalists—and the OAS and other dangerous breeds—gathered was called *Le Cintra*; *Le Chantéclaire* restaurant offered the richest French food one cared to order; upstairs was a dim, high-ceiling casino with tall, tinted windows, where sinister men in dark glasses (and, sometimes the more exotic French officers' uniforms) gambled for high stakes. The bedrooms were to match, with polished pink terrazzo floors and chandeliers.

The talk over Pernod in the bar was of the latest *attentat*, the prim word with the same meaning as 'incident' in Cyprus. Somebody would describe a shooting at a bus stop, or report seeing a corpse with a newspaper over its face—the customary shroud until the mortuary van arrived to take it away in a shallow zinc-lined bath—or just a stream of blood following the camber of the road to a puddle in the gutter that would eventually be hosed away by municipal functionaries. Next day, if interested, one might try to identify these in the long list under the heading *Attentats* in *La Dépêche d'Algérie*, giving time and place. Thus: '*6 h. Quartier Bellevue, M. Djallabak Khier a été tué.*' '*7 h. 15. A Maison-Carrée, M. Daniel Vicidomini est tué.*' '*14 h. 30. A Belcourt-Hamman, deux blessés musulmans.*' '*16 h. 45. Square Bresson, M. Mustapha El Bahar est grievement blessé.*' '*17 h. 30. A Kouba, un mort non identifié.*' And so on: fifty to a hundred killed or wounded each day in the streets of Algiers alone.

These were mostly casual killings, 'soft targets' chosen because they had presented a convenient back, or passed too close to a side alley and been of the necessary race. The OAS was killing Algerians in the hope of provoking the FLN to take reprisals, which, in turn, would force the French to intervene militarily and so disrupt the negotiations now in progress at Evian-les-Bains that were planning independence for Algeria. The FLN, although it was showing remarkable restraint at command

Algiers, 1962: defying the OAS and succeeding. Foreign correspondents escorting Prince Nicola Carraciola (arrowed), condemned to death for his defiance, through Algiers. Centre foreground are Michael Weigall of the *Daily Mail* and the author. (*Photograph: The Times-Associated Press*)

Defying the OAS and failing. Four Algerians ventured into the Rue Michelet when a gang of *pied noir* gunmen were roaming central Algiers in search of 'soft targets'. Such *attentats* had become daily routine. (*Photograph: Associated Press*)

Borneo, 1965. At Nanga Gaat, the advance base of the Fleet Air Arm helicopters
near the Indonesian border, the unveiling of a memorial to the British dead is
interrupted. Naval officers and the new Malaysian political officer look skyward
as a Hastings parachutes supplies to the outpost which can otherwise
only be reached by river.

level, could not stop its street assassins taking revenge.

More important killings were announced with formality: those of liberal lawyers, civil servants loyal to Paris and army officers, who did their duty, murdered by the OAS. Pointedly public were the wall posters upon which were a score or more of portraits—usually enlarged passport photographs—showing brutish, sometimes oriental, faces; some would be crossed out and beneath scrawled '*Tué*'. These posters, printed by the OAS, advertised their success in slaughtering their most dangerous enemies, the *barbouzes*—'the false beards'—sent to Algeria from France to fight with the same lack of scruple. Some *barbouzes* were former criminals, some Vietnamese, who had served the French as policemen, or even, it was said, torturers in Indo-China. But they were no more successful against the OAS than the regular police. Informers at police headquarters identified them or their lairs and had even provided photographs for the posters. The Vietnamese were easy to pick off as there were few orientals in Algiers, and Japanese correspondents became so apprehensive that they took to wearing small Rising Sun flags on their lapels.

The first few days proved a gentle introduction: shots heard from another street; screaming sirens as ambulances sped away to the hospitals; bullet holes in cars and shop windows; bloodstains on the pavement. Then, passing a florist's shop where orchids bloomed in the hot, damp air, I felt the *frisson* of alarm remembered from Cyprus. People in the street had stopped, or were running towards the corniche between the city and the docks. I followed and there was a group of Algerians, gathered around and looking down at something on the pavement. It was a dead man. A European dressed in a smart tweed jacket, pressed blue trousers and crepe-soled shoes, he lay sprawled and still as a dummy; face down, his spectacles splintered on the concrete. A stream of blood across the kerb and into the gutter.

The Algerians looked down at him with curiosity. Then, with shouts and the barking of dogs, a Zouave patrol burst through them, machine-pistols cocked at their hips, Alsatians on chains leaping at their sides. A lieutenant, red-faced and bright-eyed with excitement, saw me and shouted, '*Allez-vous en, c'est dangereux!*' I slid away through the crowd, chilled by the first encounter with death in Algiers. That evening I heard that the dead man had been an airman, due to leave for France that day after his tour of duty in Algeria, who had changed into civilian clothes and taken one last walk along the seafront promenade to admire the view before boarding the ship for Marseilles.

Now the *frissons* ran through the streets each day, always leading to a death and sometimes more than one. I ran with the soldiers along the wide pavement past the café tables and smart shops of the Rue Michelet to see a dozen bodies lying face down and streaming blood. All were young Algerians, who had been walking in the same direction when OAS gunmen had raced along the pavement, shooting them in the back as they passed. But here there was no crowd; the French still sat at the café tables; young secretaries in suede jackets and high-heeled shoes minced out of office doorways for their lunch break, squealed at the sight of death, then, realizing that the corpses were Algerian and not French, went on chattering as they delicately stepped over the gathering pools of blood.

Sometimes the OAS were more selective, choosing their targets not by race but by occupation to demonstrate their dominance of the city. One morning they shot five postmen, both Algerian and European; then it was pharmacists, killed in their dispensaries, their blood bright on their white coats; next came railwaymen, tram-workers and municipal electricians; women, too, in their turn; *coiffeuses*, then flower vendors, shot at their kerbside stalls; finally, cleaning-women. A crack of pistol-shots and one would run towards the sound to come upon some such horror, or, perhaps, something even more selective, like a sober-suited lawyer turning grey-green in death.

For the correspondents there was no reliable source of information; the official spokesmen in the *Gouvernement Générale* building dispensed bromides and, in any case, were preoccupied with staying alive themselves; the OAS frequented *Le Cintra* bar, but only to boast; as for the FLN, they were presumably in the Casbah, but what European would venture there and expect to return?

Among several dozen journalists staying at the Aletti, the best-informed seemed to be Clare Hollingworth, whose reports to the *Guardian* showed an easy command of the complexities and contempt for the dangers of Algeria. She was a middle-aged Englishwoman of the upper middle class with a charmingly uptilted nose and big blue eyes that were in contrast to the formidable set of her mouth and chin. In 1939 she had been assistant to Hugh Carleton Greene, the *Daily Telegraph* correspondent in Poland, and had herself seen and reported the first hours of the German invasion, then spent the rest of the war in the Middle East as one of the few women who dressed like a war correspondent and behaved like one.

When I returned to the hotel from the sight of that first dead body on the corniche I met Clare, who invited me to join her for a walk. There had been shooting in the *pied noir* district of Bab-el-Oued on the far side of the Casbah and she suggested a stroll in that direction. At the best of times these streets were uneasy: from the Aletti, an arcaded street of well-stocked shops and sometimes-busy cafés led to the Square Bresson on the edge of the Casbah. At one end stood the opera house; at the other stretched the Mediterranean; either side stood more tall, arcaded buildings; in the middle, Algerians loafed beneath the trees and around the two newspaper kiosks. On the far side another, meaner, arcaded street, Rue Bab-Azoun marked the northern boundary of the Casbah and led to Bab-el-Oued beyond.

Today the streets and the square were empty but for a Zouave patrol standing in the doorways of an arcade. A coil of barbed wire had been dragged half-way across the Rue Bab-Azoun but the street itself had the ominous emptiness of a no-man's-land. Clare walked past this as briskly as if she were going out for coffee in an English county town, talking about the chances of the negotiations at Evian and what the OAS would do if they succeeded. Suddenly she stopped, nodded to an alley (half-choked with barbed wire and rubbish) that slanted steeply into the Casbah, and said, 'Let's go up there.'

I told her not to be ridiculous; we would be killed before we were questioned. Clare replied that perhaps that was so, although only a man would be at risk; a thrown brick or an emptying chamber-pot being more likely than a bullet. So we returned to the hotel and, a few minutes later, I noticed that she had gone, only later discovering that she had returned, alone, to the alley off the Rue Bab-Azoun. Much later she told me that she often went to the Casbah, visiting friends in the FLN command.

Clare was indomitable and seemed even more so as each of us, in turn, came upon something particularly ghastly. John Wallis of the *Daily Telegraph* had seen the burning of the *barbouzes* in an ambushed car; the Reuter correspondent had seen a Zouave shot in the back; a freelance had seen a dead *barbouze* hanged high above a street in Bab-el-Oued; when we returned to *Le Cintra*, our experience was announced by an ash-grey face. Even Clare, after seeing a murder at close quarters, was unusually quiet for a few hours.

Experiences were not always like this; occasionally they were comic. One reporter, prowling the streets on the edge of the Casbah, saw, emerging from the shadows of one of its alleys an elderly couple. He wore a rumpled suit of white linen and a panama hat; she, a floral frock; they could only be English. Moreover, since the woman was carrying an old-fashioned folding Kodak camera in a brown canvas case, they appeared to be tourists. When the reporter approached and asked if all was well, the old gentleman had replied that it was indeed, except that the light in the narrow streets of the Casbah had, sadly, not been sufficient for photography. Now they would be grateful for directions to the docks, where the cargo liner, in which they were passengers, was berthed during her short call at Algiers.

My own encounter was in the same district, in the Square Bresson, whither I had walked on the chance that one of its two news-stands might have received London newspapers, some days old, as they sometimes did. Algiers was tense: the OAS had the day before killed a dozen Algerians in the centre of the city, shot a party of *barbouzes* dining in a Chinese restaurant, *Le Dragon d'Or*, and attacked the *gendarmerie* barracks; that morning, I had already seen two Algerians shot dead outside the university and another, sitting on the kerb near the Aletti, bleeding from a gunshot wound and guarded by a brave policeman.

Now there were rumours of more trouble in Bab-el-Oued. But I longed to read news from home and a walk to the borders of the Casbah seemed worth the risk.

Approaching the Square Bresson, it became apparent that no Europeans were about and the open space in front of the opera house was crowded with Algerians; there was a risk of becoming a target of opportunity for the FLN. On the far corner of the square the red caps of a Zouave patrol could be seen under the arcade; the nearest kiosk was shut but I could see newspapers hanging outside the other, near the entrance to the Rue Bab-Azoun. After hesitating in apprehension, it seemed shaming to flinch before so docile a crowd and I shouldered my way through them with a fixed, ingratiating smile. When I reached the kiosk the newspapers on display proved to be French and, with relief, I turned to retreat. As I did so, a shot cracked in my ear. Jerking round, I saw a young European collapse, a red rose of blood burst open on his temple. He had been about to open the door of his parked car as he was shot; a thin Algerian in jacket and trousers stood above him, pistol in hand. A whistle blew from the direction of the Zouave patrol; he turned and raced through the crowd towards the Casbah, the soldiers plunging after him. He had escaped; I had, too, for there had been only two European 'soft targets' in the Square Bresson. Ten minutes later, returning to the Aletti, the chill in my cheeks confirmed the pallor announcing that today it had been my turn.

There was also the possibility of becoming an identified target; of threats and assassination. Some of the seventy, or eighty, foreign journalists in Algiers had received threatening letters after filing reports critical of the OAS, and several had been told that they had been sentenced to death.

At the beginning of March such a message was delivered in person when an OAS commando—as their gangs liked to be called—tramped into the hotel, pistols in pockets, and demanded to see the Italian journalists. Trouble had been expected because several had condemned the OAS in newspapers and on television and, since some of the *pieds noirs* were of Italian extraction, this had been reported to Algiers. When some of the eleven Italians—including a charming thirty-year-old *príncipe*, Nicola Caracciolo, representing *Il Giorno*—had gathered in the lobby, the OAS spokesman berated them and gave them twenty-four hours to leave the country; otherwise they would be shot.

Witness to all this was an officer of a *Régiment Parachutiste* and Caracciolo remarked loudly to the effect that he must be deaf for otherwise he would have done his duty to uphold the law. At this the officer stepped forward and knocked him down. This roused the blood and pride of the Caracciolos—one had rebelled against the Bourbons and been hanged by them when Nelson recaptured Naples for the monarchists in 1799—and he declared that he would not be dictated to by gangsters. And so it was, next morning, that when his ten colleagues were loading their baggage into taxis, bound for the airport and the flight to Rome, Nicola Caracciolo stood calmly, with arms folded and bags unpacked, watching them go.

The journalists were now making news themselves and the prince's defiance of the OAS was inevitably going to provide more. A meeting was held and decisions taken: first, that the French Government must be made aware of their duty to protect a foreign journalist; second, that since we could not rely upon them doing so, we must plan to do so ourselves. That afternoon a dozen of us formed a phalanx around Caracciolo, walked out of the hotel and through the streets to the *Hôtel des Postes*, then up the wide steps to the *Gouvernement Générale*. There we were received by the worried spokesman, whose wrinkled brow was familiar at the few press conferences held here, and given the bland assurances we expected. We then walked back to the hotel unmolested and looked to our defences.

There were 150 bedrooms in the hotel, to which the only access was by two lifts from the lobby, since the stairs had been blocked with barbed wire as an obstacle to any assault by the OAS. Therefore, if Caracciolo was moved from one room to another each night, the OAS would hardly have time to search them all before help could be summoned from the soldiers and police always on duty at the *Hôtel de Ville* and *Préfecture* along the street. Nevertheless trouble was expected and, sure enough, it came.

All the correspondents dined at the Aletti that night because of a curfew and, because of strikes, the choice of food was limited; but I had long turned from the rich and expensive dishes my expense account could afford in favour of scrambled eggs and Perrier water. So, expecting trouble, we sat down early in *Le Chantéclaire* and speculated on the form this might take. After coffee, all being quiet, we gathered in the lobby to agree that we should all go to our rooms and lock ourselves in.

Headlights swept into the driveway and now, through the plate-glass doors, we saw figures with guns race up the steps and burst into the lobby; gendarmes, aiming their machine-pistols at us; standing, feet apart, fingers on triggers. There were, perhaps, a dozen of them and, to judge by their *képis*, of the *Garde Mobile*. Then through the open doors behind them sauntered a tall man, with black hair and line of moustache, in a pale blue suit, smoking a cigarette. We all stood and stared. The tall man whispered to the hall porter, then spoke to us in French: 'We wish to know the whereabouts of the Italian correspondent Nicola Caracciolo.'

A few voices said, 'We don't know', or 'He's not here', or 'Try the Italian consulate' but, in truth, we did not know; I had assumed that he was upstairs in one of the rooms. John Wallis of the *Daily Telegraph*, a robust Englishman with the pink cheeks and merry eyes of a Surtees squire (but also with a command of Marseillaise slang) stepped forward and said quietly that not only did we not know the whereabouts of the colleague in question but, even if we did, we would not divulge it in view of the threats against his life.

It was now apparent to all that these were not police but an OAS commando in disguise. This was confirmed as their spokesman announced that, as they could not find Caracciolo, they would take another and gave an order, at which two of his men waved John Wallis towards the door with their gun-barrels. The rest of us stood, watching and bemused, until Clare Hollingworth acted. Striding up to the tall man in the blue suit she declared in confident, English-accented French, '*Monsieur*, if you do not release our colleague at once, I will have to hit you on the head with my shoe!'

The OAS man pushed her away and followed his gang and their captive through the glass door and down the marble steps to two Jeeps parked outside. 'We must go, too!' cried Clare. 'They can't shoot all the world's press!' We followed her, pushing through the doors and down the steps to climb aboard the Jeeps. The OAS men swore and pushed John Wallis towards us and, shouting that they would be back, started the engines.

'Get down! They're going to shoot!' somebody yelled and we did; I leaping behind a pillar of the porch. They did not, and roared away into the darkened street, leaving their captive behind. Trooping back into the hotel, quiet and shaken, we discussed the next move; should we telephone the police now, or leave it until the morning? It was decided that it would be safest for all to go to our rooms and one of us to report the raid to the duty officer at the *Gouvernement Générale*. As we talked my eyes wandered to the hall porter, who stood in his frock coat with crossed keys upon the lapels behind his desk beside the doors. Suddenly he ducked out of sight. Beyond the plate glass more men with guns were running up the steps and pushing open the doors. 'They're coming back!' someone shouted. Several ran for the lift, struggled to open the sliding doors, and crammed inside. Three of these were correspondents from the brasher London newspapers, whose reports boasted of their own adventures; now they stared through the lattice of the lift as, over-loaded, it slowly rose, exposing them like chickens in a cage, their eyes round with fear.

'*Haut les mains!*' Up went our hands; up they went, high. This time, I saw, the gunmen wore the dark blue uniform of the CRS and their leader was another civilian, unshaven and with an extinguished cigarette stuck to his lower lip. Now he addressed us. 'Where have the others gone? They were false gendarmes and we are here to arrest them.' When told that they had gone, he shrugged and regretted it was necessary for us to remain where we were with hands above our heads until our identities had been checked. Slowly the CRS men came up to each in turn, allowing us to lower our hands to extract passports or identity cards from our pockets. Finally, satisfied, they wished us goodnight and left. At last we were able to queue for the lift and reach our rooms; from our windows the lights of Algiers not only glittered on the hillsides but flashed as tracer bullets flew like sparks and explosions rattled the furniture. It was not the usual *plastiquage*, but sounded like a bombardment; after eighty explosions I lost count, but somebody else reached a hundred and thirty-five.

There was fighting around the Casbah next morning. Streets, recalling European cities after bombing, were littered with broken glass and strewn with rubble. The targets had been Algerian shops in predominantly European districts and their stocks spilled on to the pavements through rent and buckled shutters, while those proprietors who dared show themselves stood glaring with hate and despair. Another to appear was the leader of the OAS raid of the preceding night, who sauntered into the Aletti at lunchtime and stood chatting with French sympathizers for a quarter of an hour.

Some of us had already bought iron rations and the bottom of my own wardrobe was stacked with tins of biscuits and sardines and bottles of Perrier. Not only had strikes and the general disruption of life in the city cut the menu in *Le Chantéclaire* to a minimum but most of the Algerian cooks and waiters had disappeared. That night the restaurant was to close early—in any case we had all agreed to be in our rooms before ten o'clock—and half a dozen of us dined frugally, listening to a street battle outside and trying to identify the different weapons: machine-guns of different calibre, mortars and grenades. Before going to bed I ran the bath and washed with the expensive *Tabac* soap I had bought, as a vague, instinctive gesture of reaction.

Next morning the British journalists met in the BBC correspondent's bedroom to form an association, which was all we could do for our own protection. But at least we would not be expected to protect Nicola Caracciolo for much longer. That afternoon, returning from a tour of the streets, I saw him sitting alone in the lobby. He was leaving, he said, having defied the sentence of death for more than two days, and was awaiting his police escort for the drive to the airport. Just then two tough men in belted raincoats stepped up to him and he flinched: the OAS come at last? The men showed him their police identity cards, took him out to a car and drove away. Would the brave Nicola ever be seen again? This time the police were what they seemed.

A measure of Nicola's triumph was our own increased sense of exposure. I began to feel not only vulnerable but doomed and became careless of the precautionary pattern of behaviour first learned in Cyprus: if it was going to happen, it would happen. In reaction to this, I stopped at a shop window near the university, attracted by something that was not subject to the dangers that dominated Algiers: a barometer. It was a handsome, brass instrument with glass to tap as the needle flickered around the dial from *Tempête* to *Beau Temps*. I bought it to stand on my dressing table as a reminder that not everything was subject to fear.

I was now dictating only short reports over the telephone to London, and they were no longer accompanied by the whooping of ambulances, or police sirens, from the streets that so excited the copy-takers. One morning my call was put through to the news editor who told me that I was to return to London. This was difficult to comprehend for such was one's concentration upon life and death in Algiers that the world beyond had faded into the shadows. When I did accept all that my instructions implied, it was hard to keep a grin of relief from my face as I shook hands with the others, silently wondering what would happen to them. For the final hours I worried that some *attentat*, or some unexpected political development in the negotiations between the French and the Algerians at Evian, would reverse the order, but it did not: the city was quiet, there were taxis about; at the airport that afternoon the flight was on time and my spirits soared with the Caravelle.

Back in London, the absence of danger enhanced small pleasures. I admired the familiar pictures on my walls with new perception; the streets of Chelsea seemed a paradise, although I half-expected to see blood stream across the pavement. As I walked to Sloane Square station on my way to Fleet Street, I noticed that I was watching for men in unbuttoned jackets, and cars that seem to creep from behind. Yet all was forgotten in the welcome at the *Standard* office, where my audience, round-eyed, asked what it had really been like and gasped at my replies. Now safely home and beyond the reach of the OAS, perhaps I could write the article that would have brought a death sentence in Algiers? I did so and it was published beneath the headlines: 'Tom Pocock comes back from the City of Terror with a grim forecast for the OAS ... YOU CAN MURDER—BUT YOU CAN'T WIN'. Believing that this would be read by the OAS in Paris that evening and in Algiers next day, there was satisfaction both in taking revenge and in the knowledge that, having put my name to so strong an attack on them, I would certainly not have to go back.

The next week was delightful: lunches and drinks with friends; the enjoyment of London; getting back into the Fleet Street routine. The *Evening Standard*'s was a happy office, its staff as envied by other journalists as those of the *News Chronicle* had been in the 1940s and the *Daily Express* in the 1950s. Charles Wintour was regarded as the best editor in Fleet Street, a possible successor to Haley on *The Times*. None of us claimed to understand him: his donnish manner and coldly intellectual approach to the affairs of the world combined with a fascination with social gossip, celebrities and the sort of news that sells popular newspapers. He could be tetchy and remote but also generous and understanding. Under his editorship the *Evening Standard* became essential reading for the well informed.

Picking up the threads of the past month's news outside Algeria, it seemed that all was well with Britain and what was now known as the

97

Commonwealth rather than the Empire; certainly, the Lifeline was intact. We still held Gibraltar and our two bases on Cyprus, although there was still tension between Greeks and Turks; the Suez Canal was open again but Egypt was still arousing Arab nationalism. There were again stirrings in the remote mountains of south-west Arabia, the hinterland to Aden, which was itself uneasy with talk of subversion and revolt. Kenya and the other African colonies were quiet in the aftermath of the victory over Mau Mau and, across the Indian Ocean, the State of Emergency in Malaya had officially ended in 1960 and plans for the Federation of Malaysia—composed of Malaya, Singapore and the Borneo territories— were advancing. Hong Kong remained an oriental Gibraltar but there was trouble in Indo-China, which on the departure of the French had been divided into the separate states of North and South Vietnam, governed by communists and capitalists respectively. Subversion of South Vietnam, inspired and sustained by the North, had become so critical that the United States military aid had been increased and now included more than two thousand American servicemen as instructors and advisers. But that, it seemed, had nothing to do with us.

News of Algeria became both better and worse after my departure. Then on 18 March agreement was finally reached at Evian with the Algerians attaining almost all the original aims of the FLN. The *pieds noirs* could stay, if they so wished, as Algerian citizens, but it was unlikely that they would; just how unlikely was now demonstrated in Algeria itself where, on the day of the official cease-fire between the French Army and the FLN, the OAS made its last, bloody stand.

General Salan ordered a general strike and declared not only that Algerians entered the European quarters of Algiers on pain of death, but that the French Army must now be considered, and treated, as an enemy. These instructions were put into effect with horrifying results: the OAS fired mortar bombs into the Place du Gouvernement, killing twenty-three Algerians; they ambushed the half-tracks which habitually guarded the Tunnel des Facultés underpass near the Aletti, killing eighteen gendarmes and wounding twenty-five; and they attacked two lorry-loads of young French conscripts, killing seven and wounding eleven. This was too much for the French commander, General Ailleret, who surrounded Bab-el-Oued with 20,000 troops, raking the tall façades with machine-guns and cannon whenever an OAS sniper fired.

I woke early to hear the first BBC news bulletin in Chelsea one morning. The reports from Algiers were of more violence and had reached the barometric point when the *Standard* would be sending its own reporter, and I felt a surge of relief that it would not be me. An hour later, as I sat in the office, reading the morning newspapers at my desk, I looked across the big, crowded room to the news desk. There sat Ronald Hyde, the news editor, an elegant man, his prematurely grey hair and well-cut blue suit immaculate; he looked up, our eyes met, he rose to his feet, began to walk towards me and I knew what he was going to say. There is a cliché about blood running cold; mine turned to iced water. Hyde stopped by my desk, wrinkled his brow and said, 'It is thought that it would be a good idea for you to go back to Algiers.'

Stiff and cold with dread, I bared my teeth in a smile and heard myself say in a strange voice, 'Yes, of course.' There was only one hope: that the crisis in Algiers was now so desperate that the airports were shut. But there was no news of this at Heathrow or in Paris. When I had a drink with Sam White confidence began to return, since we could discuss the relevant news as equals: he knew his way about the political corridors of Paris; I knew the streets of Algiers, and that was where today's news was being made.

The airports remained open and the Caravelle did fly next morning, to come down through the cloud over Algeria above the white lines of roads without traffic; descending lower, the only sign of life was a road block of armoured cars. The airport was deserted but for an occasional, wary soldier on guard and half-tracks on the road outside. After some time I discovered a car with an Algerian driver, hidden around a corner, which proved to be a taxi, and a bargain was eventually struck: he would try to get me to the Aletti, if the road was open and seemed safe, for an understandably high price, but only if I would sit beside him—for the same reason that I had sat beside the taxi driver on arrival in Cyprus.

At the Aletti, *Le Cintra* bar was crowded with the OAS and its friends: thuggish men in dark glasses, officers in *képis* of various colours, paratroopers in mottled green leotards and women with elaborately coiffed and dyed hair. As I entered one of the latter, smartly suited, her bouffant hair a startling bronze, came up, looked me up and down and asked, 'You are English? You know what we think of you English?' And, without waiting for a reply, she spat at my feet and fainted.

On this particular day the lobby was buzzing with anticipation. I had, it seemed, arrived just in time to cover a major set-piece event that would almost inevitably result in important news. The French Army still besieged Bab-el-Oued, letting nobody in or out, but tomorrow, Monday 26 March, the *pieds noirs* planned to raise the siege. They were again to gather in Belcourt, then march for a rally in the great open space in front of the *Hôtel des Postes*, below the war memorial, then march on Bab-el-Oued. The demonstration had already been banned by the French authorities and not only the police, but the army, had been ordered to prevent them from reaching their destination. Anything could happen; certainly it would, for us, be major news and, since the march would begin in the morning, one perfectly-timed for an evening newspaper like mine.

Communications with Fleet Street were good. Telephone calls initiated in Algiers were subject to the whims of the *pieds noirs* at the exchange but those booked from London were reliable. I began this Monday by dictating a forecast of the day's events: the proposed march on Bab-el-Oued and the French Government's determination to stop it with the use of troops as well as police. Then it was time to take to the streets and, in small groups, we headed towards the *Hôtel des Postes*, which was where the sequence of dire possibilities would begin. Some correspondents had arranged to watch from windows nearby and along the Rue d'Isly, which would be the direct route towards Bab-el-Oued. I opted for a more mobile plan, which would enable me to cut back to the hotel through side streets when a call from London was due. If the march got into the Rue d'Isly it would head west until it reached the Square Bresson, where I had drawn the long straw a month before; there it could either take the inland, more dangerous route to the Place du Gouvernement and Bab-el-Oued through the Rue Bab-Azoun, or the corniche above the harbour. So I decided to walk just in front of the head of the procession, keeping on the pavement, ready to duck into a doorway should shooting start.

The Rue d'Isly was not crowded, but at its far end, where it opened into the great square before the central post office, was a vast assembly, stretching to the buildings on the far side and into the streets beyond. Either the march had not begun, or it had been stopped by a line of soldiers, standing shoulder to shoulder across the street behind a few flimsy barricades of rolled barbed wire mounted on wooden trestles. It was here that the making of news would begin.

Beyond the soldiers stood the leaders of the marchers: some middle-aged men in gaberdine coats; a few toughs in leather jackets; some in uniform, including several *pompiers*; youths carrying *tricolore* banners; behind them, thousands upon thousands of Mediterranean faces, many of them much like those in a crowd of Algerians, rather than European settlers. They stood there singing *La Marseillaise*, or chanting their slogans '*Al-gér-ie Fran-çaise! Al-gér-ie Fran-çaise!*' while their leaders talked earnestly with the young fair-haired lieutenant in a white *képi* who commanded the cordon.

But it was his platoon of infantrymen who attracted the attention, for they were *harkis*, Algerians loyal to France and recruited with the assurance that Algeria would remain for ever French. They stood there in steel helmets and dusty denim battledress, fingering their weapons and nervously watching the restless mob a few yards away. They looked tired and frightened for they had, like other troops brought into the city, come straight from operations against the FLN in the *bled* without rest. It was obvious that, if the crowd started to move, the soldiers would be swept aside. But another possibility became apparent. Just behind the cordon the road forked and, while the Rue d'Isly was the main thoroughfare, a narrower street branched uphill, also leading to the gardens and the square. Should the crowd take this route, they would emerge behind the line of *harkis* and the whole length of the Rue d'Isly would stretch before them.

The roar of singing and chanting mounted, the crowd began to sway with restless anticipation and, just then, the first of them began to filter down that side street, shouting to those behind that the way was clear. Any moment the great body of the assembly would be surging after them, but it was not that which first prompted me to move. Standing on the pavement by the shuttered shops, I had noticed people in the road look beyond me, then quickly move away. Turning, I saw why. In the doorway of a smart boutique and leaning against its glass door, set back between two bay windows, stood a *harki*, feet splayed, the butt of a light machine-gun rested on his hip, its barrel waving to and fro. His eyes glared, showing white all round, his teeth bared in a defiant snarl, his forefinger crooked around the trigger. The man was at breaking point through rage, or fear, and finding myself a few feet in front of his gunmuzzle, I moved; as I did so the mob surged through the side street with the roar of breaking seas and, in a moment, the khaki helmets of the *harkis* were bobbing amongst a multitude of heads and hats. The march on Bab-el-Oued had begun.

Hurrying ahead and keeping within jumping distance of doorways, I stopped two or three hundred yards along the street and stood on a doorstep to look back at the approaching crowd. Once past the cordon it had again taken shape and was fronted by the leaders who had been asking the lieutenant to let them pass. They walked with a slow, rocking gait, roaring *La Marsellaise*, *tricolores* flying. A shot cracked; a machine-gun rattled; somewhere behind, where the cordon had been, sounded shots and bursts of shooting. But the crowd came on, nobody turned. What was happening? A rooftop skirmish, perhaps, or even a *feu de joie*, for anything more would have the marching mob turning in pain and anger. So I dodged on along the street, keeping just ahead of the marchers until the road opened into the Square Bresson: the opera house to the left; the sea to the right.

At first sight the square seemed empty. Then figures could be seen in the south-west and north-west corners. Across the mouth of the sinister arcades of the Rue Bab-Azoun ranks of French soldiers, guns held across their chests, could be seen behind another barricade of barbed wire, closing the street. The other way to Bab-el-Oued, the corniche, was also blocked; this by armoured cars parked across it, hub to hub. As the marchers entered at the south-east corner I saw, drawn up in a massive, dark phalanx in the north-east of the square, the riot police in full panoply: helmets, gas masks, machine-pistols slung and clubs in hand. Here the confrontation would come.

In the excitement I had forgotten the others; now I found myself with two companions; one British, one French. Together we walked to the centre of the Square Bresson, stopped and looked around: two corners held by the French Army; one by the riot police; the *pied noir* marchers about to debouch from the fourth. As they did so the police raised their clubs and charged. The pounding of their boots sounded like a stampede heading for us. Turning to run, we saw tall doors between shop windows standing ajar, a bright eye gleaming from within; the door was closing when the French reporter flung himself at it, bursting it open, flinging the old *concierge*, who had been watching, on to the marble floor. We followed, slamming and bolting the door behind us, while the riot police beat upon it for entry. Following the young Frenchman, we raced upstairs to the top landing, where he hammered on the door of a flat, shouting, '*Ouvrez la porte! Ici l'OAS!*' The door was quickly opened by a nervous woman in a dressing gown and we rushed inside, through the smart furnishings of a drawing room and out on to a terrace high above the square that commanded a view of the theatrical scene about to begin below.

As we had climbed the stairs the charge of the riot police had run its course, forcing the marchers back into their corner of the square but not scattering them, for there was nowhere to disperse. So the police again drew up into their phalanx and they, the marchers and the soldiers opposite stood and stared at each other. There was, however, a change at the head of the march: one of the *tricolore* flags was stained with blood;

whose we were not to know. The head of the column stood halted, still singing *La Marseillaise*, realizing that any further advance would bring down another charge and that, ahead, stood not nervous *harkis* but the French army.

A girl detached herself from the front of the crowd and was handed the blood-stained flag. Holding it in front of her with both hands, she slowly walked across the empty square until she came to the barricade and the soldiers that barred the way to Bab-el-Oued. There, in front of the soldiers, she stopped, stood and stared at them, then flung the flag to the ground at their feet. Then she turned and walked back to the silent crowd. The bloody flag lay there in the dust, a symbol of defiance, and an almost religious stillness came upon the scene. It was broken by the clatter of a helicopter, flying low over the rooftops, which circled above the trees in the square, then dropped grenades of tear gas. The white smoke swirled upwards through the trees and eyes began to smart, driving us indoors, then out into the arcade to run through the gas for the clear streets beyond. Something had happened: the bloodstain on the flag had been bright and fresh; now a Jeep roared past from the direction of the Rue d'Isly, its crew of helmeted soldiers crouched over a machine-gun trained at the crowded pavement. So we pushed through the throng, mopping eyes with handkerchiefs, to find the crowd thickening and tension verging on hysteria. There had been some killing and, assuming it to be linked with the fusillade heard earlier, we hurried to the end of the Rue d'Isly, where the *harkis* had been.

There the road and pavements were strewn with bodies, and men in blood-smeared white coats were heaving them on to the back of a lorry. Blood was congealing in pools and rivulets; on a pavement lay the top of a man's head, the wall behind splashed with his blood. The wounded were sitting on the kerbs and doorsteps, or being helped, limping, away. Broken glass from shop and car windows lay in drifts over hats, handbags and women's shoes. The bay windows of one boutique were shattered, revealing the cardboard cut-outs of yellow chicks and Easter eggs within and, in the doorway between, a dead man lay sprawled on his back: middle-aged, neatly-suited, his shoes polished; now covered with broken glass.

'*Les harkis les ont tué!*' voices were saying. Shooting had started without warning—perhaps by the soldier with the machine-gun in the shop doorway—but nobody knew why because those who might know were probably dead. How many? Again nobody knew; some guessed a hundred, maybe two hundred, and hundreds wounded. Nobody knew and nobody would know until the bodies could be counted in the mortuaries. But there *had* been a massacre and I must report it to London; a telephone call was due in ten minutes, so I ran through the side streets, dodging the wounded, bleeding on the pavements. At a crossroads, a bullet whip-cracked past my head and, as I ducked for cover, the rifleman who had fired looked down from a rooftop and for an instant our eyes met. So into the hotel to sit panting beside the telephone, scribbling my report into a notebook.

The telephone did not ring until half an hour after the final deadline for the last edition of the *Evening Standard*; for the first time communications had failed. So to spare myself the misery of hearing others dictate their reports from the telephones off the lobby, I walked back to the scene of the massacre. All the dead and wounded had now been removed but the top of the head was still there, perhaps thought to be a fragment of red fruit. Some of the scattered belongings had been collected in piles and posies of flowers laid upon them. A youth with a paint-spray was writing across the width of the road, '*Rue des Martyrs 26 Mars 1962.*' Later, back at the hotel, those who had time to write and dictate their reports at leisure to morning newspapers spoke of ghastly scenes at the mortuary where they had counted the naked, bullet-holed bodies of the dead. The final count that day was forty-six dead and more than two hundred wounded, many of whom were dying. In the Rue d'Isly, more than two thousand spent cartridge cases had been picked up.

What had happened? At the tense moment when the crowd had flooded round the flank of the cordon, somebody had fired a single shot. At this, the overwrought *harkis* had opened fire into the crowd; yells of '*Cessez le feu!*' seeming to increase their terrified rage. The crowd had been scythed by gunfire, flinging themselves to the ground, diving for doorways. Shouts from the lieutenant were unheard, or ignored, by his beserk soldiers, who fired into the crouching figures until their magazines were empty. Yet so thick was the crowd that those who had already passed the cordon did not know what was happening, assuming, as I had, the fusillade to be no more significant than those heard nightly in Algiers. News had reached the head of the column when a *tricolore* dipped in the fresh and flowing blood of a victim had been brought to them. This had been the one they had carried to the Square Bresson and flung at the feet of the French soldiers. For it was the French army, and not only the *harkis*, whom they accused of mass murder; their countrymen upon whose intervention they had pinned their hopes for a continuing French Algeria.

In the aftermath of the massacre in the Rue d'Isly the army poured into Algiers, jet fighters howled low overhead, helicopters scattered leaflets appealing for calm, and the pale grey shapes of warships appeared upon the impassive blue sea. The OAS had called for a general strike but the city was, in any case, paralysed by a massive *quadrillage* cordon-and-search operation throughout the centre of the city by soldiers, marines and the Garde Mobile, who for six days could be seen to dominate the streets. The OAS, like everybody else, seemed stunned by the events in the Rue d'Isly; so much so that, two days after the massacre, the siege of Bal-el-Oued was lifted.

There was, relatively, a lull in Algeria, and I was ordered home but, so engrossing had the death throes of an empire become, that I was almost reluctant to leave. In any case this was not easy, for reasons that immediately became apparent. The *pieds noirs* had lost heart after the massacre in the Rue d'Isly and an exodus had begun. Seeing their *raison d'être* draining away, the OAS had forbidden any to leave on pain of death and, to make their point, had blown up the Air France booking office in the city. No reservations could be made on flights but, despite the threats, thousands flocked to the airport in the hope of escaping from the country. I now joined them.

There was no euphoric lift of the spirits this time. April in Paris was delicious—the budding chestnuts, the tables outside the cafés, the summer dresses—but could not slake my nervous excitement, geared to the running feet and pistol-shots of Algiers. I walked by the Seine in the velvet-blue night, thinking only of the political predictions I could make in the *Standard*. Next day, back in London, the unwinding began in discussing Algeria and its future. Seen from London, well back from the wood and the trees, it could be seen to be over. The siege of Bab-el-Oued and the massacre in the Rue d'Isly had been the decisive defeat of the OAS and whatever outrages they could still perform were irrelevant.

The leaders of the OAS were at last being arrested and, although Salan himself was cornered and caught in a flat in Algiers a few days later, the Secret Army struck out in its final convulsions and hundreds died in the streets. But it *was* the end. The date for the formal declaration of independence had been set for 3 July and there was a stampede of *pieds noirs* to the ports and airports and, by that date, about a million Europeans had left. By any standards, it had been a ghastly war. The French Army had lost nearly 20,000 Europeans and North Africans killed or missing, and more than 3,000 European civilians had died during the seven years of war. The Algerians estimated their total of dead as one million but it was impossible to judge with accuracy; the French claimed to have killed more than 140,000 in action and believed that another 28,000 Algerians had died fighting amongst themselves and that another 50,000 could be added to those totals as missing believed killed. Yet, in the perverse cruelty of the Algerian war, some of the most terrible slaughter was still to come. Despite their assurances to the contrary at Evian, the victorious FLN turned on the *harkis*, the Algerian soldiers who had fought for France, and the others who had worked for the civil service and the municipalities, and massacred them. Disarmed and abandoned by the French, they were rounded up, sometimes with their wives and children, to be tortured and executed. Nobody knew the total but it was estimated at anything between 30,000 and 150,000.

For France it had been a total defeat and, unlike the British in Cyprus, they had not even managed to keep the strategic footholds they needed. But now they would be preoccupied with the resettlement of the unwelcome *pieds noirs* in metropolitan France and Corsica, and before the end of the year joined the rest of the world in the agonized anticipation of nuclear war when the United States and the Soviet Union came into direct confrontation. The issue was the installation of Russian missiles in Cuba and the American ultimatum in October that they be removed.

One possibility was that the Russians would react by occupying West Berlin and there I was sent, reflecting that it was, relatively, the safest place to be in a nuclear war. Looking down the Kurfürstendamm from my hotel window and telephoning the British garrison to ask for reports of Soviet tank movements on the *autobahn*, it was difficult to remember looking down from the Aletti a few months earlier at scenes that had already passed into history.

5

Far-flung Battle Line

To be back in the bar of the Ledra Palace Hotel in Nicosia at the beginning of 1964 seemed like the recurrence of a dream but no longer the former nightmare. Reports of murder—indeed, massacre—were again being announced by Savvas to many of the same correspondents as before but now there was a detachment because we ourselves no longer felt ourselves to be the targets.

It was now the Greek and Turkish Cypriots who were killing each other. Since the creation of the independent Republic of Cyprus four years earlier and the withdrawal of the British to their two sovereign base areas on the south coast of the island, tensions between the two indigenous communities had been mounting. Over Christmas fighting had broken out in Nicosia and Larnaca, the worst being in the suburbs of the capital where a reconstituted EOKA led by Nicos Sampson, the former leader of its gunmen in Nicosia, had slaughtered whole families of Turks.

Only two British battalions remained in Cyprus for the defence of the RAF airfields—the Rifle Brigade and the Gloucestershire Regiment—and these were rushed to the scene of conflict in the hope of keeping the two sides apart. During the first days of January three more battalions were flown to the island from Britain and with them came the usual posse of Fleet Street correspondents, myself among them. We were warned to avoid a blue-painted Land-Rover that Sampson often drove, because it was thought he might still enjoy shooting at Englishmen, but otherwise there was little sense of personal danger.

Horrors were spreading throughout the island. Villages were under siege; isolated farmers and shepherds were murdered; gangs of armed Greeks and Turks roamed the countryside seeking some weaker group that could be slaughtered with the minimum risk to themselves. Whenever the British soldiers could appear, peace was usually restored even if the Greeks, who were the stronger if not the most resolute of the opponents, began to blame the bloodshed and their fears of Turkish revenge on the British.

As more troops arrived from Britain another schoolmasterly figure came to take command. This was Major-General Michael Carver, who was reputed to be something of an intellectual as well as having been a ruthless wartime tank commander, and had the look of a university don combined uneasily with a soldier's hard physique, and perhaps, we speculated, a conflict between the two expressed in a stammer. He reminded me of a clever, tense Classics master I had known at Westminster School, struggling to control his irritation with the unruly, cheeky boys in his charge. Certainly, Carver sometimes seemed to have difficulty in checking his annoyance with the Greek-Cypriots who seemed bent on destroying the little republic they had so recently won.

Our own irritation matched his. Now we were meeting the social and political leaders of the Greek community, whom most of us had ignored during the earlier bloodshed, and initial pleasantries quickly gave way to mutual recrimination. Once, warning our Greek-Cypriot hosts that their treatment of the Turks was inviting invasion from the Turkish mainland, I was told that as they had already defeated the British Army there would be no problem in defeating the Turks. In vain did I explain that, whereas the killing of a British soldier was likely to have involved little more than an immediate cordon-and-search operation, followed by a few days of curfew, the Turks would react differently: killing Greek men and raping Greek women, for a start.

Fears of Turkish intervention and the danger of conflict between Greece and Turkey now focused the attention of the intelligence services of the major powers upon Cyprus and among new arrivals were many whose identities were suspect: amongst them a party of muscular priests with crew-cut hair, who announced that engine trouble had forced their airliner to stop at Nicosia on their way to the Holy Land, and vanished after a single appearance at the Ledra Palace, leaving us to wonder whether they might be Central Intelligence Agency men on their way to take up positions in the mountains. More sinister was the case of a plump, middle-aged officer wearing the uniform of the Royal Army Ordnance Corps, a Major Macey, who spoke many languages and was usually festooned with expensive cameras. He and the driver of his Land-Rover made long expeditions out of Nicosia and I instinctively refused his offer of lifts. Soon afterwards they did not return from one such journey, and no trace of them was ever found.

A delicate cease-fire having been imposed on the two sides and the

British troops entrusted with maintaining it being known as the Truce Force, the risk of fighting between them and the Greek-Cypriots was reduced at the beginning of March when the peace-keeping operation was handed over to the United Nations. Relieved at this as the British were, there was satisfaction in having been able to demonstrate that the heavy, paternal hand of the British Empire was, after all, essential to keeping order amongst such volatile people, who seemed to have proved that they were not, as they had been proclaiming for so long, able to conduct their own affairs in a civilized manner.

It was not only in Cyprus that there seemed urgent need for the re-imposition of *Pax Britannica*. In the Middle East and in South-East Asia the British found themselves called to arms in the defence of the Commonwealth. My own reporting of the new Cyprus troubles was interrupted by a recall to London and orders to fly to a battlefront that had opened in what I remembered as somewhere described in a Victorian soldier's memoirs, rather than a place I had visited: the Radfan.

Little news of any apparent significance had come out of the south-western corner of Arabia until 1962, when a republican revolution overthrew the monarchy in the Yemen. This was welcomed not only by President Nasser but by trade unionists and socialists in Aden, who demanded the merger of Aden and its hinterland with the new, revolutionary Yemen. The British response was blunt; not only was the proposed Federation of South Arabia to be completed but the British Government would not recognize the new Republic of the Yemen. The scene was set for confrontation and, next year, the action began.

An intensification of troubles on the frontier was expected and this was concentrated in the Radfan, where the tribes resented British refusal to recognize their traditional rights to levy tolls on passing trade. The five principal tribes were believed to number something between thirty and forty thousand and to be able to muster anything up to seven thousand fighting men. They were natural guerrillas for whom warfare, whether between tribes or just families, was a normal state, and this aptitude was now exploited by the Yemenis, who offered them not only rifles and ammunition but mines (often originating from the abandoned British depots in the Suez Canal Zone) and a four months' training course with the Yemeni National Guard. So there was more shooting in the mountains and more British lives were lost.

But it was not until the December of 1963 that the tension was recognized as a crisis. The High Commissioner, Sir Kennedy Trevaskis, and several ministers of the Federation were going to London for a constitutional conference and, while they stood talking on the airfield at Khormaksar, a grenade was rolled at them. Trevaskis and more than fifty others were wounded and his political adviser and an Indian woman were killed. A State of Emergency was declared and the frontier with the Yemen was closed, as much as it could be.

Calls for action now came not only from the ruling families of the Federation, who saw their inheritance threatened by Yemeni republicanism, but from London. The newly-arrived Commander-in-Chief, Middle East Command, Lieutenant-General Sir Charles Harington, was the man to take it. In these years, the British produced a number of senior officers worthy of the Empire at the height of its splendour and he was one of them. Tall and handsome, he displayed a natural elegance that would have looked well in bronze, commemorating some dashing deed of conquest. Like all senior officers and officials in the Middle East—and, indeed, the politicians in London—he was convinced that the British could, and would, remain in Aden for as long as it suited us. We *had* to stay because to leave prematurely would be to betray the trust of the sultans, emirs and sheikhs we had persuaded to join our Federation. So when General Harington made a diplomatic visit to the French in Djibouti he was surprised and given grounds for thought when his hosts told him, 'They'll have you out.'

The bomb at the airport had been taken as a warning, but the principal threat was still from the Yemen, where 40,000 Egyptian troops were reported to have arrived. Rather than await serious conflict on the border General Harington decided to deter further Yemeni aggression with a show of strength and mounted a small punitive expedition of three of the four battalions of the Federal Army—as the Levies had been renamed—supported by a modest force of British tanks, artillery and engineers with the RAF flying in support. They were to be sent to the Radfan to demonstrate the long arm of British power; the specific aim being to enter the wide fertile valleys running east from Thumier on the Dhala road, the Wadi Rabwa and, beyond, the Wadi Taym. Having driven away any opposition, the force would then build a road into the former valley so that, in future, Federal or British troops could be quickly deployed in what had been the inviolable fastness of the Radfan.

The operation, launched at the beginning of 1964, was a complete success: the enemy was driven back and fighting was over by the end of the month; the road was built and, in March, all being quiet, the force was withdrawn to continue its routine duties on the frontier and in Aden. Once it had gone the tribesmen returned, tore up the road and resumed their attacks on traffic between Aden and Dhala. Meanwhile, Cairo Radio was presenting the withdrawal as a military defeat and the tribal leaders, who had been persuaded to join the Federation, began to wonder whether they had made the right decision.

The most forceful of them, the Sherif of Beihan, tall, black-bearded and with a rascally glint in his eye, was the sort to whom the Arabists of the Colonial Office instinctively warmed. An old-fashioned autocrat, he had no sympathy with the new Arab nationalism; when news of the Suez war reached him he had said, 'Praise be to God, the old woman has woken up at last!' and it was clear that he was talking about Britannia. His liking for and loyalty to the British combined with the most robust Arab sentiments and prejudices and unexpected touches of sophistication. So when Yemeni aircraft made a sudden and unprovoked attack with cannon-fire on a village in his state, he was loud in his demands for vengeance. If the British failed to honour their promise to what had, until recently, been called a protectorate, they must either be frightened of the Yemenis or be about to abandon South Arabia. Thereupon the new Federal Government invoked their defence treaty with Britain and called for immediate action.

It was a simple matter to avenge the air attack and a squadron of eight Hunter jet fighters flew from Khormaksar to demolish a Yemeni frontier fort with bombs and rockets. But there were overland attacks too, and it was reported that a force of 500 uniformed, dissident tribesmen and another 200 irregulars, trained by the Egyptians, were active on the Federal side of the frontier in the Radfan. Something much more substantial was called for.

Britain had no wish to become involved in war with the Yemen and the Egyptians: indeed, the aim was to restore normal relations with Cairo. A second campaign in the Radfan would mean the use of more British troops and this could not only unsettle the embryonic Federation but could, at the least, sour relations with other Islamic nations. Yet to do nothing would be to lose face and that the British could not risk. So General Harington decided upon more action and his decision was endorsed by the Cabinet in London: the Radfan war had begun.

It only lasted for two months and, even while it was in progress, the soldiers and airmen—and the correspondents—involved realized that war was rarely so enjoyable as this. It was not, of course, enjoyable for those killed or wounded, or for their families, but these were few and, for the vast majority, danger added zest to what would, even in time of peace, have been an exciting expedition to explore unknown and spectacular territory. As could be seen from Thumier, or Dhala, and even more from the forward positions reached during the first advance into the Radfan, this was, for westerners, virgin country. It could be seen from the air as a wild jumble of peaks and valleys with stone villages perched on hills but, so far as was known, no European had set foot there and, as could be seen from aerial observation, the wheel was unknown.

The aim of Harington's second punitive expedition was louder sabre-rattling rather than the capture of any specific objective, but it was given the official task of bringing 'sufficient pressure to bear on the Radfan tribes to prevent the tribal revolt from spreading, to reassert our authority and to stop attacks on the Dhala Road'. This offensive was to be more ambitious than the first, with the initial aim of occupying the commanding heights, the crests and peaks that stood nearly six thousand feet high above the secret valleys of the Radfanis, and then these were to be entered and occupied. The invaders, known as Radforce, were a brigade group made up of a commando of Royal Marines, a company of the Parachute Regiment and two battalions of the Federal Army, with a battalion of the East Anglian Regiment to join them later. There would be armoured cars of the Royal Tank Regiment, howitzers of the Royal Horse Artillery and a field squadron of Royal Engineers in support, as well as a detachment of the Special Air Service Regiment, the highly-trained specialists in operating behind enemy lines. In the air would be two squadrons of Hunter jet fighters, a squadron of Shackleton bombers, a few big, twin-rotor Belvedere helicopters and some light aircraft of the Army Air Corps. In command was Brigadier Louis Hargrove, the new garrison commander at Aden, called from his desk after only six weeks in the Middle East. This would only be enough for the first attack, so reinforcements had been ordered: a full brigade headquarters to be flown out from Northern Ireland, and the strength in infantry to be doubled.

The first phase of the offensive—the capture of peaks which had been given the code-names of Coca-Cola and Sand Fly, and the seizing of the mountain-top known as Cap Badge, which dominated the valleys below—began on 29 April. While the marines advanced overland, a troop of the SAS would be landed near Cap Badge to mark a dropping zone into which the Parachute Regiment would make a descent the next night. The plan quickly went wrong: the overland advance ran into unexpectedly heavy opposition and, worse, the SAS party was discovered and attacked by the enemy. So the parachute drop had to be cancelled and Cap Badge assaulted on foot. The heights were carried in the old-fashioned way by marines led by Major Michael Banks, a celebrated mountaineer and explorer, and, at dawn on 5 May, they stood on the peak watching the sun catch the tawny summits of the Radfan, then flood with light the wide, fertile valleys. Despite the initial setback, success was complete. But the SAS men had, in fighting their way back to the British positions, lost their commanding officer and a trooper killed; and the company of the Parachute Regiment, making their approach to Cap Badge from another direction, were delayed by the roughness of the terrain and were still in open country at sunrise and had to fight at a disadvantage, suffering nine casualties, including two killed. Their little battle had been fought around the village of El Naqil, which, in the time-honoured way, they renamed Pegasus Village, after the winged horse on their regimental crest.

Such a feat would have commanded the attention of Fleet Street at any time but a macabre detail promoted it to the headlines. At a press conference in Aden on the evening of 3 May Major-General John Cubbon, the commander of Middle East Land Forces, was asked about reports broadcast from the Yemen that the tribesmen had found and decapitated the bodies of the two SAS men who had been killed in the initial skirmish, and that their heads were on display, mounted on stakes in the town of Taiz. This the general virtually confirmed, describing the report as 'reliable' and adding that, if it were true, 'I must express, on behalf of all three Services in South Arabia, our deepest sympathy with the relatives of the men and their regiments.' It was, perhaps, unnecessary to offer sympathy to anybody since the men had been dead when the mutilation took place, but this was gratefully received in Fleet Street, where it touched a responsive nerve. Severed heads had once been displayed on the arch of Temple Bar in Fleet Street, proving a popular spectacle and, perhaps, the memory of this was in the blood of the headline-writers who, in any case, kept ears cocked for news that could shock. Next morning the blackest headline announced, 'TWO BRITISH SOLDIERS BEHEADED', words that conjured up the axe and scaffold rather than a grim military practice, for British soldiers on active service in Malaya had been under orders to sever the heads of enemy dead found while on patrol and bring them back for possible identification.

Nevertheless this was seen as an outrage and, in the House of Commons, Denis Healey, himself a former soldier, proclaimed the 'horror and revulsion' of the Opposition at the news. The time had come for the *Evening Standard* to be represented in the Radfan and, before the end of the week, I was standing on the peak of Cap Badge, watching tired soldiers of the Parachute Regiment in tattered uniforms clamber to the summit they had begun to ascend before I had left London. Looking across a tremendous panorama of mountains, sharp and black-shadowed in the burning sun; and, around me, at the young British soldiers, exultant at their feat of arms and endurance; I became aware of the dreadful sweet-sour smell of death. Other young men, killed in this noble landscape, were being laid out on the summit to await a helicopter that would fly them back to Aden for burial in the parade-ground neatness of the military cemetery there.

It was a clean-cut little war. Both sides respected each other's courage; the British praising the tribesmen's skill at sniping and their ability to resist under bombardment by artillery and aircraft; and we felt apologetic when it became known that they regarded our use of helicopters as unsporting.

There was pity as well as admiration for the enemy. One morning when I was at a forward position a patrol of marines—tired and unshaven, eyes bloodshot, their sun-burned skins streaked with blood from thorn scratches—came trudging back from a nocturnal prowl with a prisoner. He was a thin, wiry little man with a tuft of beard beneath his chin, his long, black hair crimped like an Ancient Babylonian's. An Arab officer of the Federal Army questioned him and asked why he was fighting. His answer was as pathetic as it was surprising. No, he was not fighting for the Republic of the Yemen, nor for President Nasser of Egypt, nor against the British. He was fighting for his village, he said. Once they had been happy; they had tilled their fields and had levied tolls from passing camel trains. But now the soldiers had come and were building roads. There had never been roads here before and wheels had never been used. Now lorries would replace camels. Their camel herds would lose value, the makers of camel harness and saddles would no longer be needed. Strangers would come into the lands bringing new ways that they did not understand and did not want. That was why he was fighting.

By the end of the first week the first phase of the offensive was complete; the crests and peaks were occupied and patrols were being sent down into the valleys through which Radforce was now to advance. Already the correspondents had settled into daily routines that suited their deadlines. I would be called each morning at five and by seven be at Khormaksar, awaiting a light aircraft bound for Thumier; there Brigadier Hargrove, or one of his staff, would report on the events of the night and the plans for the day; next a helicopter ride to Cap Badge, fast and low over hostile country, then riding the thermals past crag and precipice to the bald, rock summit. From there the spectacle of the day could be watched through binoculars: the tiny figures of a patrol on the valley floor, burning the thorn hedges round a deserted village as a sign of imperial wrath; the howitzers thumping the mountainsides in search of hidden marksmen; pairs of Hunters diving out of the sun to blow a stone watchtower off the skyline with rockets. Lunch would be *al fresco*, from mess-tins, before the swooping flight back to Thumier and Aden to write a report and take it to the Cable and Wireless office for transmission; now, time for a swim from Tarshyne beach, then back to the hotel for a shower and a change into 'Red Sea rig' of open-necked white shirt, slacks and cummerbund before drinks in the bar and dinner with friends at one of half a dozen restaurants. It was a pleasant routine.

Clare Hollingworth was in Aden, as resourceful as ever. One evening, when meeting her for dinner, I was about to ask her why she had not been at Thumier that day, when the reason became apparent. Clare was well-groomed in a dark blue dress, her hair freshly shampooed, but red creases ran across both cheeks from the bridge of her nose. Those could only have been made by an oxygen mask and that would mean a high-performance RAF jet aircraft. Clare had spent the day flying in a two-seater Hunter, on strikes against enemy positions in the mountains.

The second phase of the offensive was about to begin, and reinforcements were arriving by air from Kenya, so that Brigadier Blacker, who had arrived from Northern Ireland to relieve Hargrove, would have a little army that included seven infantry battalions, five of them British, and Wessex troop-carrying helicopters from the aircraft carrier *Centaur*, which had arrived off Aden. Such was the air of confidence and even exuberance that Duncan Sandys, the Defence Minister, and Hugh Fraser, the Army Minister, arrived from London and were flown to the summit of Cap Badge to survey the battlefield and distant lands ripe for conquest. So must their predecessors have gazed with a sense of mission across African *veldt* and American forest, Indian highlands and Malay *padi* at territory which, thanks to their expertise, could be coloured imperial pink on the map.

The strategic aim of the second phase was even more vague than the first; it was, namely, to demonstrate the ability of British and Federal troops to go where they wished within the Western Federation and to discourage the dissidents by inflicting casualties on them. Also, as punishment, the villages in the valleys below Cap Badge were 'proscribed' so that standing crops, stores of grain and the thorn hedges that corralled their herds were to be burnt. Smoke could be seen rising from the burning of distant villages but not all the British troops were punctilious in carrying this out. Lieutenant-Colonel Jack Dye, the brawny, handsome commanding officer of the East Anglians, who were to lead the advance into the valleys, insisted that he was undertaking a military operation, not a punitive expedition. 'How can I ask my Norfolk farm boys to burn standing wheat, or pour petrol on grain?' he asked.

As the East Anglians' column rolled across the wide, cultivated floor of Wadi Taym, where no Europeans had been before, they became aware that other influences had been more effective than those of the British Empire, for almost every deserted house had a curling photograph of President Nasser fixed to the wall. Until now the British had only brought demands for loyalty and obedience to their laws and, more recently, fire and the sword. So it was realized that the military commitment to the Radfan must be a long one and a modest civil aid programme was begun in a 'hearts and minds' campaign to win these with practical help and propaganda. The drilling of six wells through the rock to the water beneath was begun; these to be left, together with pumps and tanks, when Radforce eventually withdrew. There was also talk of setting up a permanent medical mission in the Radfan.

Jack Dye's column—accompanied by Clare Hollingworth who, alone amongst the correspondents felt able to break away from the routine of daily reporting to disappear into the unknown—vanished in clouds of its own dust and the offensive began its final phase, which was to end with the capture of Jebel Huriyah, the highest peak in the Radfan.

The conquest of the Wadi Taym was not a great feat of arms, since the enemy was numbered in hundreds rather than thousands and was armed mostly with rifles and mines. But there was satisfaction in achieving it with odds in the invaders' favour of seven to one, as current military thinking held that guerrillas could only be defeated when outnumbered by ten to one. There was greater satisfaction in the performance of difficult tasks that did not involve killing; in the night marches across rough, trackless country; in scaling peaks that might never have been climbed before; in flying jet fighters with style and expertise; in piloting helicopters with field guns slung beneath and depositing them gently on mountain-tops. There was about Radforce the *élan* of the old Empire. It came naturally to a battalion commander, in explaining why he had decided to by-pass rather than assault a mountain thought to be held by the enemy, to say. 'There's really no point in doing a Wolfe and storming the heights.'

Only once did the tribesmen stand and fight and that at a place, hitherto unknown, named Saab Sharah, where a ridge commanded the approach to the Jebel Huriyah. To attack this meant that the infantry would have to scramble down 400 feet to the floor of a valley before beginning their assault up another 600 feet to the crest, without cover and, presumably, under fire the whole way. About fifty tribesmen opened fire on the advancing East Anglians and Federal Infantry and awaited their attack. But it did not come. Instead, Colonel Dye called up his artillery and the rocket-firing Hunters and it was the Radfanis who suffered. They held the ridge all that day—it would have been suicidal to move from cover—and the survivors withdrew after dark. Two days later the two battalions in Dye's column launched a full-scale night assault on Jebel Huriyah in the light of flares dropped by circling Shackletons. There was no opposition and next morning the regimental flags of the conquerors were hoisted on the summit. The battle was won and, it was decided in Aden, the Radfan campaign had been brought to a satisfactory conclusion; but, as if to contradict such an idea, the flag-raising ceremony was followed by the crackle of sniper fire. The date was 11 June and a week later the East Anglians were withdrawn to Aden; but the British were in the Radfan to stay and would have to remain there as long as they were in South Arabia.

So placid was the domesticity of garrison life in Aden that this seemed likely to be a long time, although the slow evolutions of a future Federation of South Arabia were given impetus in July 1964 by the Conservative Government during their last months in power. Sir Alec Douglas-Home, who had succeeded Harold Macmillan as Prime Minister announced that, while the British base would remain in Aden indefinitely, South Arabia would be granted independence as a federation within the Commonwealth in four years' time.

British soldiers were also fighting in South-East Asia, in one of the few territories collected by the Empire that matched the Radfan in spectacular wildness: Borneo. Upheavals had been expected in both the Middle East and the Far East but when they came the location of their epicentres took everybody by surprise. The two countries divided between communism and capitalism, Korea and Vietnam, the possibility of a Chinese attack on the surviving Nationalist stronghold of Taiwan and the widening split between Russia and China all threatened to erupt into international conflict. But it was none of these that set British generals searching for maps of Borneo.

There were still imperial ambitions in these parts and one dream of empire was nearer to implementation than any one imagined. President Achmed Sukarno had regarded himself as leader of Indonesia since 1945 and had been recognized as such, even by the departing Dutch colonialists, since 1950. A flamboyant dictator of a now-familiar type, he imagined a domain far larger than the huge, rich one that he had yet to develop. This was to be a union of Indonesia with Malaya, Singapore, those Borneo territories which were not already Indonesian—Sarawak, Brunei and British North Borneo—and the Philippines; it was later planned to include Burma, Thailand, Laos and Cambodia. The whole was to be named Maphilindo and ruled by himself. The only obstacle in his way was the British, who with their current craze for federations had already combined the Malayan states in one and now planned that it should not only be joined by Singapore but by the Borneo territories, 400 miles away, in what was to be called the Federation of Malaysia.

One problem was that the Sultan of Brunei did not wish to surrender his authority over this tiny British protectorate, or to share the riches of the oilfields which Shell were developing on his coast. Persuaded by the British to introduce a degree of democracy amongst his 85,000 subjects (half Malays, a quarter Chinese and a quarter native Dyaks), he had been distressed to find that the overwhelming majority were opposed to his rule. But they also wanted to regain the lost lands of Sarawak and Sabah, which had been ruled by the Sultan's ancestors, until one had granted them to James Brooke—'The White Rajah'—in 1841. This opposition was led by the People's Party—the *Partai Ra'ayat*—which had formed a military arm, the North Kalimantan National Army—the *Tentera Nasional Kalismantan Utars*, or TNKU—which recruited beyond the bounds of Brunei and by the end of 1962 could muster some four thousand men.

Small but unstable, this was the political explosive Sukarno chose as detonator of an eruption to break apart the component countries of Malaysia, even before the federation was formed. The main charge would be the population of the Borneo territories, which he knew as North Kalimantan, the remaining two-thirds of the island already belonging to Indonesia. Of a population just short of one and a half million, there was a large Chinese minority: twenty-eight per cent in Brunei; twenty-one per cent in British North Borneo and thirty-one per cent in Sarawak. The remainder were a mixture of Malays, immigrant labour from Indonesia and the indigenous tribes of the interior, living by primitive agriculture and fishing and, it was said, remembering their recent head-hunting past with nostalgia. Here, as elsewhere in South-East Asia, the Chinese were the most forceful and, as in Malaya, they had formed a subversive network known as the Clandestine Communist Organization—the CCO—which was said to command some sixty thousand active or passive supporters. In Sarawak alone there were believed to be nearly five thousand sympathizers. If they would rebel against the Sultan of Brunei and the British, and the Malays could be persuaded to fight for a pan-Malay Maphilindo, the Federation of Malaysia could never be brought together.

The rebellion had begun at two o'clock in the morning of 8 December 1962. The Sultan's palace and the British Resident's house were among targets attacked in Brunei town while other rebels occupied the Shell oilfield cantonment at Seria and the town of Limbang, in both of which British hostages were taken. A last-minute warning had come from the latter to alert the police and the Far East Command in Singapore.

Gurkhas, followed by the Queen's Own Highlanders and Royal Marines, were flown to Brunei and, in a series of brisk and gallant little battles, the rebellion was put down and the hostages released within four days. Of an estimated force of four thousand, the rebels had lost forty killed and about three thousand, four hundred captured. The survivors fled into the jungle.

By the first week of 1963 the British, with an alarming range of contingencies in mind, had flown a small expeditionary force to Borneo: to Brunei and East Sarawak, 99 Gurkha Infantry Brigade, consisting of one Gurkha and four British battalions; to West Sarawak, where the threat of the CCO was felt to be worst, the headquarters of 3 Commando Brigade and a small force with more to follow; in British North Borneo, a company of Highlanders. In addition were the police, local defence forces and 4,000 irregulars of Harrisson's Force; these were Dyak tribesmen raised by the remarkable Tom Harrisson, curator of the Kuching Museum in Sarawak and an authority on tribal life, who had recruited these warriors to fight the Japanese and had summoned them again by sending canoes up the rivers flying plumes of red feathers, the traditional call to arms. To command this growing force the commander of the main operational formation in Malaya, the 17th Gurkha Division, Major-General Walter Walker, arrived shortly before Christmas.

Knowing of Sukarno's ambitions, Walker was convinced that the Brunei revolt was only a beginning and he was right. On Good Friday the police station at Tebedu on the border of Sarawak, south of Kuching, was attacked and two policemen killed. The attackers were first thought to be TNKU, or CCO, guerrillas; but this had been a well-executed commando raid, the work of professionals. They proved to be Indonesian regular soldiers from Kalimantan. The revolt was over; the war had begun.

Now General Walker had to plan to defend not only the towns against guerrillas but 1,000 miles of border, almost all of it dense, often mountainous jungle, against a regular army equipped with modern weapons. But after the attack on Tebedu there was a lull until August, when two raids were made into Sarawak; yet this could do nothing to delay the formation of the Federation, since a United Nations mission had reported the majority of its future citizens to be in its favour. On 16 September Malaya and Singapore joined with Sarawak and Sabah, as British North Borneo was renamed, and the Government of Malaysia became nominally responsible for its own defence. Indonesian reaction was quick and violent: the British Embassy in Jakarta was attacked and burned and a major raid by 150 Indonesians was made on the Sarawak village of Long Jawi—but repulsed—and the surviving raiders ambushed as they fled by canoes, twenty-six being killed. Other raids followed, the most successful of them at the end of December, when Indonesian commandos crossed the eastern extremity of the border of Kalabakan and caught a detachment of the Malay Regiment by surprise, killing eight and wounding nineteen. Walker rushed a Gurkha battalion to the scene and quickly killed, or captured, most of the raiders, but the damage had been done and Malaysia had been humiliated by a resounding—if, by the usual standards of modern war, small-scale—defeat.

News from Borneo came mostly from carefully-worded communiqués issued by Far East Command, for correspondents were kept away. Until now there had been little incentive to go because what fighting there had been was in such remote jungle that one could read a report of it in London as easily as in Kuching or Brunei. In any case, it had been a busy time elsewhere. The Brunei revolt had seemed a minor affair after the events of the two previous months when the crisis over Russian missiles in Cuba had suddenly made the Third World War seem more of a probability than a possibility. The following year had also been active for me, but not with the customary wars and emergencies. In July there had been a dash to Yugoslavia to reach the ruins of Skopje as they were still shaking with the final tremors of the earthquake that had destroyed it. In October there had been a scramble to the Italian alps to report the dam disaster, which had washed away the town of Longarone. Then, the following month, came the stunning news of the assassination of President Kennedy.

At headquarters, Major-General Walter Walker (right) meets Admiral of the Fleet Earl Mountbatten, Chief of the Defence Staff, and Sir Solly Zuckerman, his Chief Scientific Adviser, on their arrival in Borneo.

In the field, the author interviews soldiers of the Royal Leicestershire Regiment after their action with the Indonesians in the Borneo jungle. Outnumbered by three to one, they had killed seven of the enemy and put the rest to flight.

The Radfan again, 1964. British troops board a Belvedere helicopter to be lifted on to a mountain peak commanding valleys held by the hostile tribesmen.

Flying into battle by helicopter, British soldiers ruminate while, at the open door, a gunner watches for enemy movement on the mountainsides below.

By the end of 1963 there was, all too obviously, what was called a 'confrontation' with Indonesia that seemed likely to escalate into full-scale war. A few correspondents—amongst them Clare Hollingworth and myself—were to be allowed into Borneo and I flew to Singapore for the preliminary briefing. There I was fitted out with a green uniform and canvas boots, which were laced to just below the knee and into which were slipped inner soles of a hard plastic mesh as protection against the poisoned bamboo spikes in man-traps, such as were being set by both sides in Borneo. Next morning I was called at four and, in the cool and sumptuous hotel bedroom, dressed myself in jungle green. Before it was light I joined a queue of Malaysian infantrymen, similarly dressed but laden with arms and equipment, waiting to board an RAF transport bound for Kuching.

Borneo had always seemed the ultimate *terra incognita* of the Empire. In London, old Cockneys still used the term 'Wild Man of Borneo' to describe what the youngsters would call a tearaway, an expression surviving from the visit of a Dyak to a Victorian freak-show. Here were unexplored jungle and rare creatures, like the orang-utan; the savages of the interior were still said to be head-hunters. It looked mysterious as we came down through rain-clouds over Kuching, the capital of the White Rajahs, with jungle and ranges of mountains stretching away into the distance. At the little grass airfield I was met by my conducting officer, who announced that we were going straight to the headquarters of West Brigade to meet its commander, Brigadier Pat Patterson, who was responsible for the defence of western Sarawak.

There was something pleasantly old-fashioned about Brigadier Patterson, although he was aged only forty-five. His well-brushed dark hair and trimmed moustache recalled an earlier military fashion; his friendliness and good manners, a time when English gentlemen tried to conform to a smart and amiable ideal. He was an officer of the old Indian Army and had recently commanded a battalion of Queen Elizabeth's Own Gurkha Rifles and that offered an explanation, too. Seen amongst their stocky soldiers, British officers of Gurkha regiments often looked like the better sort of preparatory-school masters with their small charges; particularly so when in England and wearing civilian clothes, which, for the latter, were dark blue blazers and grey flannel trousers.

Brigadier Patterson at once apologized for an unforeseen change of plan. There had been trouble on the border that morning and he had to go there; perhaps I would care to come along too? On the way to the helicopter pad he explained that a frontier position manned by a platoon of the Royal Malay Regiment had been fired upon. No casualties had been reported but, since the affair at Kalabakan, it was important that the Malays should recover their self-confidence. They must be shown that they had strong support and given praise when it was due. So we were going there, into a place called Nibong, and would collect the Malays' colonel from their base camp on the way.

From the height of a few hundred feet Sarawak looked even more exotic. As the suburbs of Kuching gave way to rice fields and pepper plantations, followed by secondary, then primary, jungle, strange, humpy hills lifted the trees between rivers which flashed as they caught the sun, their banks cleared of undergrowth, here and there, to show the thatched roof of a longhouse, where the Dyaks lived. After a while we landed at a tented camp to collect the Malay colonel, a tough man with the looks of a Gurkha and the manner of a Boy Scout patrol-leader, anxious that the turn-out of his boys will meet with the scoutmaster's approval.

Over the Radfan, I had become accustomed to the exhilaration of rides by helicopter, lurching as the pilot threw it one way and the other to avoid any gunfire from the enemy below. That had been over cliffs and chasms; now we were skimming tree-tops, brushing the leaves and sending flocks of white cockatoos streaming across the dark green canopy. The Wessex helicopter flew its zig-zag course, heeling at each turn, rotors thrashing: suddenly it reared and side-slipped into the jungle, steadied and sank past trees 200 feet tall to a jungle clearing.

Jumping out into the long grass, we saw that the ring of Malay soldiers, who should have been watching the jungle to guard against attack, were staring at the helicopter and its passengers. A Malay lieutenant marched up to Patterson and saluted nervously. 'Good morning,' said Patterson pleasantly. 'Perhaps you will tell me what has been happening?' It was a simple story that the lieutenant had to tell: a few hours before, his men had been fired upon by automatic weapons from the edge of the jungle. How many of the enemy had there been? He did not know. Well, he could have sent a patrol to look for their tracks and spent cartridge cases. Had he sent out a cut-off party to work its way behind the enemy to ambush him when he retreated to the border? He had not. Then that was something to remember next time.

The brigadier suggested that we might go and look for cartridge cases now, and wandered towards the wall of jungle, swishing the grass from side to side with his stick, with the lieutenant, the colonel and myself following cautiously, wondering whether the Indonesians might still be there. Patterson then inspected the platoon's positions and gave its commander more advice so that, when we stood by the Wessex making our farewells, the ring of soldiers guarding us were looking into the jungle, weapons ready. The helicopter's engine coughed into life and she lifted for a fast, skidding take-off over the trees, thrown this way and that to avoid fire from the Indonesians, who might be anywhere below.

The encounter with Brigadier Patterson should have prepared me for meeting the Director of Operations and Commander of British Forces, Borneo, General Walker, who was also a son of the Indian Army; grandson, indeed, because his own Gurkha regiment had once been commanded by his splendidly-whiskered grandfather who, at the siege of Lucknow in the Great Mutiny, used to 'bag a few mutineers before breakfast' as casually as a squire potting at rabbits on his lawn. This meeting involved a flight to Brunei, where the main headquarters were in a requisitioned girls' school, in which the Director of Operations occupied the headmistress's study.

I had known nothing of General Walker, beyond his experience of the Malayan campaign and that he had been commanding Gurkhas for the past three decades. Other generals I had met tended to fall into categories: the austere, with the weight of global strategy on their shoulders; the political, who looked more at ease in the suit and bowler hat of Whitehall than in battledress; the free and easy, with a developed sense of public relations, whose nicknames were quoted in press hand-outs. General Walker was none of these.

Like Patterson, he looked like a British officer from my boyhood imagination: fierce little moustache; bright blue, intelligent eyes; immaculate tropical uniform; charged with zest compounded of self-confidence and optimism. Like Patterson, he knew how to enthral a visitor and whisked back the curtain that hid a wall-map of Borneo. On it were marked the disposition of his own forces and the enemy's, and he set about describing how he was fighting and, he said, winning the war. He had to defend an area the size of England and Scotland, nearly all of it jungle, much of it mountains; with a front of 1,000 miles across which the enemy could attack at will and did.

The enemy had something like fifteen hundred trained irregulars— known as Indonesian Border Terrorists, or IBT—along the frontier supported by an increasing proportion of the regular standing army of 200,000 men. Their raiding parties numbered anything up to a hundred, sometimes more. For defence, he had patrol bases along the border but these could not stop incursions. The answer was the helicopter. Likely crossing points were watched by the SAS in four-man teams and by the locally-raised Border Scouts; when they reported an incursion and its route, helicopters lifted infantry from their camps and put down ambush parties ahead of it and cut-off parties in its rear. That was how they were stopped.

Walker's position had been strengthened by the arrival in Singapore of a new Commander-in-Chief, Far East, Admiral Sir Varyl Begg, who had commanded the *Triumph* on the visit to Leningrad. He took over a newly-unified command structure in Singapore, which reflected the merging of the Admiralty, War Office and Air Ministry into the Ministry of Defence. Quickly recognizing Walker's qualities, he gave him an independence of action allowed to few commanders in modern war.

General Walker had brought to Borneo a distillation of the Empire's military skills. As a young man he had fought the Pathans on the North-West Frontier of India; he had commanded a battalion fighting the Japanese in Burma; and he had commanded a brigade during the campaign in Malaya; he was more at home in tropical swamps and jungle, or roadless mountains, than on Salisbury Plain, where he would have felt a stranger. Now he was giving his young British soldiers the self-confidence to live and fight in this exotic but terrifying country, as I was about to see.

Reports were reaching Walker's headquarters of an action near the Indonesian border with Sabah in deep jungle near a place called Long Semado. Most recent actions had been fought by Gurkhas, but this one had involved British troops and none could have been more English than the Royal Leicestershire Regiment commanded by a Colonel Badger. I was invited to fly to meet the soldiers who had fought what seemed to have been a sharp but victorious little battle.

This time the helicopter flew high over jungle that was ruffled by hills, then ridged by ranges of mountains, rising above misty valleys, following each other like waves. At last we sank towards a clearing in the trees, felled to make a landing site near the tribal settlement of Long Semado, where other helicopters had just landed the Leicesters, fresh from the battlefield. They were all volunteers—for conscription had ended in 1960—and many were not yet twenty, but they bore themselves with an extraordinary degree of nonchalance. Their green combat dress was dark with sweat, but they were freshly shaven; strings of bright Kelabit beads were strung round their necks and at the belts of several hung *parang* swords. When asked about the battle, they described it as young men in Leicestershire might have talked about their part in a hard-played football match, but without boastfulness, or any apparent sense of surprise at finding themselves so engaged in such a place.

Their story was simple, brave and brutal. It had been known that the Indonesians were over the border and an alarming report reached the Leicesters' patrol base from the Border Scouts that an abandoned camp had been discovered in the jungle; no ordinary camp, however, for this could have been occupied by 500 men. Undeterred, the platoon commander, Second Lieutenant Michael Peele, six months out from Sandhurst, led his twenty-five men to the site and followed tracks, only a day old, that led from it to another, slightly smaller camp, also abandoned. Another fresh trail led from this towards the border and the Leicesters followed it, their Border Scouts now lagging behind, until they sighted another camp ahead of them and saw that this one was occupied. Peele guessed that he might be outnumbered by, perhaps, ten to one, but, hoping that surprise would shorten the odds, ordered his men to drop their packs and divided them into two groups, one to assault, the other to work its way round to the far side of the camp to ambush any retreating enemy. But before the cut-off party was in place they were seen by a sentry, the alarm sounded and Peele gave the order to charge. Firing from the hip, they rushed the camp and, for fifteen minutes, a furious battle was fought among the trees. Then, suddenly, it was quiet; the enemy had disappeared; all but seven, who lay dead. The Leicesters searched the camp, collecting half a ton of modern weaponry and stacks of documents and maps. The odds had not been quite as fearsome as they had expected; they had only been outnumbered by two, or three, to one.

As they stood in groups, talking and drinking cans of fizzy lemonade, or leaned against trees, reading letters from home that had arrived in my helicopter, their *sang froid* was even more impressive than their account of the small, complete victory. It was something I was to encounter repeatedly along the frontier, whether in the relaxed style of the SAS, or the formality of the Royal Marines. The latter manned another patrol base, named 'Fort Sleepless', which was so near the frontier that the helicopter pad was covered by a heavy machine gun inside Kalimantan. Here a hulking Cornish sergeant, with a curling Victorian moustache, commanded the little garrison, several of whom had left England for the first time a fortnight before. The enemy were known to be in position eight minutes' walk along a jungle track and the marines had just been under fire when I arrived, but a young corporal from Wembley was more interested in showing off the live cobra they had captured that morning, which was kept tethered to a stick in a clearing just outside the perimeter.

Such places and their little garrisons, which would have qualified as Outposts of Empire a few years before, caught the imagination with their juxtaposition of the familiar and the exotic. Nowhere was this more apparent than at a place called Nanga Gaat, so remote that it was almost off any map with a claim to accuracy. It lay some hundred and fifty miles from the sea on the headwaters of the great Rajang river in dense jungle below the hills that mounted towards the border of Kalimantan. Formerly it could only have been reached by water after many days' travel by launch and canoe; now, however, it was accessible to all with the use of a helicopter. When General Walker had decided that those embarked in the commando ship *Albion* would be more useful ashore, one of the two Wessex squadrons was based at the town of Sibu near the mouth of the river and established a forward base at Nanga Gaat, eighty minutes' flying time to the south.

This lay in the fork of the confluence of the Rajang and Baleh rivers and was thus a centre of communications; it was also the seat of the Temonggong Juggah, the paramount chief of the Dyaks in this part of Sarawak. Thus it could play a dual role: ferrying patrols and ambush parties in and out of the surrounding jungle, and carrying out the civil aid programme which Walker had initiated to win 'the hearts and minds' of the Dyaks so that here the enemy could not, as in Cyprus, hide among sympathizers. Before the Royal Navy had arrived the RAF had decided that, since the riverbanks rose so steeply, there was not enough flat ground to land helicopters. The Fleet Air Arm, however, had inherited the old individualistic dash of the Royal Flying Corps and had been excited by the prospect. Landing-pads were cut into the slopes and a petty officer, who had taken part in the annual field-gun race in the Royal Tournament at Earl's Court in London, and knew how to rig ropes and spars for swinging heavy loads across chasms, supervised the erection of such tackle here for lifting drums of aviation fuel from the canoes that had brought them up-river.

Even flying to Nanga Gaat was something of an adventure. Sitting in the co-pilot's seat of a Wessex, I studied the map spread on my knees, trying to identify hills and rivers in the enormous landscape unrolling beneath. 'You can throw that away,' said the pilot. 'We're off the map. You'll find some mountains ten miles out of place, and some rivers, as wide as the Thames at Richmond, are not even marked. Often, we can't recognize the country from the map. Most of the territory we fly over is unexplored.' Looking again at the map, I noticed that what had looked such confident cartography was less so; contours of mountains were vague and rivers faded into lines of dots.

Landing on a ledge cut in a steep green slope among the trees was the beginning of a strange interlude. The pilot switched off the engine and the only sound was of rushing water as the two rivers swept together below the headland. Dug-out canoes darted on the swirling brown surface; some bound to or from distant longhouses; others, on fishing expeditions, to catch the giant carp with bait of over-ripe fruit, for these fish lay lazily beneath trees overhanging the river, waiting for their favourite food to rot and fall from the branches. Dappled with sunlight, the rivers were not so idyllic as at first sight; they could rise thirty feet in six hours when it rained in the hills.

The aircrews and technicians of the Wessex flight were not immediately recognizable as such when encountered amongst the open-sided thatched huts where they lived. Most were bare to the waist but for their tattoos and strings of bright Dyak beads, wearing *lunghi* waist-cloths, like sarongs. Only the Gurkhas, who guarded them, remained immaculately military but they, too, seemed beguiled; the fierce little men having caught wild mouse-deer, no bigger than Siamese cats, were keeping them as pets and refusing the sailors' demands for venison as a change from curried wild boar and fried giant carp. They were also fascinated by the strange and beautiful creatures all about: the cockatoos and hornbills, the flying foxes, the butterflies, which flopped through the hot, heavy air like brilliant silk handkerchiefs, and, less attractive, the giant centipedes, striped tarantulas and snakes, emerald and poisonous.

Equally exotic were the people ruled by the Temonggong Juggah, whose wooden house stood, surrounded by brightly coloured shrines, near the point of the peninsula. The Dyaks of the longhouses had become friends of the newcomers to Nanga Gaat, due both to the success of the 'hearts and minds' campaign and the friendliness of the British and Nepalese strangers; particularly those like a pilot of a Wessex and the petty officer from the Royal Tournament, named Robertson and Hazel, who were learning the Dyak language and spent much of their spare time visiting longhouses. That day Petty Officer Hazel, curly-haired broad-shouldered and merry-eyed, invited me to accompany him on an expedition to a longhouse two hours distant even by canoe powered by an outboard motor and going with the current.

It was an exhilarating voyage, riding the river between boulders, shooting rapids and skimming deep, swirling pools. In the bows squatted a Dyak signalling the way through the rocks to the helmsman with his hands; behind him, Hazel, a rifle between his knees. On either bank, the trees of virgin jungle rose in columns, one to two hundred feet, sheer to their canopies of leaves. At last the forest gave way to the thick mesh of secondary jungle, where the great trees had been felled, then to cultivation and finally to a longhouse, stretching nearly two hundred yards along a terrace above flood level. Built of bamboo and thatched with palm leaves, it stood on stilts, beneath which chickens and little brown pigs scratched. In front of the longhouse and running its full length was a bamboo terrace, springy as a trampoline: within, a long communal hall with small rooms—one for each family—at the back; up a ladder, an attic for storage and for the unmarried girls' dormitory, the unmarried men sleeping in the hall below.

Along the shore naked children frolicked in the water and women, bare to the waist, washed clothes, all standing to wave as our motor stopped and the canoe slid across the calm water to the beach. From here, the longhouse was reached by a series of huge logs, laid end to end, in which steps had been cut and, at the top, the headman waited to greet us. Petty Officer Hazel was a friend; grunted introductions and greetings were exchanged as we were led up the ladder and into the longhouse, the headman sending some of the girls to prepare drinks and a meal and the prettiest to adorn themselves with ornaments. In the great hall we squatted on mats, exchanging nods and grins, the headman rolling us thick cigarettes from the shaggy, green tobacco he grew. Then the two prettiest girls returned, still bare-breasted, but wearing beads, bangles and intricate head-dresses, to kneel before us and sing little songs of welcome in reedy voices.

We had been joined by some of the Dyak braves, muscular young men wearing loin-cloths, their black hair cut in a thick fringe and hanging down their backs in long manes. All were tattooed and Hazel explained that the black and blue whorls decorating their throats were inflicted at an initiation ceremony on reaching manhood to demonstrate their courage in withstanding pain. If the back of a warrior's right hand bore a blue tattoo, it was a sign that he had taken an enemy's head; twenty years before, the likes of Tom Harrisson had encouraged them to collect Japanese heads and now there were rumours of decapitated Indonesians being found in the jungle. As little cups of rice wine were handed round, my eyes grew accustomed to the gloom and I saw the principal decorations of the longhouse; a faded colour photograph, cut from some magazine, of the Queen's wedding to Prince Philip, and a bunch of human heads, blackened with age, hanging like coconuts from a rafter.

Petty Officer Hazel had made friends with the Dyaks by more than speaking a little of their language. He had attended their parties, drunk his share of rice wine and, when the young men competed in horseplay and acrobatic feats, introduced them to a new game, blind man's buff. His final acceptance came when they teased him about the lack of tattooing on his throat, implying that he could be no warrior. At this he rose, turning his back to them and dropping his shorts to reveal, tattooed in lurid colours, flames roaring up his back from his anus; an angel and a devil directing fire extinguishers at them from either buttock. He was at once accepted as a fellow-warrior. Later the Dyaks had tried to teach the British how to use a blow-pipe and hunt jungle pig; the British showed them how to water-ski.

Amongst his more practical duties was the reporting of opportunities for 'hearts and minds' operations, particularly any need for medical aid. As a result the Dyaks, who had hitherto had to rely on their own medicine man, were taken to Nanga Gaat for attention by a naval surgeon-lieutenant, or sick-berth attendant, or even flown to hospital in Sibu; one girl, who had been accidentally blinded in one eye, was flow from there to Singapore for treatment. When a smallpox epidemic broke out in long-houses on another stretch of riverside, the helicopters flew 200 sick Dyaks to hospital. In consequence a helicopter cult had developed and the first understandable word that Dyaks sometimes spoke to their British visitors was 'Coptah!' Helicopters appeared in tattoed decoration and Dyak children played with toy helicopters carved in redwood.

Sick-berth attendants regularly visited the longhouses just as the young army doctor had made his calls on villages in the Radfan. In turn the Dyaks visited Nanga Gaat, bringing gifts to the British commanding officer as well as tribute to the Temonggong Juggah, who was equally happy with his guests, having visited London and sometimes showing his approval of European ways by wearing an old double-breasted jacket with his *lunghi*. He was a quiet, dignified man in middle age, wearing his hair in the usual fringe and mane but speaking a little English; enough to convey that he knew his people would have to make the difficult transition to the modern, outside world. When Dyak braves visited the British camp they were given iced beer from the refrigerator and took to arriving in time to watch a film projected on to a screen slung between trees after dark. The last to be shown had been a James Bond movie called *From Russia with Love*; next day a pilot about to take off on a jungle mission, was standing beside his helicopter, loading his pistol. A Dyak came up to him, pointed at the weapon, and spoke two words, just recognizable as 'James Bond'. But fraternization with young women was forbidden by order, guidance on this from Tom Harrisson having been circulated amongst all serving in Borneo: 'If you feel like pinching somebody's bottom, count ten and pinch your own.' Since the girls were comely, their pretty breasts were customarily bare and the longhouses had a tradition of sexual generosity to strangers, it was often difficult to obey. Such frustration apart, life at Nanga Gaat was idyllic and it occurred to me that not since the crew of the *Bounty* went ashore at Tahiti can British sailors have encountered such an earthly paradise.

It was daunting country, too. Helicopter pilots returned with more traveller's tales than stories of battle. Often they flew amongst mountains that rose to five thousand feet and more, and described scenes of grandeur and menace, of peaks and precipices, chasms and caverns, that recalled the illustrations to Rider Haggard stories. Helicopters could alight on perches that were otherwise inaccessible: one was a tower of rock with jungle upon its summit, surrounded by a wide skirt of fallen, rotting trees and vegetation, upon which secondary jungle had grown, so that it appeared solid ground; yet it would not support the weight of a man, who would be instantly swallowed up. Even the bravest regarded Borneo with awe.

Warlike operations took place away from Nanga Gaat. Patrols were flown to map references in the jungle and sometimes lowered by ropes through the canopy of leaves to the ground 200 feet below. At intervals along the border trees had been felled to clear landing sites, some only slightly wider than the span of a helocopter's rotor-blades—one, such a tight fit that it was known as 'The Funnel'. Here the four-man standing patrols of the SAS would wait for relief and evacuation after several months of living in the jungle and watching the trails leading from Kalimantan. The strategic and tactical movement of troops was the helicopters' main task and Walker disapproved of their direct involvement in battle, 'charging like Prince Rupert', but occasionally it was necessary. Once this squadron had flown Gurkhas to attack the enemy on an island in a river, suddenly appearing over the tree-tops, the down-wash of their rotors ruffling the water and blowing reeds flat, to land the assault parties under fire 'in the face of the enemy' as military phraseology has it. Most of their direct action was the cutting off of the invaders; as the commanding officer, Lieutenant-Commander Geoffrey Sherman—nicknamed 'Tank' because of the Second World War association of his name and his square-cut looks—put it, illustrating his words by chopping one hand on to the palm of the other: 'The Indonesians cross the border. We let them come; the further the better. We put an ambush party down ahead of them—*zonk!*—then we drop ambush parties in their rear—*zonk!* Then they've had it.'

The jungle skirmishes in Borneo were being watched with increasing alarm from Washington, for Sukarno's Indonesia was seen as a bastion against communism spreading south from Russia, China and North Vietnam. At the beginning of 1964 Robert Kennedy, brother of the murdered President Kennedy and his Attorney-General, was sent by President Johnson to Jakarta and Singapore on a peace-making mission. Visiting the Indonesian dictator first, he replied to the greeting, 'Have you come to threaten me?' with the assurance, 'No, I've come to help get you out of trouble.'

His confidence was based on sketchy knowledge of the risks involved as he discovered when he reached Singapore and tried to persuade the British and Malaysians to come to terms with the Indonesians. He was told that the greatest danger was that Sukarno, having annexed Malaysian Borneo, if not Singapore and Malaya, would himself be overthrown by Indonesian communists. Then it was the turn of the British to persuade Kennedy that the United States should not support the aggressor. As a gesture to the Americans a tentative cease-fire in Borneo was announced by both sides but it came to nothing—indeed, the Leicesters' action had been fought while it was supposed to be in force—and the first whispers of negotiation quickly fell silent.

Indonesian raids continued, and were repelled, but Walker warned that their weight and scope might increase and that they might be timed to coincide with attacks by the CCO. In August the Indonesians launched commando raids against Singapore and Malaya and it seemed likely that the fighting would spread and escalate, involving both sea and air forces. Then, just as full-scale war with Indonesia began to seem a probability, the background to the confrontation suddenly altered. In October 1964 the British Government changed, the Labour Party ending thirteen years of Conservative rule, winning the general election by four seats. But any apprehensions Walker had of a slackening of resolve and a hasty cutting of the last imperial ties were quickly set aside for the Labour politicians seemed even more resolute in the prosecution of the war than the Conservatives had been. The new Secretary of State for Defence, Denis Healey, had already visited the scene of action in Borneo as parliamentary spokesman, and his attitude was robust. Reinforcements were immediately flown out, bringing Walker's force up to twenty-three battalions, eight of them Gurkha and three Malay, together with supporting arms. So that he himself could concentrate on the direction of operations, Walker handed over command of the field force itself to Major-General Peter Hunt.

Walker's first request to the new administration was for permission to take the war to the enemy by attacking the bases inside Kalimantan from which the raids were mounted. This was immediately granted and, a month after Labour came to power, the first of the cross-border operations—code-named *Claret*—was launched. Initially these only penetrated a mile or so into Indonesia, but their range was gradually increased, finally to about ten miles. Instead of fighting patrols, whole battalions—usually Gurkha—were sent across. The only Victoria Cross to be awarded during the campaign was won by a Gurkha inside Indonesia.

Thereafter most of the fighting was on the Indonesian side of the frontier. Acting on reports from the SAS, the Border Scouts and intelligence sources, enemy concentrations were attacked before they could even begin their approach marches to the border. While operations remained at this level, Malaysia seemed secure; the principal risks of escalation lay in the use of Indonesian air or sea power and British retaliation against their bases. The RAF was restive; the air marshals urging that their V-bomber force, parked idle at airfields in the British Isles as part of the nuclear deterrent, should be able to launch conventional bombing attacks against Indonesian targets: a temptation resisted by Denis Healey.

The electoral victory of the Labour Party might be sustaining the young Federation of Malaysia but, on the far side of the Indian Ocean, the news had a different effect upon the prosects of the other federation designed to hold together the states of South Arabia. Even before the new British Government could formulate its policy for the Middle East the aspiring politicians of Aden and its hinterland made up their minds what this would be. Labour politicians in London would surely hasten the dismantling of the British Empire. Already the British planned to hand over South Arabia to the traditional rulers up-country and moderate politicians in Aden, who might agree to remaining within the Commonwealth. For those who had other ideas, it was time to stake their claim.

6

Imperial Echoes

The office block was half completed and, although still lacking its outer wall, it could be seen to partially obscure the view of St Paul's Cathedral from Fleet Street. Too late had come the protestations against the spoiling of the grandest and most familiar juxtaposition of stately and domestic architecture in the capital that had seemed to symbolize the nation's conception of its own imperial destiny. Now there was nothing to be done but smile at the explanation offered by the comedian Spike Milligan: that Ludgate Hill was to be made yet narrower until the approach to St Paul's could be compared with that to Petra, with visitors guided by flaring torches through a narrow gorge from which they would suddenly emerge to see the great portico and façade of the cathedral towering above them.

But today, on Saturday 30 January 1965, the new building was put to practical, temporary use as a grandstand commanding views west to Ludgate Circus and Fleet Street and east to the forecourt and steps of the cathedral. From the bare concrete of the fourth floor I and other journalists were to watch the funeral procession of Sir Winston Churchill. His death had come as no surprise at the age of ninety; the strokes that had brought about the end to his long career had allowed him time and dignity to take a formal farewell of the House of Commons the previous year. He had then retired to his house in Kensington to await the end and the implementation of the plans for his funeral, in which he had taken a close interest, code-named Operation Hope-not.

Just as the Victory Parade of 1946 had inspired sombre forebodings, and the coronation procession an optimism yet to be fulfilled, so the silent crowds and the distant beat of the funeral drums induced thoughts that ranged beyond the expected death of a great historical figure. These were the obsequies of the ideals that had been the motive force in Churchill: of the British Empire itself. It was the native British who marched through London with his coffin; those he would have known as the Queen's subjects from her Empire were present as diplomatic mourners, taking their place alongside the Europeans and the Americans of the North Atlantic Alliance. As the blocks of colour—the red and black of the tunics and bearskins of the Guards, the white of the sailors' caps, the dusty blue of the airmen's uniforms—moved down the length of Fleet Street the procession seemed something like that of a family funeral: our patriarch was gone and no other would take his place.

As the ceremonial progressed below, there was a sense of completeness in the spectacle. It was twenty years since Churchill had watched the crossing of the Rhine, the last great, set-piece battle of the war in Europe; so much had happened, so fast, since then that, had this occasion been delayed, the dignity of his departure might have been impaired. The Empire had slipped away far more quickly than expected and grandiose schemes for federations of former colonies within the new Commonwealth had encountered unexpected storms: the Central African Federation had broken apart; the Federation of the West Indies collapsed after ten years; the Federation of South Arabia faced mounting opposition from within; the Federation of Malaysia was fighting for its life against Indonesian aggression.

In London a Labour Government with a minimal majority in the House of Commons was in power but, as yet, showed no sign of wanting to abandon the global power that Churchill had exercised with the relish of the Earl of Chatham two centuries before. There was some hope that a Commonwealth bound together by sentimental loyalties might survive and the noble façade would be seen to stand despite the cracks and fallen masonry. The despoiling of the prospect of St Paul's Cathedral was itself symbolic of the change in self-regard that was overtaking the British.

For me, the signs were apparent in what was happening to two pillars of the old order, *The Times* and the Royal Navy.

The sight of Buckingham Palace being hacked to rubble by pick-axes could hardly have seemed more shocking than the demolition of Printing House Square in 1960, together with the Private House, the Lamb and Lark and the ethos of The Thunderer. Without, it seemed, a wince of sentiment, the whole came down; the great clock-face on the pediment was saved, but only to become the top of a garden table; the mutilated remains of the stone lion and unicorn from the Royal Arms that had surmounted a doorway became ornaments for James Morris who, in sympathy, it seemed, had himself put aside the masculinity that had assaulted Everest and submitted to a surgical and chemical transformation that would enable him to lead the rest of his life as a woman.

Printing House Square had now been rebuilt as a slab-faced office block at an expense that cramped the scope of the newspaper's reporting oversea (the final *s* still being forbidden by the sub-editor's Style Book). Sir William Haley's broadening of *The Times*'s appeal, in the hope of increasing the circulation from a quarter to half a million, was continuing; but at a cost that made traditionalists flinch. Ineptitude and vulgarity had joined in an advertising campaign which covered hoardings with posters proclaiming, 'TOP PEOPLE TAKE THE TIMES—DO YOU?' and the boast that seventy per cent of those listed in *Who's Who* read the paper. This not only violated the quiet gentlemanliness with which *The Times* had conducted its affairs, but contradicted Haley's own policy which was, of course, to shift its appeal away from those 'top people'.

It did, however, help to raise the circulation to 300,000, and increase production costs more than revenue, so that, in 1966, the Astors were to find it necessary to sell the paper to Lord Thomson, an elderly Canadian newspaper millionaire, of an age and upbringing to understand that he was buying an institution. The determined destruction of the traditions would continue and news, which had always seemed so confidential on the inside pages, was printed on the front page. Haley, who was later to edit the *Encyclopaedia Britannica* in Chicago—perhaps the nearest equivalent to *The Times*—was replaced by William Rees-Mogg, a young man with the gravitas that might have identified him as a leader-writer in earlier years. Indeed, his leading articles were as sonorous as of old but, before this became apparent, he inflicted the *coup de grâce* to The Thunderer by abandoning the old anonymity in favour of what Fleet Street calls 'bylines'. Thus, instead of reports from Our Own and Our Special Correspondents, they were now signed by often able, sometimes distinguished, journalists who had formerly submerged their identities in the corporate character of the newspaper. At that moment the spirit of the old *Times* fragmented and it could be seen and praised, or criticized, in its component parts. No longer were Delphic pronouncements awaited from the depths of Printing House Square; the temple of the oracle had been sundered and the priests and acolytes exposed to view; *The Times* had become just another newspaper aimed at what advertisers classified as an AB readership in the higher range of purchasing-power.

For my generation, and our predecessors, the ultimate sanction that had ensured the survival of the Empire, and its constitutions and institutions was the gun-muzzles of the Royal Navy, bound in burnished brass and, for most of the time, stopped with heraldic tompions, their message clear to all. This had undergone some technical change and the capital ship was now the aircraft carrier: floating airfields, as battleships had been floating batteries. Other weaponry—notably nuclear weapons and missiles and combinations of the two—had inspired much reconsideration of what the nation needed for its defence and what it could afford. Such were the issues that successive Conservative and Labour governments agreed that the planning and control of national defence should be centralized in a single Ministry of Defence and the four separate departments—Admiralty, War Office, Air Ministry and the small policy-making Ministry of Defence had been combined in this administrative monolith in the spring of 1964.

The new Secretary of State for Defence, Denis Healey, decided that public relations should now be coordinated by a civil servant unhampered by loyalty to one particular arm of the services. So, a year after the merging, defence and political journalists gave a dinner at the Dorchester Hotel for the departing Chief of Public Relations, Brigadier Godfrey Hobbs, who retired early. Most of us saw his removal as the consequence of a confrontation of two strong personalities rather than a pragmatic arrangement by Healey, but later it assumed a symbolic significance. Men like Hobbs, sons of the old Empire, no longer looked as if they belonged in Whitehall.

In his younger days Godfrey had been of the breed reflected in the novels of John Buchan, carrying his intelligence with a jaunty nonchalance and disguising his toughness with laughter. A visit to his office in the Ministry of Defence—both the old, small one and the new, big one—always produced news for the following day. One would call at five in the afternoon, a bottle of gin would be produced from a filing cabinet and Hobbs would start his *tour d'horizon*, touching on sultanates and people's republics, federations and colonies with easy familiarity. The exclusive news that he never failed to offer was never a gift; always, one knew, planted with a particular purpose. Perhaps Brigadier Hobbs was flying a kite or trailing his coat; perhaps he was hoping to alarm the Treasury or the Russians; always, it seemed certain, there was an ulterior motive, for he was the bluff but wily English gentleman who daunted enemies and had friends shaking their heads in admiring bewilderment.

Now Godfrey Hobbs and his kind were going; there was no place for their amused and proprietorial paternalism. In his place appeared a succession of young and able careerists, who seldom, if ever, produced exclusive news and were promoted; the first, Philip Moore, to be Private

Secretary to the Queen; two of his successors to be Director-General of the Central Office of Information. Godfrey Hobbs retired to Sandwich and played golf.

Hitherto the three services had competed with each other for their shares of the defence budget, vigorously and openly, like the electrical and gas industries; rivals in their markets but both publicly owned. Competition had always been keenest between the Royal Navy and the RAF: the former insisting that it must control all arms of maritime defence on, under and above the sea; the latter demanding that, by right, it must command everything that flew. Until 1964 the admirals and the air marshals had campaigned for their particular hopes and the final decision had been taken by the Cabinet in consultation with the Ministry of Defence. But now that they shared the same corridors (and sometimes the same rooms) in Whitehall and were ordered to show a semblance of unity, conflict was driven underground. The issues of national defence, long regarded as above political or factional dispute, became subject to intrigue.

At this time the principal choice was between aircraft carriers for the Royal Navy and strategic bombers for the RAF; the nation could not afford both. The task of evaluating the arguments and arbitrating between the rivals now faced Denis Healey, who had brought to the Ministry of Defence an incisive intelligence, administrative ability, a well-stocked mind and a tendency to bully. As a young man at Oxford he had joined the Communist Party and, although he had resigned because of the alliance between Stalin and Hitler in 1939, he had startled the Labour Party conference at Blackpool in 1945 with the violence of his radicalism and was suspected by some senior officers of remaining a clandestine communist; a suspicion only gradually dispelled by his stand against communist expansion around the world.

The campaign for the building of big ships was romantic as well as practical. There was a magnificence about those great hulls, the power of their armament and the intricacy of their machinery, inheriting names familiar to Tudor or Georgian sailors, that could affect the ways of the world by crossing horizons to hearten, or threaten, by their presence. But the Royal Navy no longer enjoyed a monopoly of such romantic symbols of power for, instead of aircraft carriers, the Royal Air Force offered islands. Their alternative proposition was that Air Power—the expression demanded capital letters, like Sea Power—could be exercised globally from a chain of islands belonging to the British Commonwealth. There would be no need to build, maintain and man large and expensive ships; airfields could be built on these islands so that reconnaissance, strike or transport aircraft could be based upon them, moving from one to another as required.

I remained a navalist, since bombers could only drop bombs and could not fulfil the other functions of warships, from giving cocktail parties to landing marines, but I was not immune to the appeal of the idea. I already knew the prototype island base—Gan in the Maldive Islands, south of Ceylon—and had heard imperial echoes there. It was a long concrete runway, with workshops, fuel tanks and barracks, set upon a coral island, one of a ring of them that formed Addu Atoll. On its shore palms tossed in the warm sea-breeze and creamy surf broke on reefs rising from the clear depths of the peacock and cobalt sea. There were other islands in the Indian Ocean and Arabian Sea, like Aldabra, Diego Garcia, the Cocos, Masirah, Perim and Socotra, where giant tortoises lived, and others, unknown to all but geographers and navigators, like the McDonald and Heards islands; there were more than enough islands available in the Pacific from Fiji across to Pitcairn, the home of the *Bounty* mutineers' descendants, which was also on the air marshals' list. In the Atlantic there were the Falklands, St Helena, Ascension, Inaccessible, Gough and Tristan da Cunha. It was this latter island that was described to me as an example of the island base of the future, and beguiling it proved.

In a small office overlooking the Thames in the Ministry of Defence a group captain showed me maps and plans of Tristan da Cunha and what might be built upon it. The importance of this particular island was that long-range aircraft could refuel there and reach the Far East and Australia without having to fly through the more sensitive skies of the Middle East or Africa. The island was a volcanic peak and an eruption was a contingency that had to be taken into account. Indeed the only level ground upon which the 3,000 feet of concrete runway could be laid was now used for growing potatoes by the few inhabitants of the Edinburgh settlement. There was no space to erect fuel tanks but there was sheltered water offshore where huge plastic, sausage-shaped containers could be moored underwater, filled with aviation fuel. So detailed were the plans for the base that they included the site of the bar for the officers' mess, where it would command a fine view of sunset over the Atlantic.

The choice between aircraft carriers and islands was a principal one, but could only be made when British commitments to the Commonwealth, to NATO and to other friends and allies in the Middle East, Africa and East of Suez had been decided upon. When the Labour

Government took office there was no doubt that Britain was to remain a global power.

Behind each eruption of trouble East of Suez lay the fear of Russian or Chinese hordes, or both; the Chinese intervention in Korea had demonstrated that such apprehension was well founded. Before 1947 the facing of such threats had been the task of the Indian Army; now, could they be faced without it?

India was still there, of course, mutilated by the partition from Pakistan but still, despite its perennial problems of overpopulation and poverty, a great power. This was gratifying because, for all its irritating ways, its smugness, its attachment to the Ancient World and its waywardness in world affairs, an affection between the former ruler and the ruled remained. The British and the Indians had a liking and a respect for each other and the legacies of the British Empire were plain to see. There was a constitution and democracy to represent people as varied as Europeans in a unified system of government; there was the legal system; there were communications—notably the railways—that physically linked them; there was English as a common language; and there was an Indian Army, the final assertion of that unity. In 1965 it was not only on the borders with Pakistan and China that the Indian Army was withstanding threats.

Since the hurried partition of the Indian Empire into predominantly Hindu India and Moslem Pakistan, there had been inherent instability in the state of Kashmir on the southern slopes of the Himalayas. It was ruled by a Hindu maharajah but mostly inhabited by Moslems, and the ruler had opted for integration with India. This had led to fighting between India and Pakistan, as a result of which the United Nations had ordered that, while some small enclaves should be ceded to Pakistan, Kashmir itself would join India, leaving the issue almost as contentious as before. So it came as no surprise when fighting broke out again between India and Pakistan in the spring of 1965.

It seemed almost like old times when trouble was first reported from a far-flung frontier with an exotic name, the Rann of Kutch. When an old India hand, who knew where and what this was, could be found and interviewed it proved to be desolate flats of mud, or sand, according to the weather, to the east of the mouths of the Indus and apparently of little use to either country. It had started as a simple case of frontier violation, unimportant except as a *casus belli* such as it now was. The armies of both nations quickly became involved and, as access to the disputed territory was easier from Pakistan, India reacted by concentrating forces in the

Punjab to threaten Lahore. Meanwhile the Pakistani President Ayub Khan had already taken the opportunity to resume attempts to annex Kashmir by launching a campaign of guerrilla warfare and subversion within its borders, involving some thirty thousand men, both regular Pakistani soldiers and irregular Kashmiri Moslems, under the command of one of his generals. Despite apparently successful efforts to solve the problem of the Rann of Kutch at the Commonwealth Conference in June, the campaign against Kashmir had already been launched and was impossible to stop. The armies and air forces of both sides were now mobilized and, in August, they fought.

The opponents were more evenly matched than they seemed. Although the Indian Army numbered about eight hundred thousand men, six of its seventeen divisions were facing the Chinese, leaving eight to defend the Punjab and three in Kashmir. The army of Pakistan could muster less than a quarter of a million men but all of these could be deployed against India and they were equipped with the new American tank, the Patton, whereas the Indians could only field the Centurion, a reliable but obsolescent British tank. In the air the Indians could put up some five hundred combat aircraft but these were mostly out of date or inadequate, including the tiny Gnat fighter, British-built and used by the RAF for training, and a few new Russian fighters. Although Pakistani strength in the air was less than half the Indian, it included a large number of American-built Sabre fighters. Capabilities became even more difficult to assess because all the senior officers on both sides had been trained by the British in the old Indian Army, they spoke English amongst themselves and called each other by English nicknames.

Skirmishes and artillery exchanges along their common frontier quickly escalated as Pakistan attempted to conjure a popular rising against India in Kashmir and at the beginning of September launched an armoured division towards the town of Akhnur on the main supply road between India and Kashmir. It was stopped a few miles from its objective and in retaliation the Indians threw three divisions towards Lahore in what they called Operation Grand Slam; but they, too, were held. The war had now escalated to the point at which the *Evening Standard* sent its correspondent, so a telephone call recalled me from holiday in Norfolk and put me on a Comet airliner flying via Rome, Damascus and Abadan to Bombay and thence to New Delhi.

The press centre at the Ministry of Information was crowded with Indian and international journalists, including familiar faces from Fleet

Street (amongst them Clare Hollingworth's), who had arrived to report the war but, so far, had been able to describe nothing but air-raid warnings in the capital. No creature is more ungainly and pathetic out of its element than a war correspondent deprived of conflict, without stimulation for the adrenalin or excuse for braggadocio. We were allowed no nearer to the war than the press centre, where charming Indian civil servants tried to soothe us with promises of expeditions to come, meanwhile offering hand-outs in English on the progress of the war and occasional press conferences, over which presided a formidable lady in a sari, Mrs Indira Gandhi, the Minister of Information. In vain did we protest that their enemies were allowing correspondents to the front, so bringing down a barrage of I-was-there reports on the war, as seen from their side, into the world's media.

Old India hands grumbled that this would never have happened under the Raj and left for a swim at the hotel pool, or a curry lunch in Old Delhi. Only Clare Hollingworth took direct action and, since Indian civil servants presented no such problems as the OAS, she pushed open doors, marched unbidden and unannounced into offices, and beat upon desks with her fist. Perhaps because of their natural courtesy, or because some daunting memory of fierce memsahibs stirred, they listened to her complaints and, finally, to put a stop to them, they told her that, because of her professional distinction and the fair-mindedness of her newspaper towards India, she—but she alone—would be permitted to travel into the war zone. To this Clare responded with gratitude and the reminder that they could hardly expect a frail woman to venture alone on to the battlefield; she felt sure that they would include on whatever pass they were to provide permission for two male bodyguards, or bearers, to accompany her. Hurriedly agreeing to this, and slightly embarrassed at what might seem a lack of thoughtfulness on their part, the Indians were not to know what effort this had demanded of Clare. She was a woman who would glare at a man who offered to carry her suitcase and, as had been apparent in Algiers and Arabia, was not only a war correspondent of intrepidity but an Amazon. The two menservants she planned to engage were an Australian journalist, Creighton Burns of the Melbourne *Age*, and myself.

We departed before dawn in a sky-blue taxi with little curtains at its windows, plastic flowers decorating it within and driven by a Sikh to whom we had offered a fare he could hardly refuse. In this we sped to war, frequently stopping at petrol stations to replenish the petrol tank since stocks were likely to have been used up by the Indian Army as we neared the Punjab. The three of us wore khaki and Clare grumbled at the unmilitary look of our taxi, although this proved advantageous as we passed Indian Army transport wrecked and riddled by cannon-fire at the roadside and Pakistani fighters howled down the road looking for more targets, spurning the taxi with flapping curtains.

We aimed to reach the city of Jammu before dark, so stopped for refreshments in Pathankot; briefly, for there was an air base nearby and even Europeans were regarded as Pakistani spies; we were watched by a surly, muttering crowd and seldom can iced, fizzy drinks have been drunk so quickly. This hastened the journey and it was growing dark, the roads unlit, headlights forbidden and the risk of hitting people, carts or cattle considerable. It was more by luck than skill that the rest house was discovered and simple food and lodging provided without any light beyond the occasional striking of a match.

In daylight, the foothills of the Himalayas hung in sunshine above the mist and we headed towards them, now in the familiar orderliness of the back areas of a war zone. There were convoys on the roads, each vehicle neatly and inadequately camouflaged with branches of dying leaves— one Hindu driver of a parked lorry watching helplessly as a sacred cow munched his camouflage—and military police directing traffic at crossroads. The nearness of battle was first indicated by a sign in English pointing down a track towards 'Burials and Cremations'. There were checkpoints, too, where Clare's papers were inspected and, at one of which, we were directed to a large house with gables, bargeboard porch and verandah that would have suited Camberley and where Indian officers recommended that we see a Major Puri. An orderly was sent for this officer and when he appeared—a plump, middle-aged figure in battledress—he and Clare cried out in delighted recognition and embraced. They had known each other twenty-three years before when Major Puri had been with the Eighth Army in the Libyan desert and Clare had, of course, been a war correspondent. From that moment there was no problem in going to war with the Indian Army.

With Major Puri we felt at ease; the British, the Australian and the Indian seeming to understand one another, feeling certain shared loyalties and attitudes; the major using that old-fashioned English slang, which, so I had heard, had been frozen in the style of 1910—the year of the King-Emperor's Durbar in India—when a sudden upsurge of nationalism put an end to the fashion for the latest colloquialisms from London. Certainly, as we sat watching the condensation-trails of Indian and Pakistani fighters chasing each other across the sky, we felt more relaxed in each other's company than did our only other companion, an Indian radio correspondent in a white *dhoti*, who seemed both wary of us and nervous of what was happening 40,000 feet above.

The keystone of the Indian defences was the threatened town of Akhnur, and Major Puri said that he would be delighted to take us there in his Jeep. With our host at the wheel, Clare beside him and Creighton, the Indian and myself in the back, we set out towards the sound of the guns that had been rumbling all morning, the distant explosions and their echoes thumping the flanks of the Himalayas. Along the way Major Puri kept up a running commentary: those unshaven men in torn civilian clothes, who squatted, bound and blindfold, at the roadside under guard were Pakistani infiltrators; those big guns under their camouflage netting had just been dug in and would shortly be knocking the enemy for six; those soldiers standing morosely by their tents were the survivors of a battalion that had taken heavy casualties in an attack but still, so he said, had their tails up.

The road ran across open, rocky country uphill to the lip of an escarpment, which fell away to reveal a tremendous view: below us, the road running towards the Chenab river and across its gorge by a steel bridge to a small sand-coloured town which, he told us, was Akhnur. Beyond it a wide, dusty plain, set with thorn trees and scrub, rolled away to the west; to the north the land rose and broke into the ridges and ravines of the foothills of the mountains. The town appeared deserted and with good reason, for it was under shell-fire and, every ten or twenty seconds, a gout of smoke and dust erupted from it, hovered then thinned in the hot air; it was not a bombardment, more as if a single long-range gun was feeling its way towards the bridge. Major Puri explained that that was the way we had to go, if we were to visit the brigade headquarters responsible for the town, and raised his eyebrows for our agreement to take our chance. The Indian radio correspondent had turned the colour of old ivory, his hands were shaking and he said something with emphasis in Hindi, to which Major Puri replied sharply, then said to us, in English, that he apologized for such behaviour and would not tolerate it from a fellow-countryman. He then explained that we would wait for a shell to explode, then drive over the bridge and through the town as quickly as possible in the hope of clearing it before the next one fell.

Watching the shells burst on Akhnur was strangely hypnotic, like watching the rhythmic breaking of surf, but the mood was broken by the major accelerating down the hill, over the bridge and through the pungent smoke of the last shell-burst. Clare swung round, eyes shining like an excited girl's, and shouted, 'This is what makes life worth living!' Beyond the town roads gave way to tracks through the scattered thorn trees and the Jeep trailed the plume of dust that has brought death to many soldiers at war in hot, dry countries. So Major Puri drove fast and the Jeep jolted and jumped over the stony ground.

Bouncing and swerving between stunted trees and tall clumps of grass, we stopped by some wigwams of camouflage netting, still in our own haze of dust and aware of heat, flies and the rattlesnake noise of machine-guns somewhere out in the scrub. A radio Jeep was parked under the netting and, from it, an elegant figure strolled towards us. He was a young major—the brigade major, Major Puri said—wearing tight, well-cut twill trousers, a wide webbing belt in regimental colours, suede desert boots, a starched khaki shirt and a snugly-fitting beret bearing the brass badge of a fashionable regiment; his face recalled the looks of a rajah of the eighteenth-century with a small, curled moustache and eyes that seemed to slant round the side of his head. He introduced himself in flawless English, spread a map on the bonnet of our Jeep and pointed out the positions of the enemy.

On the first day of their offensive at the beginning of September the Pakistanis had advanced twelve miles, until held here before Akhnur. But for an Indian counter-offensive farther south towards Lahore, which drew off the attacking armour and air support, the defences might have broken, but now they had been strengthened and should hold so long as the Pakistani tanks could be occupied elsewhere. Yesterday the Indian Army's armoured division, led by General 'Sparrow' Singh, had attacked south of Jammu and met a Pakistani armoured division head-on. Both sides were losing heavily but, said the brigade major, their own Centurions were proving more reliable than the newer and more sophisticated American-built Pattons; they were British, too, and so seemed more familiar.

The Pakistanis were still trying to take Akhnur, using infantry but, he said, 'We are giving them a thrashing.' Like a British officer, he sometimes spoke in sporting metaphors and felt no hatred for his enemies. Indeed, he spoke of Pakistani commanders by their nicknames; some were old friends and their fathers had served together under the British.

Now, perhaps we would excuse him for a moment; he had to lay on a shoot by the artillery as the enemy seemed to be concentrating in front of us. What would we like to do? The Indian radio reporter wanted to interview some *jawans*; 'The *jawan* is our Tommy, or GI Joe,' explained the brigade major. The soldiers around the command post seemed unperturbed by the sounds of battle, some squatting and scooping curried lentils from their mess-tins with folded chapattis. One was rocking on his haunches, crooning to himself and I asked Major Puri what he was singing. 'It is an old Punjab song,' he said. 'It is a wife singing to her husband that it is a beautiful moonlight night and he must come home and let us enjoy it together. But the husband replies, "No, I cannot come home because I have a duty to perform". Jolly first-class, our chaps.' It struck him that this should be recorded for broadcasting and led the radio correspondent towards the singer.

Clare said that she wanted to see something interesting; no, thank you, a captured Pakistani Jeep, or the wreckage of a Russian-built fighter, was not interesting enough; she wanted to see the battle. This was now louder and nearer and the sound of individual weapons could be identified in the clamour: the natter of machine-guns joined by nervous bursts from machine-pistols out in the tall grass; the sharp explosions of grenades and the cough of mortars. There were shouts and cries, too, and a heavy machine-gun mounted on a Jeep by the command post began to hammer the curtains of grass that hid the fighting. 'When our guns start, we may get some stick from the Pakistanis,' said the brigade major as we heard the distant thump of Indian batteries and the rush of their shells overhead; indeed, as he spoke, the enemy's counter-bombardment began with whiplash explosions among the trees. 'Would you mind taking cover?' asked our host, waving towards an empty weapon-pit. 'I'm afraid I'll be rather busy for a few minutes.'

Clare, Creighton and I sat in our sandpit, hearing but not seeing the battle around us. 'This is terribly boring,' remarked Clare after a while. 'I'm going for a walk. Coming?' This was the predicament of the Rue Bab-Azoun, except that here Clare would be unlikely to find another old friend to protect us. 'No,' I said. 'If we start wandering about it will only worry our host. If we do see anything it will probably be the last thing we ever will. We've got to stay here.' Clare's pale blue eyes stared coldly at me and she said quietly but with suppressed anger, 'You do not seem to realize how much moments like this mean to me.'

A shell exploded nearby and Major Puri came running towards us. 'Quick!' he shouted, 'I think we had better get going before this place gets too hot!' We scrambled into the Jeep as another salvo burst among the trees; he accelerated and drove breakneck through the trees and away. Looking back, shell-bursts were lifting columns of smoke and dust where we had been; ahead lay the empty streets of Akhnur and the bridge, if it still stood. It did and we were across; relief heightened excitement and satisfaction at having, at least, spent an hour or so at the war instead of in the Ministry of Information. The Indian correspondent looked on the verge of nervous collapse and Clare as if she wondered what all the fuss had been about.

We could, at least, report that we had seen the invaders halted before their objective, so we headed south, spending a night in another rest house lit only by the flicker of flames in the sky from burning aircraft and fuel tanks on the airfield at Pathankot, which had been bombed. On arrival in Delhi, we withdrew to our rooms to type the sort of graphic despatch that every war correspondent loves to write and delivered them to the cable office. Now, as the only correspondents who had managed to see anything of the fighting, we were lionized, not least by the diplomatic community, desperate for any scraps of original information to add authority to their telegrams. This involved some trading; the diplomats offering their opinions and their governments' policies in return. At the British High Commission, I was told, 'If India can hold off Pakistan, or even defeat her in battle and then sign an honourable peace and do this without foreign help—then India will give herself the self-confidence she lost when British rule ended. And it would be more than India that would gain confidence. Democrats elsewhere in Asia would become more confident, too.'

India was about to need all the self-confidence it could muster for, on 17 September, China issued an ultimatum, brutally-worded, that could, it seemed, only be the pretext and prelude to an invasion from the north-east. This demanded that India dismantle all the frontier defences in the protectorate of Sikkim, where the two Asian giants had fought briefly but bloodily three years earlier, because of what they called in the traditional jargon of the potential aggressor 'incursion and provocation'. Failure to do so within three days would bring about 'grave consequences'.

Wherever, and however, this was read, it was an announcement of intent and, back in London, *The Times* expected 'at least a border blow'. Others imagined worse: a full-scale invasion of India through the passes of Sikkim down to the plains of the Brahmaputra; since the fighting of 1962 the Indian Army had built roads up into these mountains for the movement of reinforcements but these could, of course, be used in the opposite direction. The ultimatum was obviously timed to coincide with the war already in progress so that, perhaps, Pakistan would be the anvil upon which India was stretched to suffer the blows of a Chinese hammer.

Immediately, cabled instructions from London sent Clare Hollingworth and others to Sikkim, so that the correspondents' meeting place, the swimming pool at the Ashoka Hotel—there being no bar—was deserted. The *Evening Standard* asked me to decide whether I went, too; this demanding a measure of intuition as well as the assessing of the evidence. Was China really ready to take India with its vast population, enormous terrain and manifold, cataclysmic problems? Half the Indian Army was now facing the Pakistanis, but it was disciplined and resolute and would fight hard. Certainly the Indians could resist long enough to win the time needed to summon support from the United Nations. Indeed, military aid could be expected from the United States, or even from the Soviet Union, since friction between Russia and China five years earlier had led to the withdrawal of Soviet technical assistance and the testing of a Chinese atomic weapon a year before was obviously worrying to a Politburo obsessed with the security of its Asian empire. A Chinese invasion of India would surely bring about a war on a scale that would benefit nobody. I decided that the Chinese would not attempt more than sabre-rattling on the frontier and remained in New Delhi.

The United Nations had, meanwhile, been making desperate efforts to impose a cease-fire between India and Pakistan and, as it became apparent that heavy losses in armour and about three thousand men killed on each side had brought about a stalemate, this was agreed on 20 September. Sensing that they had missed their opportunity, the Chinese extended their ultimatum and relaxed their pressure, finally announcing, despite Indian denials, that the offending fortifications had been dismantled and that the provocation was therefore at an end. On the 24th Clare returned from Sikkim, lyrical about the scenery, and next day I left for Bombay and London.

If the war had been a bloody irrelevance there had been some satisfaction in seeing that at least one legacy of the British, the Indian Army, was still functioning as its founders had intended. This had been demonstrated simultaneously on the borders of Kashmir and in the Rann of Kutch and by General Walker and his Gurkhas in Borneo. I had heard in London that a new Director of Operations had been appointed to carry on the campaign with its curious mixture of *Claret* and hearts and minds operations. This was Major-General George Lea, a hefty and enthusiastic product of the Parachute Regiment and the SAS; lacking, perhaps, his predecessor's flair for the unorthodox, but a worthy successor.

What was surprising was the nature of Walker's reward for his remarkable victory. By the standards of reward then expected, he would have been both promoted and knighted. Yet he had been sent to a staff appointment at a NATO headquarters in France, without promotion or knighthood. He had been awarded a third Bar to his Distinguished Service Order, a decoration for bravery in the face of the enemy; his citation mentioned only the risks taken in flying in light aircraft over enemy-held territory and in bad weather, and almost everybody serving in Borneo had done that. Had something gone wrong? Returning to Borneo in 1965, I tried to find out. At Labuan Island off Brunei, to which the main headquarters had been moved, staff officers were reticent; one finally muttering that Walker had been a difficult and domineering man; guilty, some said, of 'empire-building'.

Fighting was now on a heavier scale and it was a company commander's, rather than a platoon commander's war. Patrol bases had become elaborate affairs, behind minefields and barbed wire, of trenches and bunkers, dug-outs and magazines, with sandbagged positions for heavy mortars and, in each, a field gun. Their approaches were protected by man-traps, ranging from the simple, sharpened *panji* stick to pierce the feet to the Claymore mine, a flat canister, standing upright, which showered steel splinters. They owed something to the medieval castle, the trench system of the First World War and the log fort of Red Indian Country. Australians and New Zealanders were now serving in Borneo, together with soldiers from Fiji, recalling the Imperial Forces of the past.

There had been some sharp fighting around such posts—one action by the Parachute Regiment prompting talk of Rorke's Drift—but some of the earlier *élan* seemed to have gone; there were occasional signs of tension and, I was told, the British officers of the Gurkha battalions were feeling the strain of *Claret* raids. There was bad news from 'The Pirates of Nanga Gaat'—as the Wessex crews of 845 Squadron had come to be known—whose ebullience had seemed to impart invulnerability. Within a few weeks, at the beginning of 1965, they had suffered five crashes and sixteen men had been killed. The worst had been when two helicopters with a border patrol of British soldiers embarked, had collided over the base and crashed into the river; among the eleven who were drowned was Lieutenant Robertson, the Dyaks' friend. Now the squadron was to be relieved and I was invited to attend their farewells.

The helicopter was decisive in Borneo, although there were never more than a hundred of them involved and a number were always under repair or maintenance at any one time; neither Walker nor Lea was accorded the six for each infantry battalion they believed essential. The exploits of those who flew in them could recall those of other young men, the roughriders, scouts and boats' crews on the frontiers of the old

Empire. An invitation from them could not be refused.

Nanga Gaat looked much the same—the off-duty crews still in their *lunghis* and beads—but there was a wistfulness. During the past few days there had been parties for them at the neighbouring longhouses, where photographs of young Rod Robertson were pinned to the walls. When news of his death had reached them, the girls had wept and one had refused to eat for a fortnight until the dead pilot's best friend had told her that Rod would have wanted her to live and be happy. A memorial had been set up on the prow of the peninsula where the two rivers met, a short obelisk inscribed in English and the Dyak language and listing eleven British names: Morgan, Robertson, Habgood, Party, Williams, Rothwell, Johnson, McNeilly, Murray, Jack and Green. This was to be unveiled just before the last Wessex of the squadron left for Sibu and we gathered around it: the aircrews and mechanics; the sick-berth attendants and Gurkhas; the Temonggong Juggah and the Malaysian district officer; and the tattooed Dyak braves, who had come by canoe from their longhouses. As the words of dedication were spoken, the thunder of aero-engines came from the sky, but it was no ceremonial fly-past; a big Hastings transport swept over the trees; pink parachutes billowed, supply containers swinging below. Then the crews walked past the signpost pointing towards '*London 8,917 miles*' to board their helicopters, started their engines and, one by one, lifted off. Mine was the last to leave and, just as the others had gone, engine trouble was discovered. It could not be repaired at Nanga Gaat, but could the Wessex reach Sibu? Would the engine fail in flight? It was decided to take the risk and the rotor-blades whirled, the tree-tops thrashed and we were off. It was not an enjoyable flight because, although helicopters can sometimes survive engine failure in flight by fluttering to earth with free-wheeling rotors, they sometimes do not. It seemed a long eighty minutes' flight, a reminder of mortality, prompting sombre thoughts; amongst them, what would happen when the war ended and the helicopters flew away? When the Dyak children, with whom the pilots had played, were grown, there would be a legend of bountiful visitors from the sky. Perhaps the only reminder and evidence of that time would be a moss-grown obelisk on the peninsula where the rivers meet; perhaps it would become an altar.

In October 1965 further escalation of the fighting was interrupted by the sudden outbreak of political conflict, verging on civil war, in Indonesia. The failure of confrontation and its weakening of the ramshackle, if potentially rich, economy brought rivalry between President Sukarno and the communists on one side and on the other officers of the armed forces, who feared that he was now leaning more towards China than a racially-based Maphilindo. Intrigue and outbreaks of fighting led to a lessening of concentration on the war against Malaysia, and the officers, after a failure in the autumn of 1965, finally overthrew Sukarno in the following March and replaced him with General Suharto. Some feared that a military dictator would intensify the fighting in Borneo, but this did not follow. General Lea had continued to develop Walker's plans and his cross-border operations had been increasingly effective. Glad of an opportunity to disengage, Suharto negotiated with the Malaysians in Kuala Lumpur and Bangkok, and signed a peace agreement on 11 August 1966.

Victory over Indonesia had been a military and political triumph for the British. Malaysia had survived—albeit with what now seemed the inevitable loss, but not alienation, of Singapore—and a major war in South-East Asia avoided. Those subscribing to the 'domino theory' of communist expansion had expected that an Indonesian victory in Borneo would have been followed by renewed insurgency in Malaya and a communist attempt to subvert Thailand. As it was, this sphere of British influence was now more stable than it had been for a quarter of a century. This had been achieved at an astonishingly small cost in human life: although, at the height of confrontation, 17,000 Commonwealth soldiers, sailors and airmen had been deployed with another 10,000 to hand in Malaya and Singapore, only 114 had been killed and 181 wounded. Indonesian losses in killed, wounded and captured were put at about 600 but, due to the difficulty of assessing the results of the *Claret* raids, were probably far higher. The campaign was at once regarded as a classic example of the use of minimum force, for which the principal credit was due to General Walker. Yet when the war ended the laurels of a knighthood and promotion went to General Lea.

Ironically, the success of Borneo dealt an almost mortal blow to the British concept of Sea Power, which had always been seen as the means to prevail in such contingencies. The Labour Party had come to power in 1964 with British arms successful, if not triumphant, in Borneo and the Radfan, in putting down military revolts in three newly-independent African states and in stopping civil war in Cyprus by force of arms in the name of the United Nations. In Denis Healey it had a Defence Minister of high quality determined to rationalize defence expenditure by resolving, once and for all, the wrangles between the Royal Navy and the RAF. In his view the RAF had the more effective protagonists. Air Marshall Sir Samuel Elworthy, who had once been a lawyer, was Chief of the Air Staff, and proved more than a match for the First Sea Lord, Admiral Sir

David Luce, a 'blue water' sailor, without such experience of political manoeuvre. In writing a scenario to illustrate the need for aircraft carriers his staff—presumably inspired by events in and around Malaysia—set their imaginary crisis in South-East Asia, which is well supplied with airfields, instead of, say, the Falkland Islands, which were not. The Air Staff, pointing to the flexibility and success of Air Power in Borneo while operating from dry land, won their case; plans for a new generation of big aircraft carriers were discarded and a force of American-built strike aircraft ordered. The First Sea Lord and the Navy Minister, Christopher Mayhew, resigned. At Printing House Square the appointment of Naval Correspondent was no longer regarded as a full-time occupation and was combined with that of Ecclesiastical Correspondent.

The mystery of General Walker remained. At this time I did not know of his unconventional, and successful, efforts to save the Brigade of Gurkhas by privately enlisting the support of the United States Government and his consequent reprimand for disloyalty from the Chief of the Imperial General Staff. Even had I known, and known too that he had upset two successive commanders-in-chief, Far East Land Forces, by his brusque refusal to allow them to interfere with his conduct of the war, the withholding of the knighthood and promotion would have seemed extraordinary. In the time of the old Empire, Walker would have been the sort of commander whose statue was set up in Trafalgar Square. So, out of curiosity, I applied, when back in London, to visit the headquarters of Allied Forces Central Europe, which were still at Fontainebleau outside Paris, and amongst those I asked to interview was the Deputy Chief of Staff, Major-General Walter Walker. At the beginning of 1967, a few weeks before the NATO headquarters were expelled from France, I visited him. After a talk in his office about the future of the alliance and lunch at his house, we walked the gravel paths of its formal French garden in the chill of a February afternoon. I said that I assumed his appointment to a staff job at this headquarters had been to give him experience of NATO as a necessary preliminary to higher command. 'That is far from being the case,' he replied and, taking a folded sheet of paper from his pocket, said 'I've just had this letter from the Military Secretary at the Ministry of Defence telling me that I am to be retired.' Then, noting my surprise, added, 'Don't worry. I'm not going to go.'

Nor did he. By seeking the support of powerful allies—notably Denis Healey and Admiral of the Fleet Lord Mountbatten, the Chief of the Defence Staff—over the heads of the Army hierarchy, he managed to get the decision reversed, his active career continued and both promotion and a knighthood were eventually his, although neither in direct recognition of his victory in Borneo. That would come from the Malaysians, who had accorded him their equivalent to knighthood, the Order of Panglima Mangku Nagara, so that he could have called himself Major General Tan Sri Walter Walker. But, as with Nelson and the Dukedom of Bronte, awarded by a grateful ally but not recognized by his superior officers, this was for private satisfaction.

Times had changed. Those who had run their eyes down the Birthday Honours List of June 1965 in the expectation of seeing General Walker's name had not done so. Instead, they may have noticed that Dr Beeching who, as Chairman of the British Railways Board, had largely dismantled the local rail services of the United Kingdom, had been rewarded with a barony; that three vice-admirals, two lieutenant-generals and two air marshals had been knighted on reaching a certain seniority; and that the four popular young singers, the Beatles, had been made Members of the Order of the British Empire.

Ambush in Aden, 1967. A patrol of the Royal Northumberland Fusiliers
comes under fire among the office blocks of Crater. Soon after,
they were to be ambushed disastrously by the mutinous Aden Armed Police
and the district lost to British control.

Ambush in Aden (continued). A grenade, tossed from a rooftop, explodes,
wounding a soldier and blowing Donald Wise, the *Daily Mirror* correspondent,
off his feet. Both photographs on this page were taken by Stephen Harper,
correspondent of the *Daily Express*.

Arriving in Crater, 5th July, 1967, the dashing Colonel Mitchell of the Argyll and Sutherland Highlanders has recaptured Crater and left his companion, the commander of the mutinous Aden Armed Police, in no doubt as to his intentions. (*Photograph: Associated Press*)

Leaving Crater, midnight, 25th November, 1967, Colonel Mitchell receives a critical visitor, General Tower, who commanded British forces in Aden and urged them to 'play it cool'. (*Photograph: Associated Press*)

7

Into the Breach

There was a brutal professionalism about the wars fought in India and Borneo in 1965 but there was a sense of doom about that being waged in the ruins of the French Empire. Indo-China had once seemed the prize piece in their imperial collection: colonial porcelain, as envied by others as it delighted the fortunate owners. But here, as in Malaya, accounts had not been settled at the defeat of Japan twenty years before; here, too, the communists were trying to claim their inheritance from the colonialists; a major war was being fought there now. The nearest Indo-China had been to peace was five years before, in 1960, and I remembered how heavy with foreboding the place had seemed.

Headwinds had been forecast for my flight from Singapore to Hong Kong. The route ran across the South China Sea; first, between the shores of Malaya and the Borneo territories—both still coloured the reassuring British pink—then past the French purple of Indo-China. The French had left in 1954, of course, and the territory was split into the independent states of Cambodia, Laos and Vietnam, the latter divided into the communist North and the capitalist South. In 1960 South Vietnam seemed no more nor less ramshackle than most other Asian countries that had not submitted to Marxist discipline; the regime of President Ngo Dinh Diem was said to be rather more corrupt and repressive than the signatories of the Geneva Convention, including Britain, who had founded the new state, might wish; but the United States, which had subsidized the French attempt to hold Indo-China, seemed to have taken up the white man's burden and begun to support South Vietnam, with financial and military aid.

The wind had proved stronger than expected, as we flew over Saigon, which could be seen through ragged clouds—now, in 1960, an Asian capital but still displaying the avenues and squares of a French city—and it became clear that we could not reach our destination without refuelling. Again I was flying in a Valetta transport of the RAF on a routine flight and, as this one carried only freight and myself as the lone passenger, the pilot had a choice of options, one of which was to land and refuel at the former strategic air base that the French had built on the coast at Tourane. Soon, so low had fuel run, this was the only option, and there was relief on sighting the great concrete runway and the collection of hangars, barracks and control tower stretched across the dark green fields between the mountains and the sea.

The pilot called Tourane tower but received no reply. He flew in a wide arc, calling the air traffic controller below, but there was still silence. Looking down on the runway, taxi-ways and parking aprons, we saw that not only were there no aircraft, fuel-bowsers and the usual airport traffic, but no people: no sign of life. So the pilot shrugged and said that, as he had to land for fuel anyway, he would do so and he did. Taxi-ing across the concrete towards the control tower was eerie, for nobody emerged to greet us. When we had stopped, the engines were switched off and we could open the door to look and listen, there was no sound but the wail of the hot wind and the slamming of a loose shutter. The pilot and I climbed down and walked across to the buildings; all, apparently, deserted. Then, standing in the open door of an empty hangar, we noticed a tiny figure: he was Vietnamese, wore khaki uniform and a large peaked cap with a white top; since he also wore a pistol at his side, we assumed him to be a policeman and this he proved to be. In pidgin French he explained that there was nobody else there; nobody, that was, except the communists waiting in the hills—and he nodded towards the hazy, mauve shapes of the mountains. But there was plenty of aviation fuel in the tanks; we could help ourselves.

While the crew found and worked the fuel pump, I strolled about the base. It was only a few years old and far from derelict; indeed, it seemed to be waiting for something: another air force, perhaps. Then the appropriate expression came to me from lectures on global strategy and geopolitics at the Royal United Service Institution in Whitehall. This place was what strategists had in mind when they spoke of a power-vacuum. Some day, somebody would occupy and use it.

Now the aircraft was refuelled and ready to take off for Hong Kong but it was with an indefinable sense of unease that we flew away from Tourane or, as it was soon to become more familiar by its Vietnamese name, Danang. The memory of that great military airfield, temporarily deserted, and of the communists waiting in the hills came to mind whenever, in the next few years, news reached London from Vietnam, and much did. At first it had seemed that the Americans were involved in the routine support of an ally, as they might have been within NATO, or another defensive alliance; a commitment comparable to our own in Malaysia. But when, in 1959, Ho Chi Minh, the wily old President of North Vietnam, had announced that his country was actively to support the armed insurgency against President Diem in South Vietnam, the outlook became ominous, particularly so since such operations would doubtless be directed by General Vo Nguyen Giap, who had defeated the French. Nor was the problem confined to Vietnam: civil war broke out in Laos and Cambodia appeared fragile; all Indo-China quaked.

The Americans, who had originally been involved only as financial backers of the French, now found that money and arms would not be enough to defend South Vietnam. They found the enemy more formidable than expected: the brave and resourceful Vietcong, the military arm of the communist National Liberation Front (a name echoed in Algeria and, later, in Aden), who were proving themselves not only masters of guerrilla warfare and terrorism but of public relations. They were fast persuading liberal opinion around the world that they were not so much communist insurgents as patriotic nationalists fighting for their freedom against the American-operated puppets in Saigon. So the British, with long experience of South-East Asia and the successful counter-insurgency campaign just ended in Malaya, were an obvious ally: we too were signatories of the Geneva Agreement and also guarantors of the *status quo*. Soon after the Labour Government took office in 1964 Harold Wilson, the Prime Minister, made it clear that his view of the British rôle in the world was as imperial in scope and scale as that of his Conservative predecessor. 'I want to make it quite clear,' he had told the House of Commons, 'that . . . we cannot afford to relinquish our world rôle, which, for shorthand purposes, is sometimes called our "East of Suez" rôle.' His endorsement of Sea Power and traditional responsibilities rang out: 'Our maritime tradition, our reputation, our mobility . . . above all our Commonwealth history and connections, mean that Britain can provide for the Alliances, and for the world peace-keeping rôle, a contribution which no other country, not excluding America, can provide . . . None of our Continental NATO allies, nor any of our associates in the Middle East, or Asian alliances can compete with us in the range of the contribution we can make in those vast areas beyond Europe.'

The United States Government at first took that to mean that the British were ready to join them in the defence of their South Vietnamese ally, but they were wrong. During the two years following the end of the Malayan Emergency, the British might have decided otherwise; but much had happened since them: President Diem had been assassinated in the same month as President Kennedy, in 1963, and had been followed by successive military regimes; thousands of American serviceman had been sent to Vietnam as 'advisers' and, since a naval encounter in the Gulf of Tonkin during the summer of 1964, President Johnson had decided on the general use of American force, notably Air Power. Although Harold Wilson's speech coincided with an intensification of Vietcong attacks upon South Vietnamese and American forces, the British felt themselves fully occupied by the end of that year fighting the Indonesians in defence of Malaysia and facing the difficulties of cobbling together a Federation of South Arabia. Not only was there no question of any British military involvement in Vietnam but even an American request for a small 'peace-keeping force' of Royal Marines for Laos was refused. But we had offered something in which we felt ourselves richly endowed.

We had sent experience to the Americans, rather than soldiers; fulfilling our rôle as Athenians teaching Romans. This was embodied in one man, Robert Thompson, who had been Secretary for Defence to the Federation of Malaya and, a year after that Emergency ended, was appointed to lead the British Advisory Mission to Vietnam. Thompson, a vigorous, handsome man in his mid-forties, had had long experience of counter-insurgency, rooted in his time with General Wingate's Chindit guerrillas behind the Japanese lines in Burma, and had been among those responsible for the success of the defended village, or 'strategic hamlet' policy, which had cut off the communist terrorists' supplies in Malaya and led to their defeat. In 1961 when he arrived in Saigon, and in subsequent years when news arrived there of British success in Borneo, the British and their expertise were held in high regard.

By the beginning of 1965 Vietcong activity in South Vietnam had become so intense that the time for the *Evening Standard* to send its correspondent had arrived. Now, it seemed, this was not just a long-running guerrilla war but a possibility that the Government of President Nguyen Van Thieu, another general, who had taken power in February, might be overthrown. The same month saw a sharp escalation of the war; President Johnson had authorized the bombing of the Vietcong's supply routes through North Vietnam and Laos in a campaign with the evocative code-name *Rolling Thunder* and, in the same month, agreed that for the first time regular American ground forces—in the form of two battalions of marines—should be sent to defend the air bases from which this was launched. At the end of May, a few days before I was to leave for

Saigon, Thompson arrived in London for consultation with the British Government and I was able to interview him at length.

There was a sense of urgency about him and his message for London. This was: 'The South Vietnamese and the Americans have now, to all intents and purposes, lost the guerrilla phase of the war. The Vietcong are now very largely in control of the countryside and are now ready to move against the towns. The next phase of the war will be the decisive one.' The Vietcong, he said, would try to overthrow the Saigon regime by eroding, or collapsing, it: the former, largely by political means, combined with terrorism; the latter, by attacking the towns. Despite losses of between fifteen and twenty thousand men a year, the strength of the Vietcong was still growing; in 1960 they had numbered only about five thousand but now they probably had forty thousand men under arms and among the recruits were trained soldiers from North Vietnam.

The defended villages which had been so successful in Malaya had failed here. 'The strategic hamlets were set up too quickly and were far too scattered,' he went on. 'I tried to explain that they must be part of a rolling offensive to occupy and hold territory, but it was impossible to get this across. The Americans were doing it piecemeal and the result was that the hamlets could not be properly defended and the weapons that were supposed to defend them made them even more tempting objectives for the Vietcong. So, by attacking one hamlet after another, they were arming themselves with the latest American weapons and killing those who had agreed to cooperate with Saigon. About six thousand loyal South Vietnamese are being murdered in this way each year.'

Both the South Vietnamese and the Americans relied too much on the most advanced weaponry from the United States. 'I keep pointing out that it is useless to put, say, an anti-tank weapon in a strongpoint to defend it against a night rush by Vietcong armed with machine-pistols, grenades and knives. But if the Vietcong capture that weapon they can use it to blow other strongpoints to pieces. I keep telling them never to carry weapons that are of more use to the enemy than to themselves — but what general is willing to disband a brand-new armoured regiment, or battery of artillery?'

The problem in Vietnam was far more difficult than in Malaya, where the war was contained by the sea to east and west and to some extent by the Thai border in the north. Here the North Vietnamese could not only reinforce the Vietcong directly across the common frontier but through neighbouring, and ostensibly neutral, Laos and Cambodia. 'This war is not just in Vietnam, it is in Indo-China and must be fought as such.'

We talked about my forthcoming visit and the reports of correspondents already there. 'President Diem once told me, "Only the American press can lose this war,"' he said. Certainly, the media were displaying a mounting interest in Vietnam, the Americans because, although their land forces had yet to be fully committed, this was about to happen; already there were thousands of American military advisers, Special Forces units, air and ground crews for hundreds of fighters, helicopters and transports and the Seventh Fleet off the coast. In April the senior American in Vietnam, General Westmoreland, announced that American reinforcements were being sent, including nine battalions of infantry, three more of marines and various engineer and support units, which would bring the total of Americans serving in South Vietnam to 82,000. As yet only the United States Marines of the first wave were in the country, so now was the time for the Vietcong to strike, before the others arrived. June was the right time to be visiting Vietnam.

My arrival at Tan Son Nhut airport outside Saigon presented the first of many theatrical scenes of war for which Vietnam was to become renowned. Civil airliners touched down there as briefly as cats on a hot tin roof, queuing to land, and take off again, with a non-stop procession of Skyraiders, Thunderchiefs, Phantoms, Canberras, Skyhawks and grey-painted 'spook-planes' of Air America, the private airline of the Central Intelligence Agency. Once down the big white Boeings glided like swans amongst the camouflage-mottled fighting machines and disembarked and embarked passengers, while their long-legged stewardesses, standing in their open doors, waved to sweating Americans manhandling rockets on to wing-racks and pilots taxi-ing their needle-nosed jets to the runway for another bombing mission.

The ride into Saigon in a torrent of taxis and motor-scooters and a blue haze of exhaust fumes, along avenues of white villas, brought the realization that this was not, as expected, to be another agonized city like Algiers. In the squares and shopping streets off-duty Americans, unarmed and wearing Palm Beach shirts, window-shopped, towering above their exquisite little Vietnamese girls in tight brocade dresses with high necks and slit skirts. Other Americans, wearing freshly-laundered white shirts and ties, emerged, pallid, from air-conditioned offices. Vietnamese soldiers in uniform, looking fragile as frogs, walked hand in hand. Perched on high stools in the gloom of bars, girls with made-up eyes squeaked enticements to passing Americans.

I had chosen to stay at the Continental Palace Hotel, an old-fashioned, colonial establishment with a balustraded terrace overlooking a square, on the far side of which stood the tall new steel and glass Hotel Caravelle with a restaurant on the top floor commanding a fine view of the nightly pyrotechnic display of flares, tracer and explosions of the fighting around the perimeter defences of the capital. It was there that most of the correspondents stayed and where I found some friends gathered in the room of our doyen, the wise old Australian, Richard Hughes of the *Sunday Times*. They had returned from a nasty morning beside a road running through a rubber plantation, not far from Saigon, where two South Vietnamese battalions were being destroyed by the Vietcong, massed in unexpected strength. Some were drinking whisky from bathroom tumblers and Donald Wise was soaping his moustache, muttering, 'I've shampooed the damn thing three times, but it still smells of death.'

Cross-legged on his bed and wearing only underpants sat Dick Hughes, impassive as a great, pink Buddha. The most knowledgeable of all Far East correspondents, he was celebrated for his wit and the mild eccentricity of using Roman Catholic forms of ecclesiastical address in conversation. Here as elsewhere, new arrivals hoped to be 'filled in' with the current news and background by friends already so informed, and only a raised eyebrow was required to let Dick know that that was what I required. 'There is only one text that you need remember in Saigon, your grace,' he pronounced. 'This is that, whatever the preconceptions you have brought with you may be, you will quickly find evidence to prove them correct.' This was the most accurate assessment of the state of Vietnam I was to hear.

Daily routine in Saigon, I gathered, was agreeable. There was a daily press conference held by the South Vietnamese and the Americans late each afternoon, known as 'The Five O'Clock Follies', at which details of activity in the past twenty-four hours were announced. Sometimes there would be interviews with participants in the war, produced for the purpose—today it was to be some American pilots from an aircraft carrier who had shot down some North Vietnamese fighters; big, innocent, milk-fed boys, they proved to be, talking about their dog-fight like basketball—or something more thought-provoking like a briefing on the state of the economy at the house of Barry Zorthian, the principal American spokesman in Saigon. Otherwise, there were some good restaurants and shops; tropical suits and silk shirts were made to measure quickly and cheaply; there was a splendid bookshop; the night-clubs were lively and the women beautiful. As for the war, that could be watched nightly from the Caravelle restaurant, or visited by calling at the Public Information Office near the Continental Palace.

This looked like an office in any military headquarters with wall-maps and cluttered notice boards, but operated more like a travel agency. One approached a plump American sergeant, who described the excursions on offer: 'I expect you'd like to get to Danang, but the press centre there is full right now; maybe next week? But there's a whole lot to see down south, just a chopper ride from Tan Son Nhut. Now what can I offer for tomorrow? Hey, how about this? A ride to Black Virgin Mountain? Special Forces camp and radio-relay station right on top of a goddam mountain; Vietcong all round it, so you go by Huey. If you like a roller-coaster ride, this could be for you.'

Since I wanted to get out of Saigon and this was the first excursion available, I booked and arranged a call for five o'clock next morning. I was warned not to wear vacation clothes and had already seen how other journalists dressed: most had bush jackets and slacks in dark olive-green made by side-street tailors; some of the younger photographers wore elaborate uniforms with zip-up pockets for lenses, film and notebooks, with glossy leather combat boots and sometimes a pistol flapping at the hip. So I felt superior, and more professional, wearing my jungle kit from Borneo; the green canvas jungle boots with rubber soles and the shield against *panji* spikes.

Getting to war was easy in Vietnam, as I was to discover on this, my first experience of the Huey. This was the jet-powered Hughes general-purpose helicopter, which became as familiar as, and was reminiscent of, the London taxi. Out at Tan Son Nhut, the 'chopper pad' where the rank of Hueys waited was beside a sort of cabman's shelter serving coffee, doughnuts, hamburgers and frankfurters. Here I met my pilot, no introduction being necessary since his name was announced on a tape stitched to the chest of his flying-suit: 'STUMM'. Captain Stumm showed me his helicopter and pointed out the twenty patched bullet-holes in it. To me it seemed overmanned, with two pilots, both officers, and two gunners, since it carried only five passengers. There were six or seven hundred Hueys flying in Vietnam, Captain Stumm said, on communications duties, or carrying troops into action, flying in 'slicks' of half a dozen or more. A year or so ago they had been lords of the battlefield, the Vietcong fleeing in terror when a flock of roaring choppers had descended upon them. This was no longer the case.

The Vietcong had realized that helicopters were easy targets and had learned to defend themselves against 'vertical envelopment'. Their defence was not primarily the anti-aircraft cannon, which had reached them from North Vietnam, but American heavy machine-guns that had originally been sent to China during the Second World War; they could hit Hueys at 4,000 feet and the usual cruising height for helicopters was 3,000. Sometimes the Vietcong would ambush the Hueys by attacking a South Vietnamese post that was commanded by high ground, on which they could mount guns to shoot down the helicopters as they flew to its relief. Captain Stumm said that all twenty-four Hueys in his unit had been hit, most of them repeatedly; sometimes by scores, or hundreds of rounds. On average, one was lost each month.

He was a short, heavily-built man, a small moustache masking a turned-down mouth, which rarely smiled. I had hoped he was going to say that his morning's trip was an easy one, but he remarked in his formal way, 'I receive fire over this mountain once in a while.' His right gunner, hearing this, muttered, 'One day we'll sure get our ass knocked off over that mountain.' With that we climbed aboard and I was shown how to fold a spare nylon flak-jacket double as a cushion to sit on for some protection. The doors slid shut, the engine coughed and howled, the rotors thwacked and we were off.

On this and subsequent flights the view of Vietnam from 3,000 feet recalled those panoramas of battlefields by Flemish painters, showing flat green country stretching into the distance and, in addition to a battle in the foreground, towns burning here and there across the landscape. Above this panorama fighters would flash, slicks of Hueys would parade and, invisible but for an occasional silver glint in the sunlight, B52 strategic bombers would drag their white condensation-trails across the blue sky on their way to bomb a map reference.

It was a long, rattling ride towards the Cambodian border, where Black Virgin Mountain stood, and an effort had to be made to occupy the mind with constructive thoughts to deflect others about the Vietcong's point-five machine-guns down below. The left gunner, a young black, had pulled a folded copy of *Best Cartoons* out of his flak-jacket but it was some time before I realized that he had been staring at the same joke for a quarter of an hour without smiling.

Black Virgin Mountain was an isolated peak rising from the plain and, before attempting to reach it, we were to stop at the neighbouring town of Tay Ninh to collect some supplies and mail for the garrison of six Americans of Special Forces and a company of the Army of South Vietnam, known as the ARVN, or 'Arvin'. Descent into the cantonment was the first of what soon became a familiar experience: Tay Ninh seemed peaceful and busy in the early morning sunlight; bicycles sped to and fro and peasants wearing wide, conical straw hats and white cloth suits trotted to market with live chickens and produce; but the big American and little Vietnamese soldiers, waiting on the landing pad, looked tired; there had been an attack in the night and they had lost four men killed. In Vietnam the hours of darkness belonged to the Vietcong, otherwise known as the VC, Charlie Cong or just Charlie.

At the command post they said that there was no radio contact with the people on top of Black Virgin Mountain. Maybe a power failure; maybe they had been overrun by the VC in the night; we would have to find out. This time, as the Huey lifted in its whirlwind of dust, Captain Stumm gave an order and the two gunners slid back the side doors and, with graceful coordinated movements, swung their machine-guns outboard and tilted them earthward; they began to stare at the ground, their index fingers crooked around the triggers. I hugged my flak jacket around me and shifted uneasily on the other that I sat on, folded double.

Ahead, Black Virgin Mountain appeared, solitary and splendid above the lowlands, a small cloud crawling over its summit and hiding the relay station. Captain Stumm had told me at Tay Ninh that he attributed his survival to aerobatic skill and his knowledge of Vietcong tactics. He had said that he would approach the steepest face of the mountain, where machine-guns and their tripods would be difficult to handle and there was little scrub for cover. So we soared up the rocky flanks and into the cloud that hid the peak, catching a glimpse of barbed-wire perimeter defences a few hundred feet below. Stumm circled the cloud, calling on his radio, but no answer came; he flew lower around its edge, blowing the treetops with our downwash, swinging round rock bluffs and straining his eyes to see through the cloud. Then he threw the Huey on to its side and dived away from the mountain; later, down at Tay Ninh, he just remarked that we had been overstaying our welcome and somebody would have to try again later.

It had been a frustrating little expedition, but a symbolic one. All the advanced electronic communications equipment, the weaponry and the command of the air frustrated by a little white cloud and an unknown number of guerrillas hiding in the woods. I had also been impressed by Captain Stumm's skill and courage in handling his helicopter over known enemy positions but, as we flew back to Saigon, was to be less impressed by his attitude towards those for whom he was risking his life. We were approaching Tan Son Nhut along the river, flying at two or three hundred feet above its brown swirl, when we saw half a mile ahead a sampan rowed by two Vietnamese in wide straw hats. Without a word Captain Stumm dived towards the boat, lower and lower, until the two rowers turned, we saw the fear in their faces and they flung themselves to the deck as the Huey swept a few feet overhead. As we climbed again to make our descent at the base, Captain Stumm turned and grinned.

A different approach was evident next day, when the excursion on offer was to the countryside near the town of Go Cong in the Mekong river delta south of Saigon, where the South Vietnamese would be launching an offensive against a Vietcong stronghold. Again there was a start before dawn, then a flight to the headquarters of the 7 Division at My Tho for a briefing over a map marked with chinagraph symbols; then on to Go Cong and a Jeep-ride along a narrow, dusty road to the village from which the main attack was being directed.

The villagers were about their daily business and big, black water buffalo wallowed in their mud-holes behind the thatched huts; the only signs of war were a group of officers standing round a communications Jeep, the chatter of radio talk and the sound of gunfire. A huge American colonel with the name 'PRESTON' on his shirt strode across in welcome: 'I'd like you to meet Colonel Thanh. These VC will be cleaned out by evening. Colonel Thanh knows his job.' He did indeed; Lieutenant Colonel Nguyen Viet Thanh was a big, impressive man of thirty-four, half-Chinese, showing by his silence that he had no need to bother his company commanders with further orders now that the attack had begun. He explained that his infantry had just crossed the open ground in front and entered the wood from which the thud and sputter of a battle could be heard; already the artillery, half a mile back, were sending their shells over our heads into the Vietcong's second line of defence.

The offensive had been necessary because the VC company now under attack had been harassing the highway from the Mekong delta to Saigon and interrupting the trade of fruit and rice with the capital; also they had been occupying the villages—like this one—by night and mining the roads. So, early this morning, his two battalions had left Go Cong and driven the VC before them into a wooded peninsula formed by the loop of a meandering river, and more troops had been landed by boat in the enemy's rear. That had been Phase One; Phase Two, the capture of known strongpoints, was now in progress as was confirmed by a heavy explosion and a gout of dirty, yellow smoke rising from the trees; Phase Three would be the herding of the surviving VC into the killing-ground, an overgrown coconut plantation, where they could be burned by napalm bombs dropped from the air. It should be all over in a few hours.

'Care to see the local industry?' asked Colonel Preston. 'There's a while before the napalm strike goes in.' He led me into one of a group of huts from which we had heard the whine of an electric saw and the noise of chopping; inside, men, women and children were cutting, scraping and polishing wood. 'They make chopsticks here,' he explained, then called out, 'Good morning, everybody!' Only the children looked up; nobody else acknowledged his greeting, or our presence, by so much as a glance. We walked out into the sunshine, where young men in shorts were polishing the chopsticks and tying them in bundles. 'Hey, I'd better invest in their production,' said the colonel and ducked back inside to emerge, some minutes later, to ask, 'Hell, what do I do with two hundred chopsticks?' as he held up the bundle. He had wanted to make a friendly gesture, but they would only sell wholesale; it was not as if he planned to give a Vietnamese chow party back home in the States.

An armoured troop-carrier raced down the track from the wood in front of us, its crew wild-eyed from battle. Phase Two was over; the VC command post had been demolished and fifteen enemy dead found; no casualties to themselves. Colonel Thanh drew new chinagraph lines on his map and the radio operator chattered new orders. 'How about real American chow?' suggested Colonel Preston. 'You can see napalm any time.' So we jolted back along the road to the Go Cong cantonment and the adviser's mess where Florida soup, frankfurters with cheese sauce, fruit salad and coffee were on the menu. At lunch was a lean, sun-burned American in civilian clothes with a face and manner marked by danger; this was Jim Freestone, from Arizona, the representative of the United States Agency for International Development in Go Cong province, who had suddenly found himself charged with the sort of responsibilities and risks for which the British had once been eager to devote their lives on the frontiers of the Empire.

'I coordinate oil-slick pacification,' he explained. 'The idea is we spread out like oil on troubled waters. The Arvin takes a village, we move in after them and spread out into the country around, trying to establish organized society. We appoint headmen, register the villagers, number the houses. We offer aid, you name it—livestock and fertilizers; medical help; water cisterns and power plants; new roads and bridges; education for the children. I say where it's to go; Uncle Sam picks up the tab.'

Tomorrow he and his team would be following Colonel Thanh's soldiers into the chopstick-makers' village and hoping that it could be marked on a map in Saigon as 'pacified', even if only by day. Freestone admitted that only about fifteen per cent of the 180,000 people of Go Cong province were nominally under government control and only those living in towns were under this protection at night—and even there the

Vietcong could threaten. 'I get few smiles,' he went on. 'The people do not want to be seen taking sides; not until they know who is going to win. Outside Go Cong town, I just get smiles from the kids, maybe. You have to see it their way and not get too worried. You have got to think—well, maybe they would like to smile.'

Freestone estimated that about eighty per cent of the Vietnamese had little or no loyalty to the Saigon government, but neither did they want to be ruled by the Vietcong. After a quarter of a century of wars they wanted a fair and assured market for their produce and not much more. Open expression of their hopes was muted since their local leadership was subject to intimidation by both sides and outspoken originality could attract an assassin's bullet. So as he drove around the villages, alone and unarmed in his Jeep, the American could only be grateful that Go Cong was considered a quiet province.

Word arrived from Colonel Thanh that the napalm strike had gone in and that the battlefield was now clear of the Vietcong and occupied by his troops. He would now withdraw behind the defences of Go Cong town and tonight, or the next night, the Vietcong would return to the charred woodland and the chopstick-makers' village. But they would not be visible as such when Jim Freestone arrived the day after to declare that, so far as he could see, it had been pacified.

That was a typical day in the early summer of 1965. Rides by helicopter, perched on a flak-jacket folded double, to some provincial town for a briefing round a map marked with military symbols; then a jolting journey by Jeep to a village that had been attacked the night before, there to meet tall, tired American officers and sergeants who had been up all night advising the tiny Vietnamese soldiers with their big American weapons how to fight. Then back to Saigon by dusk and—unless there was a news report to type and cable—a hot bath, a change of clothes, drinks with the other correspondents and dinner at the Caravelle, watching the chandeliers of light dropped by circling American 'flareships' in the dark sky and gun-flashes flicker like summer lightning.

Occasionally a whole day would be spent in Saigon, as was one late in June, when a press conference was to be held by the Prime Minister, Air Vice-Marshal Ky, to announce the closing of newspapers critical of his Government. He was an exotic figure: a small, sleek man of thirty-four, wearing a Groucho Marx moustache as a symbol of manliness, since facial hair is rare in Vietnam, excepting wispy beards. He had been a dashing airman and led a fashion for braggadocio amongst his pilots, wearing a black flying-suit with a purple scarf and pearl-handled pistols and roaring around Saigon—particularly between night-clubs—on noisy motor-scooters. When he married a pretty air stewardess, she dressed similarly and they made tours of inspection, hand in hand. Even Ky's rank was an artifice for all Vietnamese Air Force officers bore military ranks until he took a fancy to the British rank of air vice-marshal and assumed it for himself. Ky liked to be seen as a man of action and when the Americans urged that he try to curb corruption, he announced that black marketeers and corrupt officials would be shot—possibly by himself in person—but found it difficult in deciding who to shoot. 'I have ordered my police chief to find me just one big black marketeer,' he complained, 'but he hasn't turned one up yet.'

This particular press conference ended in uproar and it was a relief to go to the quiet of Barry Zorthian's house to meet some American economists, who were studying the long-term prospects of South Vietnam. Here I heard a scrap of news that only someone with an interest in naval history was likely to recognize as important. This was that the United States was to set up port facilities at Cam Ranh Bay north-east of Saigon, a plan that most would see as a sensible move to supplement the crowded port of the capital and to avoid sending vulnerable tankers and ammunition ships up the narrow Saigon river. But naval strategists knew of Cam Ranh Bay as one of the finest natural, deep-water harbours in the world; one that had been used by the Russian fleet on its way to meet the Japanese and its own destruction at Tsushima in 1905. If the Americans were developing Cam Ranh Bay it could only mean that they were about to become far more heavily committed to the war in Vietnam.

On my way to Zorthian's house I had stopped at the Public Information Office to ask what excursions were on offer for the morning. Just one, said the smiling sergeant, if I did not mind sharing a helicopter. Morley Safer, the CBS correspondent, and his television crew, were going somewhere interesting and there was space for another passenger. Their destination had a bearing on the development of Cam Ranh Bay; it was an island, seven miles long, lying across the mouth of the Saigon river delta, from which shipping heading for the docks could be attacked. There were three villages along the beach, explained the sergeant, as if describing the delights of a Caribbean island: one was held by government troops and their American advisers; one was held by the Vietcong; and the third had changed hands four times in the past month. All the rest of the island was occupied by the VC. It was a neat little story which could be wrapped up, he said, in a few hours.

Our flight next morning was a short one and, in the few minutes before landing, the accuracy of the sergeant's description became clear. The island lay athwart the mouth of the river and shipping had to pass within range of any rocket-launchers or artillery that might be there. It was a long narrow island covered with scrub, with mangrove on the landward side and sandy beaches to seaward; there was a village at each extremity and another in the middle. Fishing boats lay on the beach by all three but, at the western village a couple of grey motor-boats lay at a little jetty and presumably belonged to the government soldiers. That was where we landed.

As the dust cleared I saw the tall, relaxed figure of an American standing with carbine slung, awaiting us. As he greeted us he could be seen to be black, wearing a captain's insignia and with the name 'DAVIS' on his chest. 'Welcome to Can Gio,' he said with a smile. 'I hope we can find something to interest you.'

This was Captain James E. Davis, of Liberty, Texas, the senior American adviser on the island. To meet the others he led us towards a prefabricated hut by the chopper pad, outside which a Vietnamese boy squatted beside a collection of big, black mud-crabs, live and trussed with string. 'You guys had lunch?' he asked, pushing open the door, 'Ice beer? How about chicken and noodles?' He waved towards shelves stacked with cans of Campbell's soup, boned turkey, peanut butter and pumpkin-pie filling above the refrigerator and water filter. Sunk in armchairs around the hut were the three other Americans, all big, crop-haired and in their twenties, listening to Beatles music and leafing through copies of *Reader's Digest*, *Playboy* and *Popular Mechanics*. They were sergeants named Dixon, Petropulos and Albright, from Chicago, Ohio and Detroit; one of them, Sergeant Robert Dixon, was black, like the captain.

The helicopter was ours for the day, so, leaving a gunner to guard it, the crew crowded into the hut with us for the promised beer, while Captain Davis relaxed in a heap of long arms and legs and explained the problems of his command. The island dominated the seaward approaches to Saigon, as we knew. His forces amounted to a company of the Regional Force—semi-regular troops for local defence and a few men of the Popular Force home-defence volunteers—here in Can Gio and in the village at the far end of the island, Dong Hoa, which had been changing hands and might be about to be lost again, for it had been under fire that morning. The rest of the island, including the big village of Long Thanh in the centre, was controlled by the Vietcong; about three hundred of them had been attacking Dong Hoa, but there were plenty more in the scrub and mangrove swamps.

The Vietcong usually attacked at night but this morning's fire from machine-guns and rocket-launchers might mean a daylight assault and Captain Davis was feeling that he should be looking to his defences rather than entertaining visitors. Could he borrow our Huey? Perhaps we would care to take a look at Dong Hoa ourselves? Thoughts of lunch were set aside, we clambered back into the helicopter, the gunners swung out their weapons and tilted them downward, the rotors churned and the pilot threw the Huey into a skidding take-off over the beach and the sea. Below, a fisherman in the surf dropped his nets and scuttled for cover in the scrub, otherwise nothing moved along the shore. In Long Thanh there was no sign of life; not even a dog or a chicken. Then Dong Hoa appeared: a big village with boats bobbing beside a jetty. The Huey side-slipped over the mangrove and banana trees, guns pointing down, gunners' trigger-fingers crooked. Then, blowing a dust-storm through the village, we were down.

The helicopter had landed between a small ruined fort which, Davis explained, had been hit by a rocket in the first attack, and a huge, symmetrical flame-of-the-forest tree in full flower. Hitching his carbine on to his shoulder the captain strode into the village beneath black fishing nets, looped across the narrow streets in funeral swags to dry. 'Hi, there!' he called, sighting two Vietnamese dressed like characters in a Wild West movie, and making introductions. One was Lieutenant Ly Cong Tu of the Regional Force, in a sombrero; the other, the commander of the Popular Force in tight black trousers, a loose scarf of parachute silk knotted around his neck and a pistol slung low on his thigh. 'How you doing?' asked Davis, grinning.

Lieutenant Tu pointed to the mangrove on the far side of a narrow creek; fire had come from there and more from the scrub on the far side of the village. Would Captain Davis like to inspect the defences? We turned into the wide, dusty lane that was the main street of the village, the helicopter crew staying cautiously close to the Huey, the television team and myself following Davis, who described what had been happening here. 'The VC came first at the beginning of the month. There were only thirty-two Popular Force guys here and five got killed. The VC burned down the headman's house, took him out in front of the people and told them that he had oppressed them. Then they shot the poor guy through the head and left him lying there.'

Otherwise they had not behaved badly in Dong Hoa, not wishing to antagonize the villagers, although they had levied taxes. They took two thousand mangoes ('I sure hope that's not one for each man,' joked

Davis) but paid for them in their own currency.

Two platoons under Lieutenant Tu and Davis himself had counter-attacked and recaptured the village. They found the headman still alive and had him flown to hospital, where he still survived. A few days later the Vietcong had attacked again and Lieutenant Tu's men had piled into the boats and escaped to join Davis at Can Gio. Finally, two days ago, he and Tu had led an assault up the beach and, once again, the yellow, red-striped flag of the Republic of South Vietnam flew over Dong Hoa. Now it looked as if the place might be about to change hands again.

In the marketplace a new loudspeaker blared martial music ('The VC took the old speaker, and set it up in the trees outside the perimeter to propagandize us') and in the shade of a little Buddhist temple the command-post radio crackled. Around the perimeter, Lieutenant Tu's machine-gunners crouched in weapon-pits and behind walls, peering nervously into the greenery beyond the wire, and a mortar had been set up in the middle of a yard, its crew keeping under cover. In the centre of Dong Hoa and by the jetty, village life went on. The children, who had never before seen a negro, loved Davis and he wrestled playfully with some boys, telling them that, lazy as they were, one day Lieutenant Tu would make soldiers of them. Down a path silvery with crushed oyster shells women in wide straw hats were unloading rice from a sampan and carrying it ashore on yokes, trotting along a swaying bamboo catwalk. In the shade the older men squatted silently, watching us, and a big, younger man with a blank face and a wall eye slowly rose and walked away. 'See that guy?' Davis muttered. 'He's never bugged out when the VC come. Could be he's an agent.'

Of the fourteen hundred people who usually lived there, all but about three hundred had left since the fighting began. 'It's difficult to know what they think,' said the captain. 'Only about two hundred of them practised any religion. It's difficult to know what they think they want. I don't believe it's communism. They want fair prices for their fish and fruit—but do they want anything else? The VC told them that their headman was an oppressor, then doubled their taxes. They just want good government, I guess. Right now they are waiting to see who's going to win. There used to be four hundred men of military age in the village; if I could persuade them to defend their homes against the VC and if the same thing could be done right through Vietnam, then the war's won.'

Davis recognized that his hold on both Dong Hoa and Can Gio was precarious. 'Sure we could defeat the VC with two battalions, maybe three. You'd clean them out, but they'd be back. They would pull out into the mangrove and just as soon as our battalions went home, they'd be back. The people know this.'

The afternoon was heavy but it was not thunder that was shaking the hot air. Across the mouth of the river an operation was in progress and there was the thudding of artillery and the reverberation of bombs. High against the overcast two Vietnamese Skyraiders peeled off into bombing runs and smoke rose beyond a tree-line. Out to sea, a freighter turned towards Saigon; an indication of the importance of this strip of mud and sand. Captain Davis was well aware of this importance and that the price to be paid for it might include his own life. 'I've been here six months,' he said. 'I've got six more to do. But I won't go on pass to Saigon. Once I saw the bright lights, this place might lose its attraction.' Then what did he do to relax? 'When do we relax?' he asked. 'Say, just what does that word mean?'

Our tour of the defences at Dong Hoa and the interviewing of Davis and the Vietnamese officers by Morley Safer had taken longer than expected and the helicopter crew were becoming anxious to leave before dusk. I too had no wish to stay longer than necessary because, if the Vietcong did attack that night, the village would certainly be overrun and I had heard what they could do to prisoners; also I was leaving for Singapore next morning and a farewell dinner party was planned for my last evening, probably at the floating Chinese restaurant, the My Canh, moored at the Saigon waterfront. But first Safer wanted to write, learn and film the introduction to his report with himself standing in front of some sandbags, barbed wire and palm trees here at Dong Hoa; punctilious reporting since the same background could have been found anywhere in Vietnam, including Saigon. He sat and wrote in his notebook; he read his words aloud; he paced up and down reciting them; then, as the sun was setting he stood in front of his camera and recited, 'To most people, Dong Hoa is just a point on a map of Vietnam, but to Captain James E. Davis it is . . .' Then he stopped and looked up the next words in his notebook; he started again and again he forgot his lines. I was beginning to wonder, as I waited in the fading light, when it would become too dark for photography so that we could leave before the Vietcong attacked. Morley Safer remembered his lines before the sun set and, hoping that our eagerness to depart before nightfall was not too apparent, we wished Captain Davis luck and clattered away towards Saigon, arriving as its lights began to glimmer.

The delay had thrown our plans for the evening slightly off schedule. After a bath and a change of clothes I had to visit the British Embassy for a drink with the air attaché, who was so well-informed and talkative that I was half an hour late in arriving to meet the others for a drink at the Caravelle before going out to dine. As my taxi pulled up at the hotel correspondents were running down the steps and piling into cars. 'Quick!' shouted one. 'The My Canh's been blown up!' He scrambled into my taxi and we sped after the others as the sirens of police cars and ambulances began to shriek. 'Just had a phone call in the bar,' he panted. 'Two bombs. Lots of casualties. First time it's happened like this. Lucky we weren't there.'

The race through the traffic was halted by police and flashing lights, so we left the cars and ran. The big white hulk of the floating restaurant looked intact but ashore, under the trees, bodies were strewn about. A street urchin, dead and green in the lamp-light; little Vietnamese and big Americans lying still; streams and pools of blood. A German photographer, chalky-faced, had been nearby and said that the first bomb had blasted the restaurant itself; the second had been a Claymore mine attached to a bicycle, leaning against a tree near the head of the gangway, timed to explode as the survivors of the first were escaping ashore. 'They are all dead at the tables in there,' he said. 'Never before have I seen soup plates filled with blood.'

Police were stopping others going aboard for fear of another bomb. They had counted seventeen dead but thought there were more and nearly a hundred wounded. The corpses were being arranged in rows along the esplanade, a dozen of them big, fleshy Americans in Hawaiian shirts, coloured slacks, decorative ankle-socks and moccasins—uniform 'vacation clothes' for a night on the town. There was just time to catch the last edition in London, so I set off for the cable office, arriving back at the Continental Palace to find the German photographer drinking whisky alone on the terrace; I joined him and we stood there drinking and staring at the now-empty streets. As we looked, a police siren whooped from the escort of a lorry speeding past, a flapping tarpaulin failing to conceal its load of big, dead Americans, whose feet, still in the fancy socks and moccasins they had pulled on so cheerfully a few hours before, protruded in bunches.

As I waited for a taxi to the airport next morning, news came that Dong Hoa had been attacked and overrun by the Vietcong at about the same time as the My Canh restaurant had been bombed. There were no details, except that Captain Davis had fought his way to the jetty and escaped by boat to Can Gio once again.

A few days later President Johnson announced that United States forces in South Vietnam were to be increased to 125,000 men, mostly combat troops; it became known in Washington that this might rise to a quarter of a million during the coming year; an eventual total of half a million was being forecast.

Could they save South Vietnam? Could they win the war? On further reflection, Dick Hughes's assessment was, as usual, right: there was ample evidence to prove any preconception correct. My own stay in the country had produced two surprises: that vast numbers of Vietnamese were ready to fight and die to resist the Vietcong, however much they might despise, or disregard, the government in Saigon; and that the Americans supporting them were often brave and dedicated men, convinced that they were defending freedom against totalitarianism, here as much as in Europe, had they been fulfilling their NATO obligations. But soldiers trained to fight with tanks and nuclear weapons could not even find, let alone defeat, guerrillas who burrowed into the earth like foxes; who hid beneath the surface of ponds, breathing through straws; who came by night to throw grenades and cut throats. Since each side was waging a war so different from that being waged by its opponent it was difficult to imagine how a decision could be reached. Probably resilience would be decisive.

8

The Last Stand

Aden was the scene of action in 1967. Only three years before it had been so peaceful; garrison life even more placid in contrast to the little Kiplingesque campaign being fought in the Radfan. In July 1964 the Conservative Government had announced that the British base would remain in Aden indefinitely but that South Arabia would be granted independence as a federation within the Commonwealth in less than four years; then came the General Election and victory for the Labour Party that would, it had seemed to Arab politicians, hasten the dismantling of what remained of the British Empire. Unless aspiring nationalists, pan-Arabists, republicans and revolutionaries took immediate action, the British would hand over power to the traditional rulers up-country and the moderates in Aden, who would maintain the political *status quo* and allow the great base to remain. So 'military arms' of political factions sprang up, varying in effectiveness but all supported to some degree by the Egyptian intelligence service and with Egyptian weapons; sometimes British weapons from the abandoned dumps in the Suez Canal Zone. In the months to come these might share the same broad aims and would form alliances, but they also became rivals and fought each other. The main rivals were the National Liberation Front (NLF), which wanted a Marxist state, linked with the Yemen and Egypt but independent, and the Front for the Liberation of Occupied South Yemen (FLOSY), which opposed Egyptian domination in favour of Saudi Arabian support but later reversed its policy to one dictated by President Nasser.

The fear of terrorism had long hung over Aden. In the spring of 1964 I had written, when reporting the euphoria over the success in the Radfan: 'Less soundly based is the optimism over the present lack of violence in Aden. It is known that quantities of weapons and explosives have arrived here from the Yemen and that potential terrorists have been recruited. Yet there have been very few acts of political violence and, in some quarters, this is put down to lack of resolution.' There was now to be no lack of resolution and terrorism was planned to begin in November to coincide with the first visit of Anthony Greenwood, the Colonial Secretary in the new Labour Government.

That autumn a domestic scene long familiar to the expatriate British came to a shuddering halt. The family life of the garrison; afternoons on the beach and bathing in the warm, sticky sea within the shark nets; lunching off mixed grill beside the swimming pool while bold crow-like birds hopped on to the tables, stealing scraps; cocktail parties and air-conditioning as a topic of conversation; shopping for duty-free luxuries; dining out of doors under the glittering stars.

Now shootings, grenade-throwing and riots began and it seemed like the repetition of the Cyprus troubles. As in the EOKA campaign it took time to gain momentum, and by the end of the year only two British servicemen had been killed and thirty-four wounded. Early in 1965 Sir Kennedy Trevaskis left and was replaced as High Commissioner by Sir Richard Turnbull, who had successfully pioneered decolonization by bringing Tanganyika to independence. But he was hampered by having to appoint as Chief Minister of Aden a certain Abdul Mackawee, who had majority support in the Legislative Council but who was an implacable opponent of British hopes for the future. So the British struggled to contain terrorism with less than half-hearted Adeni support and this ran its familiar course: the intimidation of moderates, the assassination of Special Branch police officers and British officials, and attacks on 'soft targets', including British women and children. During 1965 terrorism caused 237 casualties in Aden, thirty-five of them fatal. The occupation of the Radfan continued, despite continuing attacks by dissident tribesmen and Yemenis, resulting in 350 casualties, ten of these being British soldiers killed.

Yet the sultans, emirs and sheikhs of the federation trusted the British and, although they were wary of the Labour Government, this confidence remained unshaken. Sherif Hussein of Beihan had not taken to Anthony Greenwood, telling General Harington, 'Greenwood—*Grün Baum?* I think he must be Jewish. They tell me he likes cats. I do not trust men who like cats.'

Despite their apprehension they were unprepared for the news that reached them in February 1966. In presenting its annual Defence Estimates, the Labour Government announced, 'South Arabia is due to become independent by 1968, and we do not think it appropriate that we should maintain defence facilities there after that happens. We therefore intend to withdraw our forces from the Aden base at that time . . .' The

treaties with the Federal rulers would also be abrogated, thereby con-
demning them to extinction. So sudden and shattering was the repudia-
tion that it was not, at first, believed; even the leaders of the NLF and
FLOSY suspected that it must be some British trick of devilish
ingenuity. It was not; it was what it seemed, a betrayal.

This was confirmed when, in July, Russian-built jet fighters from the
Yemen attacked a small town in the state of Beihan and one of the houses
damaged belonged to a member of the Sherif's family. Angered by such
blatant aggression the Sherif invoked his defence treaty with Britain and
demanded protection and retaliation. But the British Government did
nothing beyond referring the incident to the United Nations, which, after
hearing Yemeni denials of their guilt, did nothing either. Finally, in an
attempt to salvage a scrap of honour, the British announced that a special
mission from the United Nations would be coming to Aden in the following year to seek a solution to its problem; a promise that inspired no confidence anywhere.

There were less than two years to run before departure and the British
devoted their energies to the vain hope of encouraging the less unfriendly
politicians of Aden to come together in some form of administration to
replace our own. But terrorism in the city and guerrilla warfare in the
mountains continued and prospects for 1967 looked even worse since the
Adeni police could not be expected to take effective action against those
who, in a year's time, would be their masters. However, the Federal
Army, which had been renamed the South Arabian Army, seemed both
loyal and effective. Since the campaigns in the Radfan it had been
expanded into a miniature army with its own artillery, armour and engineers and now numbered about fifteen thousand men, most of them in its
ten infantry battalions. The officers, including the battalion commanders,
were now mostly Arabs, but staff officers and specialists remained
British, as was its commanding brigadier. This was the doughty Jack Dye
of the East Anglians, who had returned as one of a fresh set of senior
officers who were to see the British withdrawal through to its conclusion.

The most senior of these was the new Commander-in-Chief, Middle
East, Admiral Sir Michael Le Fanu, who had come from Whitehall
where he had been Controller of the Navy, responsible for the ordering of
new ships, aircraft and weaponry. A red-haired extrovert, now aged fifty-
three, he was celebrated for his exuberant sense of humour and practical
jokes, a reputation which sometimes obscured his qualities as a leader and
administrator. He was, of course, responsible for the whole strategic

sweep from Africa to India, including the Persian Gulf, and would be preoccupied by the renewed turmoil in Africa following the unilateral declaration of independence by Rhodesia in November 1965, and the subsequent imposition of the naval patrol off the Mozambique port of Beira in an attempt to cut off its oil supplies. There was the need to keep a friendly eye on the newly independent Kenya, Tanganyika and Zambia, and preparations for the independence of Swaziland, Bechuanaland and Basutoland. Giving ominous emphasis on the need for vigilance was the growing strength of the Soviet Navy in the Indian Ocean.

Aden was only part of his responsibilities and, for this, he would need to rely heavily on an officer who was due to arrive in May. The security forces' commander was to be Major-General Philip Tower, also from Whitehall, where he had been the Army's Director of Public Relations and where I had been amongst those impressed by the deft touch he brought to his dealings with Fleet Street. He was one of those politically-minded generals often met in Whitehall, or at NATO headquarters, intelligent, suave but, his friends warned, with an unexpectedly short temper.

Under Tower's command came all the forces deployed on internal security duties in Aden and counter-insurgency operations in the Federation. The three principal formations were two British brigades: one, of four battalions, in and around Aden; the other of two brigade groups, up-country; and the South Arabian Army, in which the British element was in the process of being reduced from about fifty officers and 250 other ranks to four and ten, respectively. At the beginning of 1967—the final year of British rule in South Arabia—they were stretched to the full.

The promised mission from the United Nations was due to arrive at the end of March and, to set the scene, urban terrorists, political activists and rural guerrillas had made their maximum efforts to disrupt. There had also been riots in the Crater district of Aden, which had had to be broken up by British troops using tear gas, and in the Radfan there was continual skirmishing.

The road to Dhala was now very different from what I remembered. Now it was covered by a fortress on the scale of the great camps the Romans constructed to hold their empire, built near Thumier, but named Habilayn after a nearby mountain. This was a long rectangle surrounding an airstrip, fortified with barbed wire and minefields and defended by machine-gun posts, mortar and gun positions and, through radar, as watchful by night as by day. The command post, known as Fort

Farewell to Aden. The doughty Brigadier Jack Dye, having handed over command of the South Arabian Army to his Arab successors but still wearing its cap-badge, says goodbye to staff officers before leaving Khormaksar airfield for England.

Homeward-bound, British soldiers march aboard a Hercules transport of the Royal Air Force at Aden. When all were gone, the rearguard of Royal Marines were lifted by helicopter to warships standing offshore on 29th November, 1967.

Vietnam, 1965. Captain William E. Davis of the United States Army tries to make friends in the village of Dong Hoa in the Mekong delta, which had changed hands four times in a month and was to be taken by the Vietcong again that night.

Vietnam, 1969. The point-man. The leading soldier in an advance by the 7th Cavalry stares into the jungle for signs of the North Vietnamese troops known to be there. For obvious reasons, nobody wanted to be point-man.

Knox, was a small castle of sandbags and the tents of the camp were walled with sandbags so that life within could continue as if encamped on Salisbury Plain. Off-duty officers sat in armchairs reading London newspapers three days old, or copies of Hansard, which were stacked amongst *Country Life* and *Punch*.

Habilayn was currently manned by a commando of Royal Marines, who kept a brisk daily routine. There was the briefing of patrols, who would go out through the wire after dark, and ambush parties who were being flown into the hills in daylight (hoping to confuse the enemy as to their whereabouts, they would pretend to disembark from the helicopter at one point, but hide away from the aircraft's open door when flying on to their intended landing out of sight). Just before dusk the guns of Habilayn would open fire to range on possible targets for the night and to flaunt their power; machine-guns lashed the hillsides with tracer, raking crests and hosing into gullies; mortars kicked bombs into the dead ground beyond; field guns of the Royal Horse Artillery slammed shells against the flanks of distant mountains.

Darkness fell quickly and, for those not going out through the wire, standing by the guns, or talking to patrols and high pickets by radio from Fort Knox, a comfortable, sociable evening would now begin. Officers in freshly laundered khaki, a few in tropical mess-kit and myself in 'Red Sea rig' assembled in the tent serving as the mess ante-room for drinks before sitting down at a table, spread with a cloth, to read the menu for the evening. After dinner the colonel conducted me back into the ante-room, where chairs had been arranged in rows and projector and screen set up to show a film. He and I sat smoking cigars in armchairs in the front row to watch *Born Free*, about a worthy English couple who tame and rear a wild lion cub and finally release it to fend for itself; an apt parable for the ideals of the Empire. Just as the young lion was to be set free into the wilds, a silhouette crossed the screen and an officer in field equipment was bending over the colonel. 'Excuse me, sir,' he said, 'but Hotel Ten is under attack.'

Hotel Ten was a stone fort built to antique design for the South Arabian Army on a distant ridge that could be seen from Habilayn. 'Would you care to come and see the show?' the colonel whispered; then, nodding at my cigar, added, 'Better put that out; there are snipers about.' We walked through the darkened camp, avoiding the guy-ropes of tents and there, in the sky it seemed, were flashes and flickers of the distant battle on the mountain, From the sandbag ramparts of Fort Knox we watched through binoculars, as an officer identified the flashes: 'Rocket-launcher ... flares ... small arms ... mortar ...' Then the field guns of Habilayn opened fire, firing air-bursts to catch the attacking tribesmen in the open.

Another report came in; this time from a high picket, equipped with a new type of radar that could identify human figures moving across country. A party of the enemy were making their way towards a water-point outside the perimeter; range and bearing were given. Somewhere in the camp mortars coughed, white flashes splashed the darkness beyond and, a moment later, a report crackled through the radio speaker that the figures had vanished from the radar screen. Now reports came from Hotel Ten: the attacks had stopped but the Royal Engineers' road-building equipment, parked outside the fort, had been badly damaged.

At last the 'hearts and minds' programme had been launched and the six wells, which had been drilled three years before, increased to seventy-five. The road into the Wadi Taym had been completed, despite sniping and mining and, although no medical mission had been established in the Radfan, seriously ill villagers were often flown by helicopter to Aden for treatment.

From the military simplicities of the mountain war I moved into the sly uncertainties of political violence in the city. It was a different, more dangerous place now. Nobody went shopping in The Crescent without an armed guard, for there had been shootings even among the displays of Japanese cameras and hi-fi gear and I found myself behaving as in Cyprus and Algiers, whenever possible keeping my back to a wall. Only the Crescent Hotel, like the Ledra Palace and the Aletti, seemed to offer sanctuary as the correspondents' quarters and the link with world opinion.

It was only just a sanctuary, as the sound of gunfire and explosions after dark became so familiar that only the particularly noisy would inter-rupt conversation. But the districts of Aden around the shore of the peninsula, on which it and Mount Shamsan stood, were less dangerous than the two that became familiar battlefields: Sheikh Othman and Crater. The former was the desolate suburb of the city that sprawled across the levels to the north; through it ran the road to the Radfan and down it travelled the weapons, the explosives and those who would use them against the British; it also offered cover in its squalid streets and shanties, so was difficult to police. The latter was easy to contain since there were only two ways in and out—by the road running through the rim of the crater at Main Pass and out again at the far side to join Marine Drive, which ran beside the sea—but its grid of streets was the scene of the worst rioting, the crater no longer seeming extinct but often at the point of eruption.

It was Crater that I now visited because another riot was expected as a preview of what the United Nations mission could expect to see. The district was the responsibility of the Royal Northumberland Fusiliers, distinguished from other British troops by the red and white feather plumes of the hackles worn on their blue berets; in time of trouble their command post was in the barracks of the locally-recruited Armed Police on the road below Main Pass. Within the walled compound the Fusiliers had set up an operations room with maps and a crackling wireless, where a major monitored events in the streets outside and was able to direct me to the best vantage point.

This was at the far side of Crater, commanding a view down the main street where a crowd had assembled, chanting and waving banners. Such mobs as this had regularly rioted here, taunting the soldiers, sometimes luring them down a street where grenades would be tossed from rooftops. This morning I attached myself to a patrol of half a dozen Fusiliers led by a corporal, whose task was the interception of armed men running from the riot, of which we had a good and comfortably distant view. As we watched the banners began to sway as the Fusiliers' riot squads charged and then white wisps of tear gas began to rise. The corporal turned and said, 'See you later', gave an order, the patrol pulled on gas masks, drew their batons and ran towards the crowd, leaving me—without a gas mask—on the opposite side of a hostile mob from the rest of the British Army.

Such a problem was not new and old wiles were remembered. A correspondent from the Congo wars had once advised, 'Always smile and shake hands with everybody.' But first was the need to identify oneself as a journalist, so I slung my camera on my chest with its lens cap in place— terrorists do not like to be photographed—and held a shorthand notebook in one hand and a pen in the other. So armed, I advanced into the streets of Crater, avoiding the rising cloud of tear gas but encountering the demonstrators, similarly engaged. No British soldiers were now in sight and, as I walked alone through the fierce-eyed crowd, I tried to remember heroes of the British Empire who had faced this predicament and survived. I stopped and demanded, 'Does anybody here speak English?' There was a chattering amongst the crowd and a plump young man in a clean white shirt was pushed forward. 'Good morning,' I said, smiled, shook his hand and, notebook and pen poised, introduced myself, 'Good morning, I'm from the London *Evening Standard*. My readers would be most interested to hear your views on the forthcoming visit of the United Nations mission. Do you think it has any chance of success?'

For a quarter of an hour, surrounded by what might have been a murderous mob, but now listening attentively, I recorded the policies of the National Liberation Front, conscious that it was time well spent since it finally enabled me to shake hands all round and walk away.

The NLF spokesman had not held out any hopes of success for the United Nations and he was right. By staging the maximum number of riots and attacks, including a battle with the Parachute Regiment at Sheikh Othman, which achieved more noise than effect, the dissidents of all factions came together to prove that the British did not represent, and could not control, Aden. The United Nations delegates—a Venezuelan, an Afghan and an African from Mali—were duly scared out of their wits and cowered in the small hotel that had been fortified as their headquarters. As they had no stomach to investigate this nightmare place any further, they declared their belief in the anti-British accounts of it they had been given in Cairo on their way to Aden, refused to meet federal ministers on the ground that they were British puppets and, with mutual sighs of relief, departed.

Clearly the United Nations would not now be able to help in forming an administration capable of taking over from the British. In the hope that a fresh British mind might help, Lord Shackleton, a Minister without Portfolio, visited Aden and his recommendation was immediately carried out: Sir Richard Turnbull was replaced as High Commissioner by Sir Humphrey Trevelyan, a diplomatist with the reputation of getting near to success—if not succeeding—where others had failed. A former ambassador to Moscow, he had been ambassador in Cairo before Suez and in Baghdad after the overthrow of the monarchy; shrewd, with a gnome-like charm, his ability to communicate with an open-minded sincerity had won him lasting, and politically important, friendships. When he arrived in May the cast of characters for the final act was complete.

The most significant act of violence now took place outside Aden. On 3 June war again broke out between Egypt and Israel resulting, by the 9th, in an overwhelming victory for the latter in what came to be called the Six Day War. This humiliation prompted the Arabs to look furiously for scapegoats and amongst these, of course, were the British. Had not the British and Israelis been allies in the Suez war? Rumours that the British had aided Israel in the new war were believed and a fresh vengefulness reached the conflict in Aden.

I had returned to London because urban terrorism and rural guerrilla warfare were being contained and were not expected to worsen before the British departed at the end of the year; or so it seemed until 20 June. The tragedies of that day were caused by a misunderstanding. The choice of an Arab commander for the South Arabian Army to replace Brigadier Dye on his departure had inevitably aroused suspicions of tribal favouritism and, when four battalion commanders had protested against his appointment, they had been suspended from duty. Rumour that they had been arrested by the British spread amongst their troops and started a riot and scattered acts of mutiny in their camps. These were quickly quelled but not before prompting other rumours of conflict between the British, the South Arabian Army and the Adeni police. Where authority remained firm, the hysteria was calmed; where it did not, fighting, or rather killing, began.

The worst of it was first near Khormaksar and then in Crater. A truck-load of British soldiers passing the police barracks near the airport was, without warning, machine-gunned, killing eight and wounding eight. Hearing a garbled report of fighting there, the Armed Police in Crater prepared to defend their barracks against British attack. Trouble was widespread, a Red Alert had been declared and the Royal Northumberland Fusiliers began to deploy in Crater, their advance party going ahead to man the command post in the Armed Police Barracks. This was accompanied by another from the battalion, fresh from Britain, that was to relieve them, the Argyll and Sutherland Highlanders. As the two Land-Rovers drew level with the barrack wall, the police opened fire. Both officers and six men were killed, one escaping into flats on the far side of the road. Soon after, a motorized patrol, following them, saw what had happened and the officer in command sent two of his armoured cars back for reinforcements, himself staying behind with three soldiers. They were never again seen alive.

The alarm had sounded all over Aden and the immediate reaction of those in senior command was to do nothing that could turn the explosion into the eruption of a mutiny by the whole South Arabian Army. Yet some demanded instant action (if only to rescue any British survivors in Crater), among them the commanding officer of the Argylls, Lieutenant-Colonel Colin Mitchell, at forty-one a veteran of the Second World War, Palestine, Korea and Borneo. He had already commandeered a helicopter and seen the bodies in the road and the burning Land-Rovers outside the Armed Police Barracks, and now volunteered to lead a relief force; but it would have to go into Crater at once.

Neither Brigadier Jeffries, commanding Aden Brigade, nor General

Tower, took the decision to attempt a rescue and when Colonel Mitchell pleaded with the brigadier, he was told that the missing lieutenant was a resourceful young man who might well have managed to hide success-fully in Crater. But any opportunity for rescue soon passed. So the siege began with the two entrances to Crater sealed and British soldiers looking down into it from the rim of the cliffs above. Some said that it could only be captured in a major assault, which would cost the attackers thirty per cent casualties; others urged that it be abandoned to nationalist control; yet if there was a risk—and there was—that the terrorists within Crater had weapons such as three-inch mortars, then they could bombard the runway at Khormaksar and the place would have to be captured before the British evacuation of Aden could begin.

To report on the outcome I returned to Aden, landing at Khormaksar in the early hours of 4 July. Waiting for me at the airport was Colonel Douglas Johnson, the senior public relations officer. 'The Argylls have just gone into Crater,' he said, 'I'll take you there now.' As he drove to-wards Mount Shamsan in the light of the sunrise he described how, under cover of darkness, the Highlanders had approached Crater by the coast road and then, led by their piper playing the regimental charge, had gone in. One or two suspected Arab gunmen had been shot, but other-wise there had been no casualties; now the Argylls occupied about a third of Crater. They were, he added, the best battalion he had seen in war or peace. Soon I saw what he meant. The Argylls looked supremely pro-fessional and self-confident, as we entered Crater, waved on by a 'Jock' in his jaunty glengarry cap.

Colonel Johnson stopped beside a long, low building that had been the Aden Commercial Institute. Sitting with their backs against the wall was a row of tired, unshaven correspondents, who had been on their feet all night; on the verandah a television team was filming a number of the Argylls' officers seated around a short, pugnacious man in a glengarry. That, whispered Johnson, was Colonel Mitchell. He was taking an orders group, first asking for reports from each of the officers, 'Ian? David? Nigel?' as the camera peered over their shoulders. Then the television sound-man swore: the tape was not running. 'Don't worry,' said Colonel Mitchell, 'We'll start again.' And they did.

This was a first experience of the Argylls' flair for public relations that helped to make Mitchell a national hero and saved the regiment from its planned extinction under the Labour Government's reduction of the Army, but also made them enemies amongst the British as well as the NLF and FLOSY. The events of that day were seen on British television screens within twenty-four hours and the dashing Colonel Mitchell was redeeming the shame of the past fortnight. There he was ordering the craven commander of the Armed Police to hand over to him those responsible for the murder of British troops, then turning to the camera and explaining, 'They know that if they start trouble again we'll blow their bloody heads off.' That evening in the bar of the Crescent the *Daily Mirror* correspondent returned from the cable office and announced, 'I've called him "Mad Mitch".'

Next day the Argylls were to take the rest of Crater, including the Armed Police barracks, but they had already cowed the opposition and a battle was thought unlikely. Their advance up the road towards Main Pass was accompanied by the armoured cars of the Queen's Dragoon Guards, with the red and white plumes of the Royal Northumberland Fusiliers, who had flown home to England, tied to their wireless aerials. The column began to move, the Jocks racing ahead to take up firing positions, with myself following in a bright blue taxi. But the *Evening Standard* deadline was near and, from professional necessity rather than bravado, I told my driver to accelerate past the Argylls, so leading the final advance into Crater, past the two burnt-out Land-Rovers, still lying where they had been wrecked outside the barracks, and up the hill to Main Pass, where I was lucky not to be met with a burst of fire as a terrorist trying to escape.

Then began the Argylls' occupation of Crater for, unlike their predecessors, they lived there, gripping it so tightly that terrorism almost ceased. But there was conflict between Colonel Mitchell and General Tower: Mitchell blamed Tower for failing to attempt a rescue of any survivors of the massacre whose charred and mutilated bodies had finally been recovered; Tower regarded Mitchell as an unruly subordinate who could not understand political realities. Mitchell was appalled when the general took the salute at a reconciliation parade of the same Armed Police who had mutinied on 20 June. When Tower ordered him to ease his grip on the streets of Crater he told his battalion what he thought of the general's instruction to 'play it cool' and was soon able to support his argument with reports that, after he had had to carry out this order, the number of terrorist attacks in Crater multiplied twentyfold.

By autumn Aden was attracting international attention as the last stand of the British Empire, and the correspondents from London were joined by foreigners for whom the experience was a diverting historical curiosity.

In the city the atmosphere had changed again; there was a tighter strain of tension, suggesting that all concerned were bracing themselves for the final act. The Argylls dominated Crater, the Parachute Regiment commanded Sheikh Othman and other troops held their own sectors, but soon they would leave; the Argylls would go, the Parachute Regiment would go and finally the rearguard of Royal Marines would fall back on to the airfield. Would there be a battle if only as a symbolic expulsion of the British by force?

The killings increased and those we reported included friends. The young Arabist from the High Commission had been killed as he started the engine of his sports car, and the retired Royal Marines officer, working in public relations, shot in one of The Crescent shops. Now it was the German television correspondent, shot through the back of the head as he posted a letter to his wife. An hour after this murder, as we stood in the lobby of the Crescent Hotel, pale and shaken from the sight of a friend's corpse reminding us—as we sometimes needed reminding— that we were not only privileged spectators of other people's troubles, Colonel Johnson arrived with orders to pack immediately and move to some empty flats near the beach at Tarshyne where we could be given some degree of protection.

The evacuation was to be complete by the end of November, civilians and families were leaving Khormaksar daily by the hundred and over the horizon appeared the reassuring shapes of the Royal Navy. A strong force, including three aircraft carriers, one carrying helicopter-borne marines, had been assembled, as they always had been when the Army had to leave; this was as striking a demonstration of Sea Power as the presence of the navy off Corunna, Dunkirk or Crete. Meanwhile, ashore, plans were advanced for the gradual withdrawal of British troops and their replacement by the South Arabian Army. That this was possible was due to the calm courage of Brigadier Dye, whose responsibility it would remain until the final day.

On 20 June a full-scale mutiny by the South Arabian Army had been narrowly averted; thereafter any spark could ignite one, and Jack Dye's task had been to keep the temperature down; 'playing it cool', as General Tower insisted. Dye had visited all his battalions in Aden and the Federation, accompanied by one Arab staff officer, to calm them and demonstrate, by mixing with them without an escort and apparently unarmed, that he trusted them. In fact he wore a small pistol, concealed in its holster under his armpit, but that would not have saved him; what did save him, and their discipline, was his nerve. This was tested when he arrived by light aircraft at the up-country garrison of Ataq, where the battalion greeted him with a riot, chanting slogans in praise of Nasser and the Yemen and firing their weapons into the air. Here the chief trouble-maker was seen to be the Arab adjutant and Dye told him that he was to be transferred elsewhere immediately; indeed, that he would fly him out of Ataq in his own aircraft. When the officer refused, Dye told him that, unless he complied, he would shoot him then and there. The adjutant had another excuse: the airstrip at his own tribal capital had been mined, so they could not land there. So Dye marched him to his aircraft through excited crowds, which only dispersed from the runway as the pilot opened the throttle for take-off. When they arrived over the airstrip where they had hoped to land, there was no obvious sign of mine-laying from the air but Dye was taking no chances: telling the pilot not to land but to skim the ground with the wheels, he opened the door and, as the aircraft touched the sand, pushed the adjutant out.

Dye made a point of living alone at his official quarters in the South Arabian Army's lines, guarded and served only by Arab soldiers. I visited him there as he began a long, lonely night, surrounded by the usual fur-nishings of such quarters: floral loose-covers on the furniture, framed photographs of wife and children; dog-eared copies of *Country Life*; him-self as calm as an English gentleman passing a quiet summer evening at his country house. He had taken the precaution of making sure that his nightly guard of eight soldiers were drawn from four different tribes; otherwise he could only lock his bedroom door when he went to bed and hope for the best.

The South Arabian Army might not only rebel against the British; they might fight amongst themselves, split into tribal factions, or between supporters of the NLF or FLOSY. Since neither the British nor the United Nations had been able to find an Arab administration to take over the government of Aden and the Federation, it was at last realized that, as the place had to be given to somebody, this would have to be one or other of the two principal terrorist organizations. Of these, the National Liberation Front seemed the stronger and more efficient. This was finally decided when Brigadier Dye assembled his senior officers in a conference room, locked the door from the inside and told them that they must now choose allegiance to either the NLF or FLOSY because one of them was going to be the government. After a debate lasting for twelve hours, they chose the NLF.

Jack Dye's final act had to be the rescue of the tribal rulers—the sul-tans, emirs and sheikhs, who had believed the British assurances that they would stay and protect them—for they could expect short shrift from the Marxists who would soon take power. He managed to rescue them all, flying most, together with their families, to Saudi Arabia.

The attacks on the British had abated after a flurry of shooting on 11 November. Now that the NLF was the undisputed heir to Aden, there was no need to harass the preparations for departure, which was planned to be complete by the 29th. But there remained the chance—some said the probability—of a set-piece assault on the rearguard, or even upon the Argylls, to support a claim of a military victory. Meanwhile, district by district, the city was handed over by the British to the South Arabian Army; the major evacuation, which was to include Crater, was to take place in the early hours of the 26th.

In the Argylls' mess that night it seemed as though they were ready to stay for another six months: there were coffee and sandwiches and a stack of hand-outs summarizing their achievements. On the flat roof television lights were switched on as their flag was lowered and a lone piper played the lament *The Barren Rocks of Aden*, while I, half-expecting a sniper to take advantage of such a target, watched from a sandbagged look-out position. In the street below the lights were switched on again while Colonel Mitchell gave a final interview before the cameras. As he spoke a Land-Rover swept up and a furious voice shouted, 'Put those bloody lights out! This isn't Hollywood!' It was General Tower. Mitchell walked away while another Argylls officer took the general into the mess, where the sight of the hand-outs further annoyed him. 'Typical of the Argylls', he muttered.

It came as a surprise to those who had been in Aden that, unlike other battalion commanders who had distinguished themselves, Mitchell was not awarded the Distinguished Service Order that most of us thought he and the Argylls deserved. The newspaper correspondents had come to know and like him and sometimes forebore to quote his impromptu remarks that would have looked embarrassing in print; as when he made a jocular comparison between the killing of gunmen in the streets of Crater and grouse-shooting: 'a good left and right'. There was no false modesty, pandering to liberal opinion nor mincing of words; his panache came naturally and, on television, seemed an echo of the time when British officers did not have to explain or apologize.

Each day saw a ceremonial departure from Khormaksar, Trevelyan himself leaving on the 28th as the band of the Royal Marines from the aircraft carrier *Eagle* played, presumably at the suggestion of the humorous Commander-in-Chief, the tune of the Cockney song, *Fings Ain't Wot They Used ter Be*. By now the British only occupied the airfield, which was held by a rearguard of two battalions: the Parachute Regiment and a commando of Royal Marines. The correspondents remained in flats at Tarshyne after the replacement there of British troops by Arab soldiers of the South Arabian Army. Before this an intelligence officer from the High Commission called to wish us luck and hope that the dire prediction of a political officer named Figgis, that there would be a massacre of any remaining Europeans, would not be fulfilled. If trouble was expected the new High Commission, which had now moved from Government House, together with a statue of Queen Victoria, to a new building on the coast just outside the city, would try to warn us. If we received a message saying 'You are under starter's orders', we were to pack one suitcase each and walk, not run, to the new High Commission. But if the message was 'Figgis was right', we were to run for our lives. Once at the High Commission, we were told, helicopters from the task force, which would be waiting just over the horizon for several weeks, would try to save us.

The strain of the past months showed heavily in some who had been in Aden throughout. Several drank heavily: one kept playing with a loaded pistol; another would drive his car at breakneck speed through the crowded streets and markets of Maalla and Sheikh Othman; the correspondent of a staid British newspaper—mild-mannered, pink-cheeked and clear-eyed at mid-day—was known as 'The Strangler' because of his occasional contribution to late-night debate. Several of the younger photographers were often exhausted, having found that one of the last British girl secretaries to leave had, like themselves, reacted to the tension with a high sexual fever.

Two days before the last, we were moved to a block of empty flats on the edge of the airport and within the perimeter defences of the rear-guard. From our windows we could see Arab crowds looting British quarters outside the barbed wire and tearing the air-conditioners from walls. We even ventured back into the city to see Government House deserted and goats on the lawn, nibbling the roses; the vast headquarters and barracks complex was deserted and silent but for doors banging in the wind. This had not yet been looted, for the mob, like the Goths on entering Imperial Rome, were perhaps too awe-struck at the scale and majesty of their prize.

Next day we packed our bags, to be flown out to the ships—keeping only an overnight pack—and I was struck by the waste of leaving these well-furnished flats, built for British families, to the looters. In my room there hung a pair of cheerful yellow curtains, which would look well in my kitchen at home; as I began to unhook them from their rail, the door opened and there stood Colonel Johnson. 'What on earth are you doing?' he asked. I guiltily explained and was sternly told that, under the terms of our withdrawal from South Arabia, *all* the infrastructure of the base was to be handed over to the new administration. Sheepishly, I hung the curtains back on their rail; but, when the colonel had gone, took a beer tankard from the kitchen and furtively packed it.

Oddly, our group produced a remarkable act of courage. The *Daily Express* had kept a reporter, Stephen Harper, and a photographer, Stanley Meagher, in Aden throughout the year; when they left with the rest of us, another reporter, Donald Seaman, would take over, having volunteered in London to stay after the British had left. He was a tough and experienced correspondent but could hardly have realized the risk he was to take. Most of us expected violent reaction to our departure: the burning of the British headquarters and the lynching of those left behind, perhaps. So Seaman was teased with gallows humour: mock-serious farewells and requests for last words for us to tell England. Understandably, he came to look apprehensive.

Stanley Meagher had not packed and neither, of course, had Donald Seaman, who had left his bags back at Tarshyne. Asked why, Stanley replied, 'Old Don will be on his own. I don't want him to get lonely, so I think I'll stay.'

At last we assembled at 'Fort Alamo', the Royal Marines' sandbagged command post on the airfield, to await final departure. Helicopters were clattering to and fro from ship to shore stirring up whirlwinds of dust as marines in full battle order ran up to them, climbed aboard and were flown away. Even now the NLF might open fire for the symbolic battle we feared and the final withdrawal might have to be a rush across the airfield to the shore, where landing-craft were waiting. At last only three helicopters stood on South Arabian sand. We clambered aboard one and strapped ourselves in while General Tower stood beside another, perhaps hoping to be the very last to leave. That honour was for the commando colonel: our helicopter lifted a moment before Tower looked round and jumped aboard, then followed us out to sea.

A last look at Aden showed it hot, ugly and unlamented. Two small and diminishing figures stood alone on that vast airfield: Donald Seaman and Stanley Meagher. We never expected to see them again. We did, happily, and Stanley told me how they had made their way back to Tarshyne through jubilant, rather than bloodthirsty, crowds. By the swimming pool they had sat down with glasses of the only drink, they could find, a liqueur. The beach was now deserted; indeed nothing moved but the palms threshing in the wind; even the crows had gone. Then along the beach a big dog came racing, a Doberman Pinscher, an expensive dog, abandoned by its British owners. In its jaws was a pet cat. As dusk fell they heard the whine of mosquitoes for, now that there was no spraying with insecticide they, like much else, were coming back.

9

Recessional

The war in Vietnam had, by 1969, become so familiar a serial on television that no new twist in the plot or spectacle could surprise. Even when I flew back to Saigon at the beginning of that year, reintroduction to the war was as slick as an advertising commercial. Seated in a wide first-class seat of the Royal Thai Orchid Service from Bangkok, I was listening to the burble of light orchestral music on my headset, cooling myself with a little paper fan presented by the stewardess and finishing my second Bloody Mary, when I happened to glance out of the window. Below spread the woolly, dark-green carpet of the jungle with, here and there, a gleam of water. Then, just below us, an arrow-shaped aircraft slid into view, as neatly and brightly painted with American insignia as a plastic toy, and loosed a salvo of rockets, their smoke streaming from its wings, towards some unseen target on the ground. This was not so much an indication that we were now over the Vietnam battlefield as that another episode of this long-running programme was about to begin.

The war, and reaction to it, had come to a head a year before when the Vietcong, directed by the North Vietnamese General Giap, had thrown all its forces into a violent offensive throughout South Vietnam just as the country was relaxing for its annual Tet holiday. The Americans and South Vietnamese had been taken by surprise and suffered heavily, but recovered quickly and broke the offensive; the last Vietcong stronghold—the citadel in the former capital, Hué—fell a month later. When it was over the reckoning had been made: about one thousand Americans and twice that number of South Vietnamese had been killed but their victory seemed to have been decisive because the number of Vietcong and North Vietnamese dead was assessed at thirty-seven thousand. Indeed so shattered was the Vietcong that a belief later arose that Giap had planned that this should be so in order to remove indigenous rivals for the eventual control of South Vietnam once the Americans, sickened of the war, departed.

The Tet offensive coincided with a combination of revulsion at the bloodshed and anti-American propaganda throughout much of the world. The youth of Europe and North America, freed from its inhibitions by the loosening of ethics and morals, the vaguely bohemian cults of the hippies and the availability of drugs, was in search of a cause and this was seen to be the brutal repression of Vietnamese peasant-patriots by President Lyndon B. Johnson and his generals. 'Hey, hey, LBJ, how many kids have you killed today?' they chanted. Huge demonstrations against the American involvement surged through capitals and university cities; the Americans, who had initially seen themselves as the saviours of an ally's liberty, were reviled by many of those whose freedom they had also guaranteed.

In London, these had reached a climax with two demonstrations outside the United States Embassy in Grosvenor Square in March and October 1968, both of which I reported. I had been part of great London crowds whenever they had gathered over the past quarter-century for national celebrations, or mourning; the uneasy emotions of the Victory Parade, the mass optimism of the coronation and the pride and sorrow of Churchill's funeral in 1965. But, since the year of Suez, another head of emotional steam had been gathering power: the fear of nuclear war and a panic of anxiety to rid the nation of its own nuclear weapons in the hope of lessening the risk and setting an example to others. I had watched several of the pilgrimages from the nuclear research and production establishment at Aldermaston and was depressed by what I had seen. The earnest columns, chanting their slogans and led by firebrands of the Left and various worthies, had not learned the lessons of history and seemed bent on upsetting the balance of power that had kept the peace since 1945, their motives often idealistic, sometimes subversive. These now had a new cause and new companions from the young who had found relief for their frustrations in political violence.

So, chatting with a middle-aged police constable, who was wishing he could be at home pruning his roses instead of guarding a foreign embassy, we watched Grosvenor Square fill with a vast, roaring mob, such as I had seen in Paris and Algiers but never in London. It surged against the police lines; it charged them; it flung clods of earth and branches of trees from the gardens; it threw fireworks at police horses. Policemen's helmets were tossed high to cheers, like heads by a revolutionary mob. When the mounted police rode into the crowd, their horses were stabbed or burnt with cigarettes; as one reared, his rider was dragged from his saddle. The 800 policemen in the square had to face 10,000 demonstrators, it was said, but they held and at last the crowd dispersed. Nearly 100, a quarter of them policemen, had been injured, and 200 arrested. Afterwards a Labour Member of Parliament protested against 'police violence'.

The demonstration in October was expected to be bigger and more violent, and a phalanx of West German students, who used the poles of their banners like pikes in a charge, were to lead the assault on the police lines. Again I was in Grosvenor Square, listening to the approaching chants of 'Ho, Ho, Ho-Chi Minh!' and, in praise of the recently-martyred Cuban revolutionary Ché Guevara, 'Ché, Ché, Ché!' This time the police were ready with unexpected tactics to divide the crowd before it could mass for a decisive charge, and this never came. But when a policeman could be isolated he would be felled and kicked and one suffered brain damage. Nobody died in either demonstration but they shocked me as much as anything I had seen—more, perhaps—because they happened in London, which I had always known as a tolerant, humorous, warm-hearted city.

The mob demonstrated against the Americans because, in 1968, there was nothing that could be denounced as British imperialism. The wars in Malaya and Borneo had been won and South Arabia evacuated; British troops were not on active service anywhere. Moreover, Denis Healey's defence review, which had halted the building of the aircraft carriers two years before, had reached its final decision: the British were coming home to Europe; by 1971 there would be no British soldiers East of Suez. Modest garrisons would be maintained in a few of the remaining colonies including Gibraltar, the sovereign base areas on Cyprus and in Hong Kong with a detachment of Gurkhas hired out to the Sultan of Brunei; a few marines embarked in a survey ship would be in Antarctica. Otherwise, that final moment at Khormaksar at the end of 1967 could probably be regarded as the last sounding of the cease-fire. The Royal Navy seemed to have lost its flexibility along with the big aircraft carriers, and now the order for American bombers to rearm the RAF was cancelled too. But although the admirals had been out-manoeuvred by the air marshals, they had not lost all their wiles. Just as they had been able to build a new class of light cruiser by calling them destroyers, so they had now won approval for the construction of three 'through-deck cruisers' to carry anti-submarine helicopters and act as command ships but which were, in fact, small aircraft carriers which would be able to operate the new vertical-take-off Harrier jet fighters.

The Brigade of Gurkhas would survive with a strength of between six and seven thousand men, mostly for use in Hong Kong and Brunei, but there would otherwise be no special military capability for operations East of Suez. Concentration would now be upon the demands of NATO and the maintaining of the bulk of the British Army on the Continent. The final American call for practical military help in Vietnam, which had brought contingents from Australia and South Korea to fight there, had been refused by their fellow-guarantor of that country's independence and security. But the British would continue to offer the services of Robert Thompson, who had been knighted in 1965, and who would now advise President Johnson's successor, Richard Nixon, although his advice would not be put to effective use.

In the aftermath of the Tet battles the war was not going so badly for the Americans, and General Westmoreland was pressing for a counter-offensive that would include an amphibious landing in North Vietnam, the extension of the war into Laos and Cambodia and the intensification of air attacks. But although the Tet offensive might have failed in its military objectives, it had succeeded in breaking the American will to fight, and now their main objective was no longer to defeat the Vietcong but to extricate themselves. Sir Robert Thompson, who had been urging that the war must be seen as covering all of Indo-China if it was to be won, still believed that this was possible. It would not only involve making as free use of Laos and Cambodia as was the enemy, but making the continuation of the war too costly for North Vietnam by selective air attacks, using such precision weapons as laser-guided bombs, possible targets including the dikes of the Red River, which, if breached, would flood the rice-growing plain of Hanoi. But, just as the British had been swept away by the tide in their attempts to dismantle the Empire in an orderly, unhurried manner, so the Americans, who had reluctantly taken up the old imperialists' rôle in Indo-China, had been caught in the currents of their own revulsion. The surprise and scale of the Tet offensive had seemed to show that their well-meant efforts and sacrifice had been useless.

Yet this loss of will was not apparent when I returned to Saigon at the beginning of 1969. The South Vietnamese and the Americans had never been stronger, with 820,000 and 540,000 men committed to the war, respectively. The main threats were now to Danang in the north of the country from enemy concentrations inside North Vietnam and to Saigon itself by some fifty thousand men of five North Vietnamese and Vietcong divisions, two of which were already on the march; three, still waiting to invade from Cambodia. At the 'Five O'clock Follies' it became apparent that the battlefields to visit were no longer the scattered skirmishes and sweeps against the Vietcong but massive defensive actions against armies advancing on Saigon from the west.

Everything was being thrown against the invaders, including, surprisingly, the United States Navy. One of the natural barriers facing the North Vietnamese divisions was the Song Van Co Dong river, about a hundred yards wide, and the defence of this waterway was the responsibility of River Division 553 which I now flew to join. A little naval base had been established in a derelict sugar mill on the riverbank beyond Tay Ninh and, from the approaching Huey, the only sign of war was the glint of sunlight on the myriad pools dug in the riverside fields by carpet-bombing.

Down in the dock and out on the river—known with endearing American exaggeration, as 'The Big Blue'—lay the little fleet, and a strange one it proved to be. Low and sinister in the water as crocodiles lay six monitors—like Civil War battleships—encrusted with eighteen inches of armour plate; one of them was armed with a flamethrower and named the *Zippo* after the cigarette lighter. In contrast were the delicate little fibreglass patrol boats, manned by four men and powered by water-jets which enabled them to skim the surface at thirty-five knots, turn in their own length at speed or stop dead in their tracks.

Plenty of naval warfare was going on. In the six weeks they had been on the river the flotilla had fought thirty actions and suffered more than twenty-five per cent casualties. The first the speedboats usually saw of the enemy was when they were ambushed from the reeds and willows along the bank. 'When Charlie hits us,' explained the lieutenant in command, 'we head straight for him. We hit him with everything, turn to let the rear gunner take him, and lam out of it.' So cruising the river was a queasy mixture of showing off the speed of an elegant power boat and becoming the target for a machine-gun or rocket-launcher. As a blood-soaked sailor was lifted ashore after one such encounter, the whole concept seemed ridiculous: the enemy could see and hear the little warships a mile or so away and, should they wish to cross the river, could do so before they arrived or after they had gone.

Here as elsewhere in Vietnam it seemed that the Americans could not believe that a combination of their technology and courage could fail to win. Thus the United States Navy had pressed into service a gigantic, obsolete battleship brought out of reserve to shell the coast, almost as useless as these brilliantly-designed boats on the Song Van Co Dong river.

This particular campaign would be decided where soldiers met to fight and for this the scene of action was in the jungle just east of the Cambodian border where one of the Americans' best fighting formations, the 1st Air Cavalry Division, with 19,000 men and 400 helicopters, was fighting the vanguard of the invaders.

At the Public Information office in Saigon, the duty sergeant said that there would be no problem in riding a chopper next morning to Phuoc Vinh for a briefing and thence to one of 'The Cav's' fire-bases in the jungle. There was dinner that night at the Caravelle with a new set of younger correspondents but the view from the windows was the same: the flicker of artillery, the floating flares and sudden red streaks of tracer as the big gunship, 'Puff the Magic Dragon', circled Saigon above the flares hunting targets for its battery of super-machine-guns. Not only the news-agency, newspaper, television and radio correspondents were here now but magazine writers, freelance photographers and a variety of 'war freaks'—voyeurs, who had been accorded accreditation on the strength of a letter from a friend in the media and swaggered through Saigon in elaborate uniforms of their own design. It was a dangerous game for them, too, even in Saigon as was suggested by the marble memorial slab to three journalists killed in the streets of the city during the Tet fighting. This was propped against the wall on top of a cupboard in the South Vietnamese press centre as nobody could decide what to do with it; so there would be no such memorials for the other sixty-three correspondents and photographers killed in the war.

The ride in a Huey next morning showed a changed countryside. From vast encampments, ordnance depots, supply dumps and vehicle parks around Saigon, the roads ran between verges shaved of scrub and trees to reduce the risk of ambush and through swathes of country laid waste by chemical defoliant and napalm, poisoned and burnt to brown and black. Sometimes the plain was cratered as far as the eye could see after carpet-bombing by B52 formations and, the water level being high, these had become those thousands of circular ponds. The sky was more crowded too: slicks of Hueys (some of the three thousand or more helicopters now fluttering about Vietnam) bearing troops on some search-and-destroy mission; tight formations of shark-shaped, high-performance jets, built to fight in the stratosphere but now directed against suspicious huts and sampans; out of sight and hearing the fleets of B52 bombers until their loads were spread across the distant countryside, shaking the earth and the air.

At Phuoc Vinh stood ranks of Hueys as in horse-lines, for 'The Cav' wore a horse's-head insignia and liked to regard itself as airborne cavalry, some of its pilots affecting heavy moustaches and Civil War hats. Indeed, the briefing officer, having shown on the map how he thought the North Vietnamese vanguard was being held within a ring of artillery fire-bases, and corralled by a contracting ring of airborne infantry, so that it could be burned and bombed in a compact killing ground, said, 'Hey, how about seeing Custer's old outfit? They're right in there at Fire Base Jill. There's quite a battle going on there but this time it's the Indians getting zapped.'

From 3,000 feet the chain of fire bases could be seen as a succession of bare circles cut in the green spread of the jungle, some miles apart but with overlapping arcs of fire for their artillery. We fluttered into Fire Base Jill, which proved to be a circle some three-hundred yards in diameter of red earth dug and heaped into gun-pits, foxholes, trenches and bunkers walled with green sandbags, all surrounded by a thick hedge of barbed wire and the jungle immediately beyond. It presented a scene of warlike activity: guns slamming shells over the trees; soldiers, stripped and brown to the waist, heaving ammunition; others, helmeted, armed and in full battle order, filing out through the wire to begin a patrol. A beefy major, the colour of chestnut, strode up and said, 'Welcome to the 7th Cavalry'; then pointing to a neatly-painted sign reading, 'Headquarters. 2Bn. 7th Cavalry. "Garry Owen"', asked, 'Know your history? Sure, this was General George Custer's outfit, but you know who Garry Owen was?' I shook my head. 'We're taking no chances, we've named this place after the only survivor of the Little Big Horn. Garry Owen was a cavalry horse. He got away.'

Standing in the hot sun, buffeted by gun blast, we looked at a map and the major explained that his men were in contact with the North Vietnamese three miles away, trying to corral them into the killing-ground where he could use his gunships and napalm strikes. 'That's where the action is,' he said. 'Take a ride out there.' This was like the tree-top flights in Borneo, lurching to avoid ground-fire and lurching again as a fighter flashed past, tumbling a napalm canister into the trees to erupt in red flame and black smoke. The Huey pulled up, hovered and lowered into a tight landing zone of felled trees just wider than the rotor-blades. The pilot shouted that he would be back in two hours, told me to jump out and run for the trees; then he had soared away, the fading thwack of his rotors merging with rip and tap of machine guns close at hand. Groups of tall young Americans, green denims red with dust, stood, or sat, under the trees and one, wearing a lieutenant's insignia, detached himself. Through the sweat, dust and stubble could be seen a smooth, unlined face that one might expect to see on the tennis court of an American country club. 'We have, as they say, made contact,' he said in a slow Bostonian voice. 'My modest command is about to move through these trees in search of combat. Would you care to accompany us?'

The seated soldiers struggled to their feet and heaved each other's packs on to their shoulders, and I noticed that the black soldiers had been sitting together, apart from the rest; the whites all had cropped hair, theirs was frizzed like that of Queen Victoria's African enemies whom her soldiers called Fuzzy-Wuzzies. Then a less sophisticated voice called to the officer, 'Say, lootenant, the sergeant says I'm point-man. I was point-man yesterday, godammit.' 'Nobody wants to be point-man,' replied the lieutenant with a weary smile. 'Do like the sergeant says.' Then, to me, 'The point-man is the first to get hit, as you may see.' As his men, now helmeted and carrying their rifles across their chests, shuffled into line and then into a loose, V-shaped formation, the complaining soldier took his place at the apex and they started to walk through the trees. I remembered Borneo and how the British soldiers—particularly the SAS and Gurkhas—had melted into the jungle and moved without the rustle of a leaf, or crack of a twig. These young men just walked forward, sometimes stopping and looking about them, or sinking to one knee and staring between the tree-trunks into the dim glades. 'Hey, sir!' one shouted. 'Two enemy KIA right here!' The two North Vietnamese had all too obviously been killed in action, as the initials implied, and the lieutenant thought that the Cobra gunship, which had just been zapping the woods, must have seen them through the canopy of leaves. They were small men in brown uniforms, lying twisted in their last agony, teeth bared, fists clenched; around them was a litter of weapons and ammunition, entrenching tools, white enamelled mess-bowls and letters from home.

The lieutenant gave the order to halt and pointing forward to where we could hear the thump of shell-bursts, muffled by trees, said, 'I guess we have their battalion boxed in right there. I have orders to wait awhile so the Saigon shrinks can try a little psychological warfare before the next napalm strike.' As he spoke a big sergeant lumbered from the rear bringing two tiny Vietnamese, wearing enormous American helmets. 'Those kids are North Vietnamese soldiers,' explained the lieutenant. 'They changed sides a few hours ago and they are perfectly willing to tell their buddies that American chow is great and we don't cut off prisoners' hands as they have been told.' While the sergeant was rigging a loudspeaker to a branch, I questioned them through a Vietnamese interpreter, who had followed them. They said that they were aged eighteen but some of their fellow-soldiers were younger and there were porters and messengers of twelve. When they had been conscripted, they had been given two weeks' training and taken to a base camp in Cambodia. There they had been told that they were to march south for fifteen days to attack Saigon. One of the deserters was led up to a microphone and the other back to a loudspeaker-helicopter, which had just arrived to fly him over his battalion. A few minutes later it clattered overhead, dangerously low, chattering amplified Vietnamese; this, the interpreter had explained, was telling the enemy below that they were trapped, and would, unless they surrendered, die. His words were interrupted by the howl of jets and the sun-dappled woods darkened as the napalm smoke billowed. Later, back at the chopper pad, the deserter's escort, who had flown beside him, shook his head and said, 'That guy beats me. When he saw his buddies burn, he laughed his ass off.'

The guns from Fire Base Jill were to put down another barrage before the infantry moved forward again, but my Huey had arrived and, watched by envious eyes, I ascended from the battle towards a bath, clean clothes and dinner in Saigon. 'The Cav' was fighting a successful blocking action; since it had begun three weeks before they thought they had killed about two thousand, five hundred North Vietnamese for a loss of two hundred men themselves. My brief visit seemed to confirm that a Frenchman I had met in Saigon was right when he said, 'The Americans are brave soldiers, but they are stupid soldiers. They are too brave. If the French, British or Germans were fighting this war, they would only suffer half the casualties.'

Back in Saigon that night there were, as usual, parties. At one I was introduced to, and left with, the captain of an American freighter, then discharging her cargo of fragmentation bombs at the docks. He was a square-set, red-faced man with a shaven skull and starched white uniform and he was drunk. Hearing that I was English, he fixed me with a bloodshot eye and asked, 'Do you know what you people are doing to my nation? Do you? You know the Beatles, that crap? You know what that's doing to us? It's destroying our youth.'

For a while it had seemed as if it was over. The war might stagger towards a conclusion in Vietnam, but for the British the long recessional seemed to have ended and there were no more beleaguered outposts to visit. In 1969 I married and settled down to writing books and weekly articles about London. But in that same year other troubles did begin and, at first, seem to be soluble by political action. They were not and in the spring of 1973, twenty years after the excited preparations for the coronation of Queen Elizabeth, I was again with the British Army in the field.

I had not seen John Macmillan since the last days at Aden. He had been a brigade major then; now a lieutenant-colonel, he was again detached from his own regiment, the Argylls, and was again on active service, commanding a battalion of the Gordon Highlanders. Colonel Macmillan was occupying another fort, differing in structure from those manned by the British Army over the past twenty years, in being built mostly of sheet metal and steel mesh rather than stone blocks, or earthworks and barbed wire.

The morning had been spent listening to expositions of strategy and tactics before talc-covered maps marked with chinagraph and it had been suggested that, after lunch, I might like to accompany a patrol for a couple of hours. Then, in the officers' mess, where young men in khaki denims and pullovers sat in armchairs leafing through *Country Life* and *Punch*, we talked about Aden. I told him of the remark made to me by the head of a department in the Foreign Office: 'In South-East Asia we handed over to Benchers of Lincoln's Inn; in Africa we handed over to bus conductors—and not very good ones at that; only in Aden did we surrender totally to the enemy.' It was sad that 1967 had seen the grand finale for now it seemed unlikely that a more seemly departure would mark the final fall of the imperial curtain.

The following year had been remarkable in that British soldiers had not been fighting anywhere. True, two companies of infantry had been flown to Mauritius for fear of rioting when the island's independence had been celebrated, and a ceremonial visit by Princess Alexandra had been cancelled. Then there had been the continuing naval blockade to stop oil reaching Rhodesia, and its rebellious, still-dominant white minority, led by Ian Smith, the Prime Minister.

The Russians had invaded Czechoslovkia in that year to repress the emerging liberalism and, in France, near-revolution ended the rule of de Gaulle, but the remains of the British Commonwealth and Empire heard no new call to arms. There had been belligerent mutterings over the Falkland Islands in the South Atlantic, where sovereignty had long been claimed by Argentina; in the House of Commons, Conservatives had worried about this and Michael Stewart, the Foreign Secretary, trying to assure them that fears were groundless, had said that there was no immediate transfer of sovereignty in prospect.

The agony of Indo-China now appeared to be ending. The Americans, having lost the will to win, were to leave the fighting to the South Viet-namese. In January 1973 a tentative cease-fire agreement had been signed in Paris and, under its terms, the last Americans had left Vietnam by the end of March. (The optimism was not justified for the North Vietnamese were to launch a final offensive a year later and in April 1975 Saigon fell and the war ended.)

We talked of old friends and the Army's domestic politics. Colin Mitchell, who had commanded the Argylls in Aden with such dash and been so reluctant to 'play it cool', had not only been denied his DSO but been passed over for promotion and had resigned his commission. I told Macmillan that walking through London with Colin Mitchell must have been something like it would have been to accompany Nelson: strangers greeting him, shaking his hand and taxi drivers refusing to let him pay his fare. The Army had wanted him to stay; he did not, stood for Parliament and, in 1970, had won West Aberdeenshire for the Conservatives. The other controversial soldier of that period, Walter Walker, had success-fully defied the Army Council's decision to get rid of him, which had finally been over-ruled by Denis Healey, and, despite offending more generals and politicians by grasping the problems of defensive alliances with a mailed fist, had won promotion and honours. General Sir Walter Walker had just retired as the Allied Commander-in-Chief, Northern Europe, and there had been almost audible sighs of relief from the more sensitive capitals of NATO. He had returned to a Britain hardly recog-nizable as the motherland he had left for the farther frontiers of the Em-pire four decades before: now a country that dismayed, and sometimes disgusted him.

Over lunch such talk was interrupted by the appearance of an officer to tell Macmillan, 'Excuse me, sir, the sniper's back. He's fired at our patrol. Aimed for the sergeant. A near miss.' As he gave more details the prospect of my own sortie with the next patrol took on a new complexion: the sniper was still there and might shoot at us. So, dressed like a soldier but unarmed, I listened to the briefing with added attention and to the corporal, who was to command the patrol, as he explained where we were going, what we were going to do and that I should try to stay beside him until we got back. I stood close behind him as we waited, like men-at-arms about to make a sally from a castle, inside the gates of the fort. They opened and the first two gripped their rifles and dashed out. The corporal tapped my arm and we followed, sprinting across the road to fling our-selves against a grassy bank and peer over it at Andersonstown in the suburbs of Belfast.

He had explained how we would move: running from cover to cover; those going first, or following, keeping watch and ready to shoot; the last two, twirling as they ran, never presenting a back as a target. Along hedges, over walls, through gates, from tree to tree we ran, then stopped and stared about. It looked a pleasant place: red-brick council houses and a few low blocks of flats; above them the bare, green shoulder of a hill; below, in the haze, Belfast. 'See them flats?' the corporal panted. 'That's where the sniper is. Watch out.' We hurtled across another road and squeezed through a fence into an overgrown garden; then we raced up the path and pressed ourselves against the wall of a house. I peered into a ground-floor window: just what one would expect, inside: three-piece suite and television, but on the glazed-tile mantelpiece, where a clock would be, a model tommy gun carved in wood on a little stand.

'It's the next house.' muttered the corporal. 'I got to go in there, see the lady. One of the lads knocked a brick off her wall. We sent a brickie up to mend it yesterday. Have to see she's happy.' We ducked round to the back of the next house, where washing was flapping from a line and the kitchen door stood open. Inside, a young woman was washing dishes, a baby crawling on the lino. She was a nice-looking girl with clear skin and gently waved hair. The corporal straightened, lowered his rifle, clumped up to the door and smiled. ' 'Afternoon, love,' he said. 'That brick all right? Just wanted to make sure.' The young mother turned blue eyes to him, put down her dishcloth and screeched obscenities till her face flushed and veins stood like cords in her neck. 'Okay, dear,' the corporal sighed. 'Just thought I'd ask.' He tapped my arm and I ran after him down the garden path and through a gap in the hedge.

Nobody shot at us and we were back at the fort in time for tea. Colonel Macmillan said that the sniper would almost certainly take a second shot, then changed the subject: how were the correspondents he had known in Aden? I told him what I knew, adding that none of them was reporting this war. In Belfast the Europa Hotel was what the Ledra Palace, the Aletti and the Crescent had been, yet when I had arrived in the bar it had been crowded but there were no familiar faces. The barman, asked where the journalists were, nodded towards a group of young men with collar-length hair, talking earnestly. After four years of reporting the activities of the Irish Republican Army, the Royal Ulster Constabulary and the British Army, they seemed as nonchalant as we had once been. Outside the plate-glass window the street was empty, cleared because a twenty-pound bomb had been planted by the IRA in a shop a couple of hundred yards down the road and was to be blown by the bomb-disposal squad.

Nobody wanted to watch; when it exploded and smoke blew past the window, only one of the men at the bar strolled over to glance down the street.

It was as if one generation of war correspondents had gone with the rearguard from Aden and another was taking their place. There was nobody here with whom I could swap stories of EOKA, CTs, the OAS and FLN, the TNKU, FLOSY, the VC and the rest. There had been change in Fleet Street, too. *The Times* was now a different newspaper, competing on equal terms with the *Daily Telegraph* and the *Guardian*; there was even talk of a move from the desecrated site of Printing House Square to join Lord Thomson's *Sunday Times* in Gray's Inn Road. Lord Beaverbrook had died, aged eighty-five, in 1964 when the British had showed something of their old dash in Borneo, the Radfan, Cyprus and East Africa. The newspapers which reflected his optimistic, Victorian views began to lose impetus in his absence and many in Fleet Street were surprised to miss him so much.

Twenty years after the coronation of Queen Elizabeth II the Empire she had inherited had all but disappeared. The ceremonial of its dismembering had been conducted in style, with members of her family in attendance as the bands played, the saluting guns fired and the Union Jack lowered. During that time there had been half a dozen small wars on a nineteenth-century scale along the old Lifeline of Empire in Cyprus, Suez, South Arabia, Malaya, Borneo and in Kenya. Suez was best forgotten but, otherwise, the British had only failed disastrously in Aden and its hinterland, which had become a protectorate of the Russian Empire as the People's Republic of South Yemen. In Cyprus the British still occupied their strategic bases; Kenya had developed into a friendly African nation with comparatively little racial tension; Malaya and the Borneo territories still formed the Federation of Malaysia with a wholly independent Singapore remaining an independent city-state, a new Venice, binding itself and its neighbours and trading partners together with ties of commerce. These former members of the Empire now belonged to the Commonwealth, with other former colonies and dominions; an international club with relaxed rules, no subscription and still presided over, on formal occasions, by the Queen. None of the new nations that had achieved independence within the two decades might present much more than a superficial likeness to the intended pattern for their political system at Westminster and several already bore no resemblance whatsoever. But whatever influence the Commonwealth retained was benevolent and that was an achievement.

The cost of these wars seemed high. The bloodiest had been in Kenya and Malaya, which had each cost at least 14,000 lives: fighting men of both sides, police and civilians. The loss of life in the other four conflicts amounted to a total of less than 5,000 and the number of British and Gurkha soldiers killed in all these campaigns over twenty years was about a thousand.

The cost did not seem so high when compared with that paid by those who had tried harder to hold their inheritance: the French, and their successors in Indo-China, the Americans. In Algeria the total loss of lives, military and civilian, on both sides and of all races, was said to have reached a million; the most conservative estimate put it at about half that number; the French Army lost nearly 20,000 men killed. In Indo-China it had lost more than 75,000 men killed, nearly a third of them from metropolitan France, but a grand total for both sides of about half a million has been suggested. The war waged by the Americans in support of South Vietnam was far more costly; estimates of numbers killed came close to two million, of whom more than 58,000 were Americans.

Thus, the conflicts in the final years of the British Empire had cost something of the order of 33,000 lives, whereas those fought to hold only two subject nations for France and one of them, latterly, for the West, had taken between two and three million. The most that could be claimed for this slaughter was that, in the case of Vietnam, it had probably acted as a lightning conductor by attracting such violence, so giving some of its vulnerable neighbours a decade of near-stability. So the British could feel relief and some satisfaction that the growing realism of their politicians and the resolution of their soldiers had saved them from such calamities. They had had to start thinking of themselves as Europeans, bound to the continent by military and economic alliance. The excitements of the past two decades could, surely, be consigned together with all the memories of the British Empire, to history and nostalgia.

It had not quite ended. Since leaving the Gordon Highlanders at their fort in the suburbs of Belfast I had been waiting for the news that would almost inevitably be made by the sniper. It came next day, and opening *The Times* in London the following morning, I saw the headline announcing another death in Northern Ireland and read, 'The soldier of the 1st Battalion, the Gordon Highlanders, died instantly while on foot patrol in the Andersonstown housing estate. Private Michael Marr, aged 33, was married with a child, and came from Aberdeen.'

Other than Northern Ireland, there now remained a few more places around the world — Gibraltar, the Falkland Islands, Hong Kong among them—to be ruled from Westminster and Whitehall, stranded high amongst the historical flotsam and jetsam by the ebbing tide. In October 1973 another war would be fought and have tremendous consequences but Britain would not be involved, only suffer from it. The once-despised Egyptians stormed across the Suez Canal and the Syrians attacked Israel from the north in a surprise assault on the Jewish holiday of Yom Kippur. The Israelis recovered and were finally victorious but the Arabs took their revenge against the West. While Jews and Arabs were engaged in the greatest tank battle ever fought, the Organization of Petroleum Exporting Countries decided to raise the price of oil and, just before Christmas, doubled it. The economic consequences were catastrophic but neither the British nor the French, by whom the Arab countries involved had been ruled or dominated so recently, could do anything about it.

The British Empire, assembled over two centuries and dismantled in two decades, will survive a little longer in memory.

Index

205